COMPLETE DIGITAL
PHOTOGRAPHY

COMPLETE DIGITAL PHOTOGRAPHY

Ben Long

CHARLES RIVER MEDIA, INC.
Hingham, Massachusetts

Production: ElectroPublishing
Cover Design: The Printed Image
Printer: Malloy Lithographing, Inc.

CHARLES RIVER MEDIA, INC.
20 Downer Avenue, Suite 3
Hingham, MA 02043
781-740-0400
781-740-8816 (FAX)
info@charlesriver.com
www.charlesriver.com

This book is printed on acid-free paper.

Complete Digital Photogaphy
Ben Long
ISBN: 1-58450-007-7

Printed in the United States of America
01 7 6 5 4 3 2 First Edition

Library of Congress Cataloging-in-Publication Data

Long, Ben, 1967-
   Complete digital photography / Ben Long.-- 1st ed.
     p. cm.
   ISBN 1-58450-007-7 (paperback with CD-ROM : alk. paper)
   1. Photography--Digital techniques--Handbooks, manuals, etc. 2.
Digital cameras--Handbooks, manuals, etc. 3. Image processing--Digital
techniques--Handbooks, manuals, etc.   I. Title.
   TR267 .L66 2001
   778.3--dc21

                    2001001241

CHARLES RIVER MEDIA titles are available for site license or bulk purchase by institutions, user groups, corporations, etc. For additional information, please contact the Special Sales Department at 781-740-0400.

Contents

Acknowledgments

This book could not have been written (at least, not by me) without the help of a number of people, including:

Gina Prescia at Olympus America, Mary Resnick and Chuck Westfall at Canon USA, Kendall Anders at DigiEffects, and Susan Doering at Adobe.

If you ever get a chance to see any of Paul Winternitz's photographs, you are very lucky. I am doubly lucky to also have him as a friend and he contributed invaluable photographic advice and consultation, as well as slogging through readings of early drafts. You can check out his photographic work at www.completedigitalphotography.com/winternitz.

Sonja Schenk is a great writing partner, whether we're writing together or not. She is always ready to offer creative or editorial advice and is a great commiserator during periods of pathological procrastination.

Special thanks to Regina, Adelle, Michael, Reed, and all of the others who agreed to be models and guinea pigs for a number of photographic explanations in the book.

Finally, Kalonica McQuesten offered editorial, critical, creative, and personal advice throughout the writing of this book. This text could not have been finished without her contributions and help.

1

Introduction

IN THIS CHAPTER

- Who this Book is for
- What Counts as "Digital Photography"
- What Else do You Need?
- Digital 101: a Few Basic Ideas

"I photograph to find out what something will look like photographed."

— Garry Winogrand

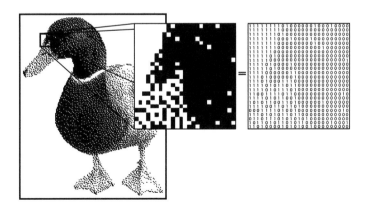

In the roughly 150 years since its invention, photography has gone from being treated as a curiosity to being accepted as a legitimate art form, to becoming what is possibly the most successful form of communication ever created. Look around the room you are in right now and consider just how many photographs you can see – from book covers to food packaging to advertising circulars. Needless to say, there have been a lot of important technological breakthroughs on the way from daguerreotypes to 8 x 10" glossies. Color *film*, sophisticated light meters, *zoom lenses*, autofocus cameras, Polaroid-Land photography, simple point-and-shoot cameras, and 1-hour photo processing are just some of the technological milestones that have helped to make photography both a powerful and ubiquitous medium.

Despite all of these changes and improvements, though, today's typical 35mm film cameras are not fundamentally different from the cameras of 100 years ago.Sure, the optics in a camera's lens, the *metering* and control systems provided by a camera's electronics, and the chemistry available in modern film and processing technology allow for higher quality and more creative control than ever before, but a film camera still records an image by exposing a piece of film to light.

Digital photography, therefore, represents the first fundamental change in photographic technology since the mid-1800s. Although the lenses, metering systems, and controls on your digital camera might be identical to those found on a film camera, the simple fact that the camera does not record images on film makes digital photography a very different process than traditional film photography.

Practically, of course, the digital photographer has luxuries the film photographer can only dream of: instant feedback, the ability to immediately discard unwanted images, no film processing, no scanning of prints or slides, and no environmental or financial concerns over film and chemicals. Artistically, the digital photographer can take advantage of unique in-camera features such as panoramic shooting, automatic image processing, and the fact that one can shoot and shoot and shoot, trying many different settings, framings, and *exposures* without worrying about wasting film.

Despite these advantages, most photographers have been waiting for the answer to one question: can digital cameras produce images that are comparable to film? Until recently, the answer was "yes, but it'll cost you upwards of $20,000." But finally, after years of waiting, film-quality digital cameras have gotten down to the $1,000 range. They're not perfect, and many of them lack features that experienced photographers have come to depend on, but whether you're an occasional hobbyist, dedicated amateur, or serious professional photographer, if you've been waiting to make the jump to digital photography, now is the time, and this book will help you take the leap.

WHO THIS BOOK IS FOR

Complete Digital Photography covers all of the technical details that you need to understand to produce high-quality digital photographs. This book is for photographers of all skill levels who want to use digital cameras to produce images. If you're an amateur or hobbyist photographer who wants to take better pictures and have decided to use a digital camera instead of a traditional film camera, this book will explain the fundamental technical concerns of shooting good pictures. If you're an experienced film photographer who is interested in making the switch to digital photography, and you want to understand the new technology, this book will help you understand what is different about working with a digital camera.

Using a film camera is really a two-step process. First you shoot your pictures – with the goal of getting as much color, contrast and tone into your image as you can. Then you develop and print the images in a way that takes maximum advantage of the information in your shot. Shooting digital photographs is no different. As with a film camera, you first shoot your subject – after carefully calculating the proper exposure. Then you digitally process and print your image.

Although cameras may change, the physics of light remains the same (fortunately!). Consequently, digital photographers share all of the same concerns that film photographers have over *apertures, shutter speeds,* and metering techniques. Chapters 2 through 5 and Chapter 7 will cover these questions and show you how a digital camera works. This information will help you choose a camera, and will form the basis for much of the practical shooting and editing information that will be covered later.

All of your additional shooting concerns, from choosing the right exposure, to using *filters* and flash, will be covered in Chapters 7, 8 and 9. Although experienced photographers might already be comfortable with much of the information presented in these chapters, they'll still want to take a close look at these chapters for information on the particular idiosyncrasies of shooting with digital cameras.

Although it is difficult to separate the artistic and technical concerns involved in creating a good photo – after all, it is your technical control that allows you to achieve your artistic goals – this book will not cover certain "artistic" issues. Composition, artistic intent, photographic narrative, and many other concerns are not covered herein, mainly because there are so many good books already available on this subject. See Appendix A for a list of suggested reading.

Just as a film camera requires a good darkroom, a digital camera requires a computer and a few select pieces of software. Chapter 6 will help you select and assemble a computer system that's right for your photo processing needs.

Chapter 10 will give you some tips on transferring your images to your computer and organizing them. Chapter 10 will also help you configure your computer's *color management system (CMS)* and prepare your images for editing.

ON THE CD

Adobe Photoshop is used for all of the image editing examples and tutorials in this book, and demo copies of Photoshop are provided on the CD-ROM. Most of the tools and functions used in the tutorial are fairly generic so you should be able to follow along using any image editing program, provided it includes a reasonable assortment of editing tools. Your editing efforts will start in earnest in Chapter 11 where you'll learn about *histograms*, and make your first tonal and contrast corrections. Editing continues in Chapter 12 when you will be introduced to some of the basic editing tools that you'll need to correct and adjust your images.

Chapter 13 details the image editing workflow that you'll typically use. It also expands on your editing know-how with discussions of color and *saturation* adjustment, resizing, and *sharpening*. In Chapter 14, you'll perform some of the more complex edits that often face digital photographers - fFrom correcting distortions, to simulating *depth of field*, *stitching* panoramas, and converting images to *grayscale*

Finally, with your images corrected, massagededited, and tweaked, you'll be ready to output them using the techniques presented in Chapter 15. Whether your final image destination is print, the web, or video, Chapter 15 will cover the details of getting your image out of your image editor and into the real world.

Finally, because Complete Digital Photography is intended for users with a variety of experience levels, many terms have been defined in the Glossary, rather than within the main text.

WHAT COUNTS AS "DIGITAL PHOTOGRAPHY"

Many people use the term "digital photography" to cover any photographic process that involves correcting and editing a photograph using a computer. By this definition, shooting with your film camera, and then scanning your film or prints, editing them digitally, and then printing on a desktop printer counts as digital photography.

In this book, digital photographs are photographs taken with a digital camera. This is an important distinction because shooting with a film camera and shooting with a digital camera involve different concerns and practices. The simple fact is: there are a lot of things you must do differently with a digital camera. But don't worry, this book covers them all!

WHAT ELSE DO YOU NEED?

Chapters 5 and 6 will help you choose a digital camera, a computer, and some editing software. Besides that, you don't need much else to be able to understand the theories, examples, and tutorials in this book. Nothing in this book is platform-specific so you should have no trouble following along, whether you use a Macintosh (also known as Mac), Windows, or Unix. Most of the samples and tutorials are built around Adobe Photoshop but you can use a different editing package as long as it provides equivalent features. Demo versions of Photoshop, as well as many other handy utilities, are included on the CD-ROM in both Macintosh and Windows formats.

ON THE CD   In addition, all images necessary for the tutorials are included in the Tutorials folder on the CD-ROM.

DIGITAL 101: A FEW BASIC IDEAS

In the old days, photographers made their own photographic papers, films and *emulsions*. Whether it was to achieve a particular style or texture or to gain more control over their printing processes, photographers like Ansel Adams, Alfred Stieglitz, and Eduard Steichen had to know a good deal about chemistry to create their prints. Similarly, to really understand how to get the most out of your digital camera, it's important to understand some of the technology behind it. Chapter 2 will cover the details of how a digital camera works but a basic understanding of the "digital" process will make things easier.

These days, the word "digital" is being added to a lot of different technologies from digital photography, to digital audio and video to digital cellular phones. In each case, the term "digital" refers to a process of breaking something down into chunks that can be represented by numbers ("digits").

The "real" world that we live in is an *analog* world. Light and sound come to us as continuous analog waves that our senses interpret. Unfortunately, it's very difficult to invent a technology that can accurately record a continuous analog wave. Storing a series of numbers, on the other hand, is simple. You can carve them in stone, write them on paper, burn them to a CD-ROM or, in the case of digital cameras, record them to small memory chips.

The process of converting something into numbers is called *digitizing*. The first step in digitizing is to divide your subject into distinct units. In the case of an image, this is a simple process of dividing your image into a grid of *picture elements* or *pixels*. How fine your grid is (that is, what *resolution* it has) varies depending on how sophisticated your equipment is.

Next, each pixel in the grid is analyzed to determine its content, a process called *sampling*. Each sample is then measured to determine how "full" it is. That is, a corresponding numeric value is assigned which represents that pixel's contents, a process called *quantizing*. Finally, these numeric values are stored on some kind of storage medium.

Take a look at Figure 1.1, a simple image composed entirely of *black and white* pixels. As you can see, it's very easy to assign a one or a zero to each pixel to represent the image. Because it only takes a single bit to represent each pixel, this image is called a *1-bit image*.

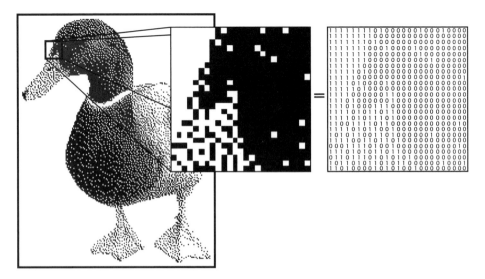

FIGURE   *Each pixel in this 1-bit image is represented by a one or a zero.*
1.1

In the example shown in Figure 1.1, our individual samples can only be 0 or 1 (that is, they have a very small *dynamic range*) because we are only storing one bit of information per pixel. If we want to be able to record more than simple black and white, then we need to be able to specify more colors. That is, we need to have more choices than just 0 or 1. By going to a higher *color depth* (*bit depth*) – let's say 8 bits, which allows for 256 different values – we can record more information, as seen in Figure 1.2.

With 256 shades to choose from, we can represent a finer degree of detail than we could with only two color choices. To store full-color images, we must go to an even higher bit depth and store 24 bits of information per pixel. With 24 bits, we can represent roughly 16 million colors, allowing us to store photo-quality images.

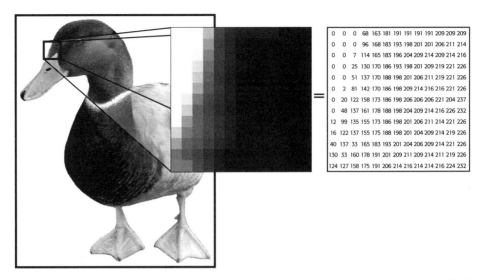

FIGURE **1.2** *By storing bigger numbers for each pixel, we can store much more than simple black and white dots. With the ability to use gray pixels the image looks much more realistic.*

To sum up, two of the factors that determine the quality of a digitizing process are: resolution (that is, the size and number of your individual pixels), and dynamic range (or, how big a range of color choices you have for each pixel).

There are many other factors that affect the quality of a digitized image - from optical quality to compression. Before exploring these questions, though, it's important to consider what makes a good image.

2

How Good are Digital Photos

IN THIS CHAPTER

- A Word About the Images in This Book
- What's Wrong with Digital Cameras
- Why you Want a Digital Camera

Many people are still wary of digital photography – they question the claims that digital cameras can produce results that are competitive with film. Given the rapid advancement of the technology, and the low level of quality produced by the first few generations of consumer-level cameras, these concerns are often valid, particularly if one is up against a deadline or shooting for pay.

In the next few chapters, you will be spending a lot of time reading about the technical details of how a digital camera works. These concepts will help you better understand how to choose – and get the best results from – a digital camera. Because of their underlying technology, digital cameras are subject to very particular imaging problems. In this chapter, you're going to learn what those problems look like, and how to identify them. This should make your technical forays a little easier to understand.

Finally, at the end of this chapter, you'll see a direct, head-to-head comparison between two digital cameras and a film camera. The results may surprise you.

A WORD ABOUT THE IMAGES IN THIS BOOK

Although a lot of hard work has gone into ensuring that the images in this book are accurately printed, some of the issues discussed herein are very subtle and may not be easy to see in the book's figures. The printing process and paper used in this book are not what one would normally choose for a high-quality photographic reproduction, so you shouldn't take the prints in this book as examples of the best that can be done with a digital camera. Rather, think of some of these images as reference images that will, hopefully, help you understand the concepts that are covered.

ON THE CD

For closer, more accurate examination, many of the images in this book are included on the Complete Digital Photography CD-ROM in the Images folder. Images are organized by chapter and are stored in both TIFF and Photoshop format.

Although examining the images on-screen will be very informative, for the truest understanding of image quality, it's best to look at the images using your chosen output device. If that device is your monitor, then by all means, keep looking at the images on-screen. If you intend to print to a particular printer, however, then it's best to judge image quality by studying prints from that printer. In addition to providing a "real-world" sample of image quality, you'll begin to get an understanding of what your printer is capable of, and how its colors look different from what's on your computer screen. You may be pleasantly surprised to find that *artifacts* and problems that are very annoying on-screen, don't appear at all on the printed page.

Printing will be covered in great detail in Chapter 15, and the tips in those chapters should help you get better printed results. Until then, simply printing the images straight off the Complete Digital Photography CD-ROM should at least help you follow the concepts in this chapter.

WHAT'S WRONG WITH DIGITAL CAMERAS

First of all, this section is not about how digital cameras are a bad choice for your photographic pursuits. Rather, in this section, you'll simply learn about some of the problems that digital cameras face and how those problems show up in your final images. Just as film photographers have to worry about everything from *reciprocity* failure to the color balance of their film, digital photographers have their own set of concerns.

When you evaluate a camera or your own images, it's important to know what types of image problems you're likely to encounter. By learning how to recognize and identify these problems it will be easier to avoid them when you shoot, and you'll have a better understanding of how to correct them afterwards.

DID YOU HEAR SOMETHING?

One of the easiest problems to identify in any digital image is *noise*. Unfortunately, all current digital cameras are susceptible to noise, and they manage to produce many different kinds. Some noise is more acceptable than others, but even if you're okay with the noise in your image, it's still important to know it's there as it can affect some editing operations.

Figure 2.1 was shot with an Olympus C2100 UltraZoom using the camera's default automatic settings. No exposure adjustments were made and no edits were performed.

If you look closely at any of the shadowy areas, you'll see that they are pretty noisy. In fact, even some of the middle tone areas have a marked amount of noise in them. Although in this grayscale figure, the noise may look simply like texture, if you look at the image in color (Color Plate 2), you'll see that the noise is far more than simple variations in the natural tone or color in the image. Rather, the noise appears as light-colored speckles – mostly magenta or green – spread throughout the shadow areas. In particular, take a look at the gray wall along the right-hand part of the curve of the street.

Noise typically occurs in darker parts of an image, although even some of the lighter shades on the pink building are suffering from a little too much noise. This particular image is free of noise in the sky, a problem that plagues some digital cameras.

FIGURE *Like many digital camera images, this street scene has some trouble with noise,*
2.1 *particularly in the shadow areas.*

Different cameras produce different amounts of noise and some digital cameras produce "prettier" noise than others. In some cases, the noise has less color in it, and almost looks like nothing more than film grain.

On the positive side, depending on the quality of your printing process, this noise may not be a problem. If you're using a somewhat coarse, noisy printing process – such as on some inkjet printers – then the printer may produce enough artifacts of its own that the noise in your image will be obscured. This is a bit of a gamble, though, and it's better to try to get a camera that produces less noise, especially since you might one day upgrade to a higher-quality printer.

Although you can reduce noise through some simple editing tricks, it's difficult or impossible to get rid of all of it. And, certain editing operations can actually make the noise more pronounced, so it's a good idea to stay aware of the noise in your image.

COLOR TROUBLES

There are many different kinds of color problems that can come up in any image, whether digital or film, but digital cameras have a few problems that are all their own. Learning to spot them will give you a better idea of where to start making corrections.

Downright Incorrect Color

Color Plate 3 shows two scenes shot with two different cameras. Both cameras were set on full auto and no exposure adjustments were made. As you can see, the two cameras produced very different interpretations of the colors in the scene. In the image on the left, the reds lean too far in the magenta direction while the greens are much too yellow.

For the record, the colors in the image on the right are much more accurate than the colors in the image on the left. The left-hand image was shot with a Nikon Coolpix 990, while the right-hand image was shot with a Canon EOS D30.

Color Casts

Some cameras have a tendency to produce images with particular color casts – overall color tones that make the image appear as if it was shot through a colored filter of some kind. Sometimes a camera will have a tendency to cast only the colors in a particular range. For example, shadows might appear too blue or yellow while the midtones and highlights are fine.

Although color casts aren't very attractive, they're usually not too hard to remove, as they typically present themselves in just one range of colors in an image. You'll learn more about removing color casts in Chapter 13.

Bad White Balance

As you'll see, before you shoot with a digital camera, you need to calibrate it to your current light source, a process called *white balancing*. If improperly white balanced, the camera will not be able to accurately reproduce colors.

Images with bad white balance are similar to images with color casts, except that white balance color damage usually goes through more areas of the image. Color Plate 4 shows the same scene shot with a variety of white balance settings. Notice the shift from red to blue throughout the image as the white balance changes.

Color Artifacts

You're probably familiar with the *red-eye* phenomenon that can turn people's eyes into demonic red circles, but there are many other types of color artifacts.

Figure 2.2 shows a color artifact that's so weird you can see it even in grayscale. If you look closely at the pen in the middle of this image you can see that's it's very strangely fuzzy. If you look at the color image included on the Complete Digital Photography CD-ROM, you'll see that the pen is positively glowing. For some reason, the camera got very confused when it was rendering the red of the pen and produced a weird halo.

ON THE CD

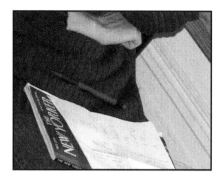

FIGURE *The fuzzy red pen in this person's lap is the result of a strange, unpredictable color*
2.2 *error on the part of the digital camera.*

If you look closely at the color version of this image, you'll also see some colored noise in the wall, in the wood, and in the denim of the jeans.

2- and 3-*megapixel* digital cameras are susceptible to a kind of color artifact that you don't have to worry about with lower-resolution cameras and film cameras. Sometimes referred to as *chromatic aberrations,* the weird *purple fringing* that you can see on the edge of the building in Color Plate 5 is actually the result of a computing problem within the camera. In Chapter 13 you'll learn more about these artifacts and how to avoid them.

Many color artifacts, such as purple fringing, seem to occur in the boundaries of high contrast change, or in areas of sharp color change. When you are evaluating a camera, or when you are assessing the quality of an image, pay attention to these types of areas.

EXPOSURE PROBLEMS

As with a film camera, if you set the wrong exposure on a digital camera, you'll get a bad image. Although modern automatic light metering systems are very sophisticated and often do a very good job, they can still make mistakes, particularly if they aren't used properly. The meters in most cameras have definite tendencies – they might handle similar situations in similar ways – and experience will usually help you to better predict how your camera might respond to a metering problem.

Figure 2.3 shows an image that was *underexposed* by the camera. As you can see, there are no visible details in the shadow areas of the image. Exposure and detail is a matter of taste, of course, and one could easily argue that it doesn't matter that there are no shadow details.If you were hoping for a different level of contrast in the image, however, - one which might reveal some detail in those dark areas - you'd be out of luck with this picture.

Figure **2.3**   *The camera's automatic meter underexposed this image, resulting in loss of shadow detail and badly posterized shadows.*

Posterizing occurs when the number of shades or tones in an image has been reduced. If you look closely at the edge of the shadow (Figure 2.4) you'll see that what should be a smooth gradation has turned into a very *pixellated,*

Figure **2.4**   *Looking closely at the shadow areas reveals the lack of midtone information in the edge of the shadow.*

posterized mess. Rather than a smooth transition from shadow to midtones, you see a very high-contrast, speckly transition.

Figure 2.5 shows the same image shot with an exposure that revealed the shadows and didn't posterize, but unfortunately the image is *overexposed* enough that all the color in the sky is gone. If you look at the color version on the Complete Digital Photography CD-ROM, you'll also see that the image has a yellowish/greenish cast.

ON THE CD

FIGURE *Now we've got shadow detail but no sky!*
2.5

These problems occurred because the wrong type of metering was used in these images. However, even when you use the right meter, your camera can still get confused. In Chapter 7 you'll learn more about using your light meter.

TOO MUCH OF A GOOD THING

Most cameras perform some kind of sharpening after they take an image. Sharpening serves not only to improve detail and the sharpness of edges, it also tends to deepen the saturation of colors and boost the contrast of an image. It's important to realize, though, that too much sharpening can be a bad thing. Better cameras offer a choice of sharpening levels which let you adjust the camera to your sharpening taste.

Everyone knows what an out-of-focus image looks like. In Figure 2.6 you can see an image that's too sharp.

FIGURE *This image has been sharpened too much by the camera's built-in sharpening*
2.6 *routines.*

As you can see, the contrast in the highly-detailed areas has gone way too high, resulting in dark blacks and white whites and almost nothing in between. In addition, many textures are now surrounded with halos of black or white (you'll learn why in Chapter 13). The in-camera sharpening has also accentuated the noise in the sky. This image was shot at the same time as Color Plate 5, but the sharpening setting in the camera was turned up.

"REASON?! WE DON'T NEED NO STINKING REASON!"

Sometimes an image just looks bad, and there's no real reason for it. Sure, you can look for color casts and *aberrations* and contrast troubles, but often there are simply indefinable combinations of all of these things that cause an image to just look "wrong." Similarly, you might have an image with bad contrast and horrible noise and be surprised to find that it is very compelling.

The point is that, when you judge image quality, an image might be full of technical mistakes, but still be a good image. Before you spend too much time obsessing over technical details, step back from the image and examine it as a whole. You may find that your technical concerns are irrelevant.

Nevertheless, it is important to know a camera's technical shortcomings so that you can work around them or, sometimes, exploit them as in Color Plate 6, a low-resolution, grainy, technically bad image that is still nice to look at.

WHY YOU WANT A DIGITAL CAMERA

Don't let the previous discussion discourage you. Yes, digital cameras have their idiosyncrasies, but so do film cameras (you could very easily come up with a list of "What's wrong with film cameras?").

Many of the problems discussed above are infrequent and won't necessarily be pronounced enough to show up in print. What's more, as you'll see later, all of the problems can be fixed with some simple image editing techniques.

The fact is, unless you're a professional photographer with very specific, high-end concerns, today's digital cameras can provide image quality that's every bit as good as what you'll get from film. Certainly not every camera will deliver such good results, but if you choose the right camera and learn how to use it, there's no reason that going digital should feel like a compromise.

Whether or not you already have a camera, if you've bought this book, you've probably investigated digital photography enough to already understand the practical and creative advantages of shooting digital photographs. From immediate review of images to being able to delete unwanted pictures on-the-fly, digital cameras offer creative flexibility that film photographers can only dream of.

One of the biggest advantages to digital photography, however, is the elimination of the scanner. You may have a great film camera, and a very good photo lab, but without a good scanner and the knowledge of how to use it (and patience to do it right) then all that extra film quality may not count for much.

Yes there are hassles and concerns when you shoot digital photographs. If you have any experience with photography, though, you know that there are also plenty of hassles and concerns when you shoot film. With the current level of digital camera and printing technology, it's safe to say that once you go digital, you won't go back to film!

NEXT STEPS

Now that you've seen what a digital camera can do, it's time to get started doing some digital photography. Although we won't get to any actual shooting for a while, the next few chapters will give you the groundwork and understanding that you need to get the most from your camera. Whether you have a camera already or are still shopping, Chapters 3 through 5 will help you understand just what's going on inside of all of those silicon chips.

3

How a Digital Camera Works

IN THIS CHAPTER

- Something Old, Something New
- A Little Color Theory
- How a CCD Works
- Compression and Storage

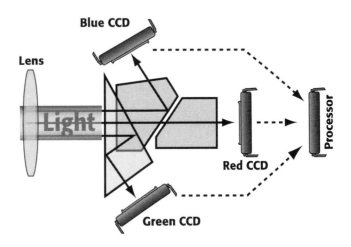

As we discussed in Chapter 1, the only real difference between a digital camera and a film camera is that a digital camera does not use film to record an image. However, this one fundamental change affects all the other systems on the camera, from the lens to the light meter. Consequently, it's important to learn just what exactly is going on under the hood of a digital camera.

SOMETHING OLD, SOMETHING NEW

Just like a film camera, your digital camera records an image by using a lens to focus light onto a *focal plane*. In a film camera, light is focused by a lens through an aperture and a *shutter* and onto a piece of film held on the focal plane. By opening or closing the aperture, and by changing the amount of time that the shutter is open, the photographer can control how the film is exposed. As we'll see later, exposure control lets the photographer change the degree to which the camera "freezes" motion, how well the film records contrast and color saturation, and which parts of the image are in focus.

Your digital camera works the same way, but instead of a piece of film sitting on the focal plane, there is a special chip called a *charge-coupled device (CCD)* sitting on the focal plane. (Also, as we'll see later, most digital cameras don't have an actual mechanical shutter.) When you take a picture with a digital camera, the CCD *samples* the light coming through the lens and converts that light into electrical signals. After the CCD is exposed, these signals are boosted by an amplifier and sent to an analog-to-digital converter that turns the signals into digits. These digits are then sent to an on-board computer for processing. Once the computer has calculated the final image, the new image data is stored on a memory card.. (Figure 3.1)

To really understand how a digital camera functions, though, you need to know a little color theory.

A LITTLE COLOR THEORY

In 1869, James Clerk Maxwell asked photographer Thomas Sutton (the inventor of the SLR camera) to take three black and white photographs of a tartan ribbon. Maxwell wanted to test a theory he had about a possible method for creating color photographs. He asked Sutton to place a different filter over the camera for each shot: first a red filter, then green, then blue. After the film was developed, Maxwell projected all three black and white pictures onto a screen using three projectors fitted with the same filters that were used to shoot the photos.

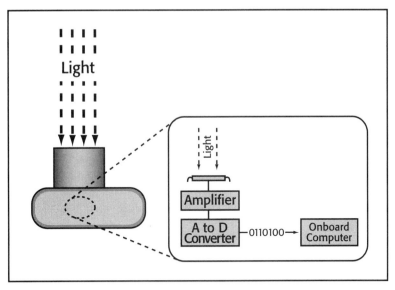

FIGURE *Light passes into a digital camera just as it would in a film camera. However,*
3.1 *instead of hitting a piece of film, it is digitized by a computer chip and passed to an*
on-board computer to create an image.

When the images were projected directly on top of each other, the images combined and Maxell had the world's first color photo!

Needless to say, this was hardly a convenient process. Unfortunately, it took another 30 years to turn Maxwell's discovery into a commercially viable product. This happened in 1903 when the Lumiere brothers used red, green, and blue dyes to color grains of starch that could be applied to glass plates to create color images. They called their process "Autochrome" and it was the first successful color printing process.

In grammar school, you probably learned that you could mix primary colors together to create other colors. Painters have used this technique for centuries, of course, but what Maxwell demonstrated is that, while you can mix paints together to create darker colors, light mixes together to create lighter colors. Or, to use some jargon, paint mixes together in a *subtractive* process (subtracting color to create black) while light mixes together in an *additive* process (adding color to create white). Note that Maxwell did not discover light's additive properties, Newton had done similar experiments long before, Maxwell was just the first to apply the properties to photography.

Take a look at Color Plate 1 to see a quick example of how the three additive primary colors of light can be combined to create other colors.

Your digital camera creates a full-color photograph using pretty much the same process that Maxwell used in 1860: it shoots three different black and white images and combines them into a color image.

The image shown in Figure 3.2 is called an *RGB* image because it uses red, green, and blue *channels* to create a color image. As we'll see later, it's possible to perform sophisticated corrections and manipulations by editing the individual red, green, and blue *color channels* directly.

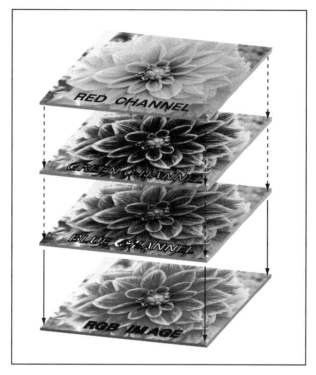

FIGURE *In a digital image, three separate red, green, and blue channels are combined to*
3.2   *create a final, full-color picture.*

 You say "black and white," I say "grayscale." *Although film*
photographers use the term "black and white" to denote an image
that lacks color, in the digital world it's better to use the term
TIP   *grayscale. As we saw in Figure 1.1, your computer can create an*
image that is composed of only black and white pixels.
Consequently, it's sometimes important to distinguish between an
image that is made up of black and white pixels, and one that is
made up of pixels of varying shades of gray.

In the century-and-a-half since Maxwell's discovery, many other ways of representing color have been discovered. For example, another model called *L*A*B color (also known as Lab color)* uses one channel for lightness information, another channel for greenness or redness, and a third channel for blueness or yellowness. And, of course, there is the Cyan, Magenta, Yellow and Black (*CMYK*) model that printers use.

Each of these approaches is called a *color model* or *color space* and each model has a particular *gamut*, or range, of colors that it can display. Some gamuts are more appropriate to certain tasks than others and all of these gamuts are smaller than the range of colors that your eye can perceive.

We'll deal more with gamuts and color models in later chapters. For now, it's important to understand that digital photos are comprised of separate red, green, and blue channels that combine to create a color image.

How a CCD Works

George Smith and Willard Boyle were two engineers employed by Bell Labs. The story goes that, one day in late October, the two men spent about an hour sketching out an idea for a new type of semiconductor that could be used for computer memory and for the creation of a solid-state, tubeless video camera. The year was 1969, and in that hour the two men had invented the CCD.

Roughly a year later, Bell Labs had created a solid-state video camera using Smith and Boyle's new chip. Although their original intention was to build a simple camera that could be used in a video-telephone device, they had soon built a camera that was good enough for broadcast television.

Since then, CCDs have been used in everything from cameras to facsimile fax) machines. Because video cameras have pretty low resolution, the CCD worked great for creating video-quality images. For printing pictures, though, you need much higher resolution. Consequently, it wasn't until recently that CCDs could be manufactured with enough resolution to compete with photographic film.

Counting Electrons

Photographic film is covered with an emulsion of light-sensitive, silver-laden crystals. When light hits the film, the silver atoms clump together. The more light there is, the bigger the clumps. In this way, a piece of film records the different amounts of light that strike each part of its surface. Color film is composed of three separate layers, one sensitive to red, one to green, and one to blue.

The CCD in your digital camera is a silicon chip covered with a series of small electrodes called *photosites*. (Figure 3.3) Arranged in a grid, there is one photosite for each pixel in an image. Consequently, it is the number of photosites that determines the resolution of a CCD.

FIGURE *This Kodak CCD is typical of the image sensors found in most digital cameras.*
3.3

Before you can shoot a picture, your camera must charge the CCD's surface with electrons. When light strikes the CCD, the electrons cluster together over the grid of photosites. The more light that strikes a particular photosite, the more electrons that will cluster there. After exposing the CCD to light, your camera simply has to measure the voltage at each site to determine how many electrons are there, and thus how much light hit that particular site. This measurement is then converted into a number by an analog-to-digital converter.

Most consumer cameras use an 8-bit analog-to-digital converter. That is, the electrical charge from each photosite is converted into an 8-bit number - or, a number between 0 and 255. Some higher-end cameras have 10- or 12-bit analog-to-digital converters meaning they can use values up to 1024 or 4096, respectively.

However, an analog to digital converter with a higher bit depth doesn't give your CCD a bigger dynamic range. The brightest and darkest colors that it can see remain the same but the extra bit depth does mean that the camera will produce finer gradations *within* that dynamic range.

The term charge-coupled device (CCD) derives from the way the camera reads the charges of the individual photosites. After exposing the CCD, the charges on the first row of photosites are transferred to a *read-out register* where they are amplified and then sent to an analog-to-digital converter. Each row of charges is electrically coupled to the next row so that, after one row has been read and deleted, all of the other rows move down to fill the now empty space. (Figure 3.4)

FIGURE **3.4** *Rows of photosites on a CCD are coupled together. As the bottom row of photosites is read off of the bottom of the CCD, all of the rows above it shift down. This is the "coupled" in Charge-Coupled Device.*

After all of the rows of photosites have been read, the CCD is recharged with electrons and is ready to shoot another image.

Photosites are only sensitive to how much light they have received. They know nothing about color. As you've probably already guessed, to see color your camera needs to perform some kind of RGB filtering similar to what James Maxwell did. There are a number of different ways to perform this filtering, but the most common is through a *single array* system, sometimes referred to as a *striped array*.

ARRAYS

Consider the images in Figure 3.5.

Figure 3.5a

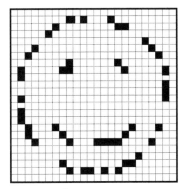

Figure 3.5b

FIGURE **3.5** *Although you have no idea what pixels belong in Figure 3.5a, you can probably hazard a guess as to what the missing pixels are in Figure 3.5b.*

If asked to fill in any "missing" pixels in Figure 3.5a, you'd probably say "What are you talking about?" If asked to fill in any "missing" pixels in Figure 3.5b, though, you probably would have no trouble creating the image in Figure 3.6.

FIGURE *If you were asked to fill in the "missing" pixels in Figure 3.5b, you would probably*
3.6 *come up with an image something like this.*

You would know which pixels you needed to fill in based on the other pixels that were already in the image. In other words, you would have interpolated the new pixels based on the information that was already there. You may have encountered *interpolation* if you've ever resized a photograph using an image editing program such as Photoshop. To resize an image from 4 x 6" to 8 x 10" your image editor has to perform a lot of calculations to determine what color all those new pixels should be.

The single array system used in a typical digital camera uses a form of interpolation to create a color image. As we saw in the previous section, the CCD in your camera is able to create a grayscale image of your subject by measuring the amount of light that strikes each part of the CCD's sensor.

To shoot color, your camera performs the same type of RGB filtering that Maxwell used in 1869. Each photosite on your camera's CCD is dyed with a filter - either red, green, or blue. This combination of filters is called a *color filter array* and most CCDs use a filter pattern like the one shown in Figure 3.7.

With these filters, your CCD can produce separate, incomplete red, green, and blue images. The images are incomplete because the red image, for example, is missing all of the pixels that were covered with a blue filter, while the blue filter is missing all of the pixels that were covered with a red filter. Both the red and blue images are missing the vast number of green-filtered pixels.

To create a complete color image, an incredibly sophisticated interpolation method is used. Just as you used the partial pixel information in Figure 3.5b to calculate the missing pixels, your digital camera can calculate the color of any

FIGURE *To see color, alternating pixels in a CCD are covered with a different colored filter.*
3.7 *The color filter array shown in this figure is called the Bayer pattern.*

given pixel by analyzing all of the adjacent pixels. For example, if you look at a particular pixel and see that the pixel to the immediate left of it is a bright red pixel, the pixel to the right is a bright blue pixel, and the pixels above and below are bright green, then the pixel in question is probably white. Why? As Maxwell showed, if you mix a bunch of red, green, and blue light together, you get white light. (By the way, if you're wondering why there are so many more green pixels than red or blue pixels, it's because the eye is much more sensitive to green. Consequently, it's better to have as much green resolution as possible.)

Needless to say, this type of interpolation is incredibly complex. Figuring out a single bright white pixel is one thing, but calculating all of the subtle shadings required to make a photograph involves a lot of really gnarly algorithms. Differences in these algorithms are just one characteristic that separates the quality of different digital cameras.

This process of interpolating is called *demosaicing* and different vendors employ different approaches. For example, while many vendors' cameras look at only immediately adjacent pixels, Hewlett-Packard cameras analyze a region up to 9 x 9 pixels. Fuji's SuperCCD, on the other hand, eschews the grid pattern of square photosites in favor of octagonal photosites arranged in a honeycomb pattern. Such a scheme requires even more demosaicing to produce rectangular image pixels, but Fuji claims this yields higher resolution.

Other companies use the familiar rectangular design, but use a different color filter array. Canon, for example, uses cyan, yellow, green, and magenta filters on the photosites of their CCD. Because it takes fewer layers of dye to create cyan, yellow, green and magenta filters than it does to create red, green, and blue filters, more light gets through the CYGM filter to the CCD. More light means a better signal-to-noise ratio which produces images with better *luminance* and less noise. Canon cameras do, in fact, produce images with very low noise levels.

 Still more interpolation. *In addition to the interpolation a camera performs to calculate color, some cameras perform still more interpolation to achieve a higher resolution. For example, the Fuji FinePix 4700z has a 2.4-megapixel CCD, but can interpolate the image upward to produce a 4.3-megapixel image. We'll have more to say about this kind of interpolation in Chapter 5.*

CCD's themselves are often very small, sometimes as small as 1/4 or 1/2 of an inch (6 or 12mm, respectively). By comparison, a single frame of 35mm film is 36 x 23.3mm. (Figure 3.8) The fact that CCDs can be made so small is the main reason that digital cameras can be made so tiny.

From smallest to largest:
1⅛" CCD - 5.52mm x 4.14mm
EOS D30 CMOS - 22.7mm x 15.1mm
APS Film - 30.2mm x 16.7mm
35mm Film - 36mm x 23.3mm

FIGURE *Most CCDs are very small, particularly when compared to the size of 35mm film.*
3.8

The only downside to this whole CCD scheme is that it doesn't work right all the time. For example, if too much light hits a particular photosite, it can spill over into adjacent photosites. If the camera's software isn't smart enough to recognize that this has happened, then you will see a *blooming* artifact – smearing colors or flared highlights — in your final image. Blooming is more prevalent in a physically smaller CCD and in higher-resolution CCDs, because the photosites are packed tighter together.

As you might expect, interpolating the color in a camera with millions of pixels on its CCD requires a lot of processing power. Such power (and the memory needed to support it) is another reason that digital cameras have stayed so pricey. A lot of fancy chips are necessary to make a digital camera.

NOTE

Extra pixels. Not all of the photosites in your CCD are used for recording your image. Some of the photosites, for example, are used to assess the black levels in your image. Others are used for determining white balance. Finally, some pixels are masked away altogether. For example, if the CCD has a square array of pixels, but your camera manufacturer wants to create a camera that shoots rectangular images, they will mask out some of the pixels on the edge of the CCD.

"ONE CCD, HOLD THE INTERPOLATION"

The system described above, which is used in most digital cameras manufactured today, is called a single array system because it uses a single CCD to image all three color channels. Although this scheme is the most prevalent, there are other ways of getting a CCD to see color. Many high-end, medium format digital cameras use a *three-shot* array that takes three separate exposures, one for each color. These three shots are then combined into a full-color, RGB image.

Because they use no demosaicing, three-shot arrays are free from some of the artifacts of a single array system. Unfortunately, taking three pictures in succession can take a few seconds, so your subject has to be stationary and your light has to be constant. Consequently, these cameras are only useful for shooting inanimate objects in a studio situation.

A *linear array* system consists of a single row of sensors that make three separate filtered passes over the imaging area. Because there's only one row of sensors used, manufacturers can pack a lot of resolution into the sensor without greatly increasing the price. Obviously, as with a three-shot array, the linear array is only good for studio work. Like the three-shot array, however, no interpolation is used.

Trilinear arrays are a simple variant on the linear array, consisting of three linear arrays stacked on top of one another. With each array filtered separately, the camera only has to make one pass over the image area. However, because of the single pass , some manufacturers have actually been able to create trilinear systems that are fast enough for shooting moving objects.

Finally, some cameras use *multiple arrays*, a collection of three separate CCDs (Figure 3.9). As the light enters the camera, it is passed through a prism that splits the light into three copies. Each copy is sent to a separate CCD that is filtered for a different color. Multiple array cameras have all the flexibility of a single array system, but with none of the interpolation troubles. Unfortunately, because they have three times the number of CCDs as a single array camera, they often cost three times the price.

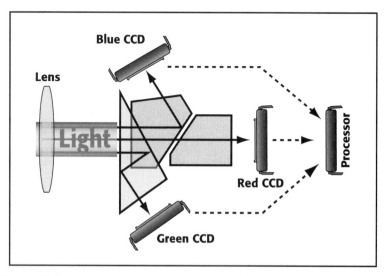

FIGURE **3.9** *In a multiple array system separate CCDs are used to record separate red, green, and blue channels. This system eliminates the interpolation required by single array systems.*

Unless you're planning on spending tens of thousands of dollars, you'll be looking at single array cameras.

SOME ASSEMBLY REQUIRED

The description provided above may sound complicated. In reality, though, the process that a CCD employs to capture an image is even more complex.

First, the light coming through the lens is passed through an infrared filter (some cameras use a very slight infrared filter, making them ideal for infrared photography as we'll see in Chapter 7). After being processed and interpolated by the CCD, the image data (which is now in full color) is passed to an on-board computer that makes a number of adjustments. For example, the image will be adjusted according to your camera's *white balance* and *exposure compensation* settings (we'll discuss these in more detail later).

Next, the camera might apply color adjustments to tweak the image's contrast and brightness. These tweaks often reflect the aesthetics of the camera's designers. For example, Olympus tends to make digital cameras that produce very saturated, contrasty images while Nikon digital cameras often produce images that look a little bit flatter, but are more color accurate.

Finally, many cameras perform some sort of noise reduction algorithm to reduce unwanted noise in your image, and almost all cameras perform some sort of *sharpening*. All of this processing takes place inside your camera, and is one reason that it can take a while for a digital camera to store an image.

NOTE

Raw images. *Some digital cameras, ranging from the prosumer Canon G1 to the high-end Nikon D1, let you download raw, unprocessed data from the camera. This is the information that comes right off the CCD. Through special software, you can specify how the raw data should be processed with full control of white balance, sharpening, and contrast. For the user who demands a high-degree of control this is a great feature. In addition, Raw images are not compressed.*

CMOS

CCDs are not the only type of image sensor available. A few vendors are beginning to work with Complimentary Metal Oxide Semiconductors (*CMOS*) sensors. Because these chips can be manufactured in the same way as most other computer chips, they are much cheaper than the difficult-to-make CCDs found in most cameras. CMOS chips also consume much less power than a typical CCD, making for longer camera battery life and fewer heat problems. CMOS also offers the promise of integrating more functions onto one chip, enabling manufacturers to reduce the number of chips in their cameras. For instance, image capture and processing could both be performed on one CMOS chip, further reducing the price of a camera.

At the time of this writing (Fall, 2000) CMOS is trying to shrug off a lackluster reputation. Known for producing rough images with inferior color, CMOS has not been widely accepted. However, Canon's new EOS D30 is changing that reputation. Priced at $3,000, the camera not only lowers the price of a high-quality SLR digital camera, but its CMOS image sensor produces images with practically no noise, something no CCD camera can do. By the time you read this, CMOS may have made a serious challenge to the dominance of CCD-based cameras.

COMPRESSION AND STORAGE

After your image has been processed, it's ready to be stored on whatever storage medium is provided by your camera. There are currently a number of competing storage options and we'll discuss these in detail in Chapter 5. All of these options have one thing in common, though: they're finite. Consequently, you'll want to make the most use of your camera's on-board storage and the best way to do that is to perform some kind of compression to reduce the size of your images.

To do this, most cameras use a form of compression called *JPEG*. Created by the *Joint Photographic Experts Group*, JPEG is a powerful algorithm that can greatly reduce the size of a photo, but at the cost of image quality. Consequently, JPEG is referred to as a *lossy* compression format.

Most cameras offer two forms of JPEG compression, a low-quality option that visibly degrades an image but offers compression ratios of 10 or 20:1, and a high-quality option that performs a good amount of compression — usually around 4:1 — but without severely degrading your image. In most cases, you'll probably find that any artifacts introduced by the higher-quality JPEG compression are obscured by your printing process. For those of you who are very picky, though, many cameras offer a completely uncompressed mode that stores your images as very large TIFF files.

JPEG compression works by exploiting the fact that human vision is more sensitive to changes in brightness than to changes in color. To JPEG-compress an image, your camera first converts the image into a color space where each pixel is expressed using a *chrominance* value and a *luminance* value.

Next the chrominance values are analyzed in blocks of 8 x 8 pixels. The color in each 64-pixel area is averaged so that any slight (and hopefully imperceptible) change in color is removed. This process is called *quantization*. Note that because the averaging is only being performed on the chrominance channel, all of the luminance information in the image — the information your eye is most sensitive to —is preserved.

After quantization, a non-lossy compression algorithm is applied to the entire image. In the *very* simplest terms, a non-lossy compression scheme works something like this: rather than encoding AAAAAABBBBBCCC, you simply encode 6A5B3C. After quantization, the chrominance information in your image will be more uniform, so there will be larger chunks of similar data, meaning this final compression step will be more effective.

So what does all this mean to your image? Figure 3.10 shows an image that has been over-compressed. As you can see, areas of flat color or smooth gradations turn into rectangular chunks while contrast in areas of high detail gets boosted too high. Fortunately, most digital cameras offer much better compression quality than what you see here.

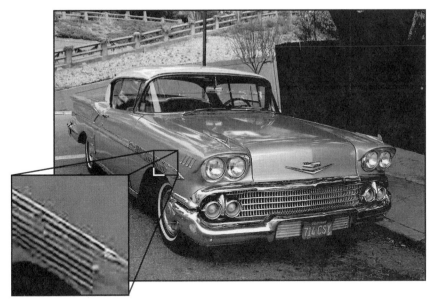

FIGURE   *This image has been compressed way too much, as can be seen from the nasty JPEG*
3.10   *artifacting.*

MEANWHILE, BACK IN THE REAL WORLD

If the information in this chapter seems like a lot of unnecessary gibberish, it's probably because when you buy a film camera you're not used to having to worry about imaging technology. However, if you're serious about photography, you probably do spend some time considering the merits of different films. And, just as you need a little knowledge of film chemistry to assess the quality of a particular film stock, the topics covered in this chapter will help you better test a particular camera.

Your camera is more than just a CCD, of course, so in Chapter 5 you'll learn about the other components and concerns that you'll need to weigh when choosing a camera.

4

Basic Photography: a Quick Primer

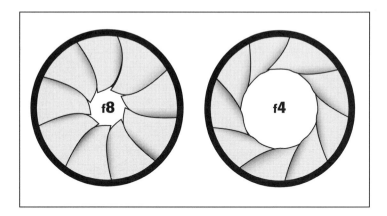

If you slogged through the technical details of the last chapter you've seen how radically different a CCD is from a piece of film. So why do we keep saying that there's really little difference between a digital camera and a film camera? Because no matter what kind of camera you use, the physics of light always work the same way. Consequently, everything from a camera's lens to the method of calculating an exposure works the same way - whether you're shooting digital or film.

In this chapter, therefore, we're going to take a quick trip through the basics of optics, apertures, and exposures. Simply put: to understand most of what will follow in this book, you need an understanding of a few photographic principles. So, if you don't know an *f-stop* from a hole in the ground, you'll want to spend a little time with this chapter. Those of you with more experience will probably be able to skip ahead to Chapter 5.

In its most basic form, a camera is really a fairly simple apparatus. A lens focuses the light from an image onto a focal plane where it is recorded by a piece of film or a CCD. An aperture and shutter placed between the lens and the focal plane allow the photographer to control how much light reaches the focal plane and how long the focal plane will be exposed to that light.

An understanding of lenses, apertures, and shutters is not necessary to take simple snapshots using a modern, fully-automatic camera. However, if you want more creative control over your image, knowing how these systems work together is essential.

LENSES

If the name Willebrord Snell doesn't sound familiar, don't worry, you're not losing your memory; most people aren't too familiar with Snell. Nevertheless, in 1621 he got the ball rolling for digital cameras when he performed the first experiments with *refraction.*

Light travels through space in straight lines. However, when it passes through a transparent object such as water or glass, it gets slowed down and bends, a process called refraction. How much the light bends is measured by the *refractive index* of the transparent substance. Air has a refractive index of 1, water 1.3, and most glass 1.5. In other words, glass bends light more than water.

A lens is simply a piece of transparent material (usually glass or plastic) that has been shaped to bend light in a particular way. A convex lens focuses light inward while a concave lens spreads light rays apart. (Figure 4.1)

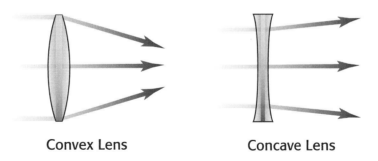

Convex Lens   Concave Lens

FIGURE **4.1** *As you may remember from science class, convex lenses bend light inward, while concave lenses bend light outward.*

Unfortunately, making a perfect piece of glass or plastic for a lens is impossible. Consequently, the surface of a lens may have defects and irregularities that can result in a number of different types of aberrations in the resulting image. Further complicating lens-building matters is the fact that not all frequencies (colors) of light bend the same amount as they pass through a lens. So, a lens might bend red light more than yellow light, resulting in color aberrations (or chromatic aberrations) in your final image.

A camera lens is actually an array of concave and convex lenses that are designed to create a specific magnification (Figure 4.2). As lens designers find aberrations, they add more lenses to the array to eliminate as many problems as they can. Each additional lens is called an *element* and some elements are cemented together to form *groups*. Although you might think that more elements

FIGURE **4.2** *If you look at a cross-section of a camera lens, you will see that it is not actually a single lens, but a complex series of multiple lenses.*

and groups are inherently better because they will remove more aberrations, be aware that each new element increases the chance of reflections within the lens. These reflections will make the lens more likely to create *lens flares* in your final image.

In the next chapter you'll learn how to test and examine a lens to determine its quality.

FOCAL LENGTH

Focal length is a measurement of the magnifying power of a lens. Technically, focal length is the distance (usually measured in millimeters) between the lens and the focal plane, the area upon which the lens is focusing. The higher the focal length, the more magnification a lens will provide. However, as magnification increases, *field of view* decreases. This is best shown with an illustration. (Figure 4.3)

FIGURE *As focal length increases, the field of view decreases. So, a long lens has a very*
4.3 *narrow field of view.*

If you've ever used a 35mm *SLR* camera, then you're probably familiar with a 50mm lens, a lens that provides a level of magnification and a field of view that is roughly equivalent to the human eye (50-55°). A lens with a smaller focal length, 28mm for example, produces a "*wide-angle*" image while "long" lenses – say, 200mm – are considered *telephoto* lenses. That is, they provide a lot of magnification and a very narrow field of view.

ZOOMS AND PRIMES

Prime lenses are lenses with fixed focal lengths. *Zoom lenses*, as you might already know, are lenses whose focal length can be varied. When you "zoom in" on a subject, you are increasing the focal length of the lens. A typical point-and-shoot 35mm camera will have a zoom lens with a range of around 35 to 110mm. (Figure 4.4)

FIGURE *Same image shot with focal lengths of 35 and 110mm.*
4.4

Until eight or nine years ago, it was pretty safe to say that prime lenses were always higher quality than zoom lenses. Advances in design and manufacturing techniques, though, have so improved the quality of zoom lenses that they can now be almost indistinguishable from prime lenses.

EXPOSURE: APERTURES, SHUTTER SPEEDS, AND ISO

As we saw in the last chapter, a CCD – like a piece of film – is sensitive to light. Although not as sophisticated as the human eye, it still takes only a fraction of a second for the CCD to get all of the light that it needs to create an image. By changing the amount of light that falls onto the CCD, you can control a number of characteristics of your final image.

For example, Figure 4.5 contains four different images of the same subject. Each image was shot using a different exposure on a Nikon Coolpix 990. The first image is a straight snapshot with everything in the frame – both foreground and background – in focus. In the second image, we used a different aperture to cause the background to be rendered out of focus, bringing the viewer's attention to the foreground. In the third image, we chose another exposure that enabled us to blur the motion in our subject's hand. Finally, in the fourth image, we chose an exposure that would increase the contrast and color saturation in the image with a little post-processing. (Figure 4.5)

FIGURE *Same subject, different exposure, different resulting images.*
4.5

As with a film camera, if you subject a CCD to too much light, you will have an image that is overexposed. If you overexpose an image enough it will turn completely white. Conversely, if you don't expose the image to enough light, you will have an image that is underexposed. If you underexpose an image too far you will have an image that is completely black. Finding the right exposure is a complex process involving light meters and a lot of theory. We'll discuss exposure in more detail in Chapters 7 and 8.

Your camera has two controls that enable you to change the amount of light that strikes the camera's CCD. You can change the size of the aperture in your camera's lens, and you can control the length of time that the camera's shutter stays open.

The aperture in your camera is usually an *iris* composed of thin, sliding, interlocking metal plates. As you close the iris down to a smaller aperture, it stops more light from passing through to the CCD. The size of the aperture, therefore, is measured in *stops* or *f-stops*. The higher the f-stop rating, the more light your aperture is stopping. So, a lens set on f8 has a smaller aperture than a lens set on f4. (Figure 4.6)

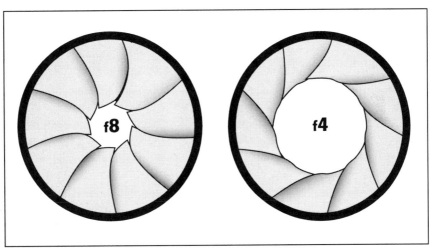

FIGURE   *The iris on the left is stopping more light than the iris on the right, consequently,*
4.6   *it has a higher f-stop value..*

TIP   ***F-Stop Defined.*** *Just in case you're wondering where those weird f-numbers come from, f-stop values are simply the ratio of the focal length of the lens and the diameter of the opening in the aperture.*

RECIPROCITY

Traditionally, each aperture setting on a lens stopped twice as much light as the previous setting. So, a lens typically had a range of f-stop settings that went something like f2, f2.8, f4, f5.6, f8, f11, f16. (The presence of some odd fractional numbers has to do with the fact that apertures are circular, and halving the area of a circle involves some fractional numbers.)

Shutter speeds are simply measurements of how long a shutter is open. Shutter speeds can vary from as fast as 1/16000th of a second to several seconds or minutes. Like apertures, shutter speeds typically double with each setting. So, a list of possible shutter speeds on a camera will often progress as follows: 1/500th, 1/250th, 1/125th, 1/60th, 1/30th, 1/15th, 1/8th, 1/4th, 1/2, 1, 2, 4, 8, etc. (all times are in seconds).

The reason for all of these doubles is very simple. Let's say you are shooting a picture of a very fast-moving race car and your light meter has told you that the "correct" exposure for the image is f16 at 1/60th of a second. (That is, your light meter says you should set your aperture to f16 and your shutter speed to 1/60th.) However, because your subject is moving so fast, you have decided that you want to use a higher shutter speed to guarantee that you will be able to stop the action.

If you increase your shutter speed to the next setting – 1/125th – then the shutter will only be open for half as long and the amount of light hitting the CCD will be cut in half. If your light meter was correct, then your new setting will result in an image that is underexposed. To correct this, you simply open your aperture from f16 to f8. Your aperture is now twice as wide, lets in twice as much light, and compensates for the faster shutter speed. This relationship between apertures and shutter speeds is called *reciprocity* because of the reciprocal relationship between the two values.

Reciprocity is a very powerful function because it means there are any number of different shutter speed/aperture combinations that all yield the same exposure. In Chapter 7 you'll see how different shutter speed or apertures affect your final image. Because of reciprocity, you can select the settings that are appropriate for your creative goals.

Digital cameras and many new film cameras expand on this traditional approach by allowing aperture settings that progress in one-half or one-third of a stop. And, with the electronic, computer-controlled shutters on modern cameras, you can have odd shutter speeds – 1/252nd, for example. We'll cover the uses and implications of these new settings in Chapter 7.

LENS SPEED

Another way to understand a lens is to think of it as a device for gathering light onto the focal plane. Depending on its quality, one lens may take longer to gather the same amount of light as another lens. Simply put, it's going to take more time for the same amount of light to shine through a lens made of murky glass then it will to shine through very clear glass.

The speed of a lens is measured by the widest aperture (and therefore, the most light) that it can gather. So, a lens that can be opened to f2 is a faster lens than a lens that can only be opened to f4. (A lens that can be opened to f2 has better glass and more refined engineering than a lens that can be opened to f4.) Faster lenses enable you to shoot in less light and provide a greater ranger of apertures, and therefore more creative freedom. A faster lens is also more difficult to build and, therefore, more expensive.

Zoom lenses usually have different speeds at different focal lengths. That is, at full telephoto, your lens might have a maximum aperture of f5.6 while at full wide, it might have a faster aperture of f4. Engineering a lens in this way allows lens designers to reduce the size of the front element of the lens, making for a physically lighter, smaller lens.

ISO OR "TRY TO BE MORE SENSITIVE"

Different types of films have different sensitivities to light as measured by their *ISO* rating (ASA is another measure of film speed, but most photographers now use the more common *ISO* system). The higher the ISO rating, the more sensitive the film is to light. Because it is more sensitive, a film with a higher ISO rating doesn't need as long of an exposure to make an image. Consequently, films with high ISO ratings are often referred to as "faster" films. Because faster films need less light to make an image, they facilitate shooting in low-light situations, and offer the ability to shoot in bright daylight with faster shutter speeds and smaller apertures.

The downside to a faster film is that it produces images with far more grain. Although grain can be stylish and attractive, it can also be problematic if you want to enlarge your image a lot, or blow up just a part of it.

The sensitivity of CCDs is also measured and rated using the ISO system. And, as with film, a CCD with a higher ISO rating produces images with more noise. Because the ISO rating on your digital camera can be changed on a shot-by-shot basis, (unlike film, where ISO is fixed for the whole roll) ISO is a third factor that you can control when choosing an exposure.

MOSTLY THE SAME

For the most part, all of the terms and topics we have discussed here apply directly to digital cameras. However, because of differences between film and CCDs and because of features made possible by new digital technology, some of the systems and functions we've discussed in this chapter work a little bit differently in the digital world.

In the next chapter you will build on the basics you've learned here by taking a look at the features and capabilities of the modern digital camera. In the process, you'll hopefully learn how to choose the camera that's right for your needs. In Chapters 7 and 8, you'll learn more about using your camera's exposure controls.

CHAPTER

5

Choosing a Digital Camera

IN THIS CHAPTER

- Basic Anatomy
- CCDs, Resolution, Image Size, and Compression
- Camera Design
- Lenses and Viewfinders
- Exposure Control
- Shooting Modes
- Camera Performance
- Flash
- Playback Options
- Storage and Input/Output
- What's in the Box
- Special Features
- "Enough Already! What Should I Buy?"

45

A good camera doesn't guarantee that you'll take good pictures, but it certainly does help. However, buying a digital camera is a bit more complex than buying a film camera because, in addition to all of the concerns about optics, features, durability, and comfort, you also have to worry about the camera's imaging quality. With a film camera, that's left up to the film. In this chapter you'll learn about all the maniacal little details that must be considered when you are choosing and buying a digital camera.

Digital cameras currently run the gamut from inexpensive ($100) low-resolution cameras, to very expensive ($45,000) digital backs for medium and large-format cameras. Most of the technical details discussed here apply to the entire camera spectrum. For the most part, however, we will be focusing our discussion on the $500 to $5,000 range. In this market, you can find any number of cameras that produce excellent images – and image quality should be your primary concern. Choosing the camera that's right for you involves balancing the features you want with your particular image aesthetic.

BASIC ANATOMY

Just as all film cameras have certain things in common – shutter button, film advance, aperture controls – digital cameras all share some basic external anatomy. Although there are variations in implementation, the anatomical characteristics shown in Figure 5.1 are typical of most of the digital cameras you'll see, no matter what their cost or body design.

CCDs, RESOLUTION, IMAGE SIZE AND COMPRESSION

There are a lot of digital cameras out there, but you can quickly winnow the field by determining how much resolution you need for the type of output you'll be creating (desktop printer, world-wide web, commercial press, etc.). In general, cameras fall into groupings based on the resolution of their *CCD*. So, you'll typically find cameras categorized as sub-*megapixel*, single-megapixel, 2-megapixel or 3-megapixel cameras. Each category denotes a CCD resolution – the higher the pixel count, the greater the resolution.

Obviously, more pixels means more resolution which means more detail which should mean a better picture. However, it doesn't always work this way. The *quality* of the pixels being captured is every bit as important as the *number* of pixels being captured, so resolution alone is not a measure of a camera's quality. Consequently, it's important not to get caught up in the "resolution wars" that many vendors wage with each other. As you'll see, more resolution is not necessarily better.

FIGURE   *Although body designs and feature sets may differ, almost all digital cameras will*
5.1   *share some variation of the features shown here.*

Resolution can be a tricky number because most vendors will make their resolution claims based on the total number of pixels on the camera's CCD when, in fact, the camera doesn't use all of those pixels! For example, Nikon claims that their Coolpix 990 delivers a resolution of 3.34 megapixels. The CCD in the camera *does* contain 3.34 million pixels, but the maximum image resolution that the 990 can actually deliver is 2048 x 1536 pixels, or 3.1 megapixels. (Figure 5.2) Where did the other 240,000 pixels go? Some are masked away to deliver the image proportions that Nikon wanted, while others are needed by the camera for functions such as determining black levels when you are shooting. So, if you're really a resolution stickler, be sure to check the number of pixels being used, or the *effective pixel count.*

Total CCD Area

Actual area used or
"effective pixel count"

FIGURE *The actual number of pixels that a CCD uses is often smaller than the total number*
5.2 *of pixels that the CCD provides.*

CAMERA CATEGORIES

As we mentioned earlier, CCDs can be very small — as small as 1/4". Should
you be concerned about the physical size of the CCD if it packs the resolution
you want? In many cases, yes. Building a lens that can focus onto a very small
area can be difficult, so lens quality becomes more important when the CCD is
very small. When a CCD's pixels are packed closer together, there's a greater
chance of electron spillage and blooming. Consequently, it is *ideally* better to
have a physically larger CCD. Also, a CCD with a larger area sports pixels that
are physically larger. The Nikon D1, for example, has a CCD that is roughly
eight times the size of the CCD found in a Nikon Coolpix 990. Although the D1's
sensor is lower resolution than the 990's, the D1's pixels are 2.5 times the size of
those found on the 990's CCD. This results in a CCD with higher sensitivity, and
a much better signal-to-noise ratio than you'll find on smaller CCDs.

Unfortunately, CCDs are very difficult to make so it's more cost effective for a
manufacturer to create physically smaller chips. The Nikon D1's large (23.7 x
15.6mm) CCD is the main reason that the D1 body sells for $5,000. If you're in
the sub-$2,000 price range, then you're probably not going to have many op-
tions when it comes to CCD size.

Here's what you can expect from each resolution class.

Sub-Megapixel Cameras

For as low as $100, you can find a digital camera that offers a resolution some-
where between 640 x 480 pixels and 800 x 600 pixels. These cameras can provide enough resolution for the web, video, or computer display, but it's

important to realize that they don't provide enough resolution for quality print work.

No matter where your pictures will be displayed, at $100 don't expect great image quality as these cameras sport inferior optics and offer lower-quality image processing. In addition, you won't have any extra resolution to play with, so enlarging an image, or just a section of an image, will be impossible. And finally, it can be very frustrating to take a great picture that's good enough for web display, but that you simply can't get a good print of.

Single-Megapixel Cameras

At the time of this writing there are a number of very good single-megapixel cameras available at very reasonable prices. Single-megapixel cameras typically offer resolutions around 1280 x 960 pixels – enough resolution to print a decent quality 4 x 6" print on a desktop inkjet printer. However, if you want to enlarge the print, or enlarge an area of it, you may find that a single megapixel doesn't provide enough information. Many single-megapixel cameras, such as the Olympus D460Z, now provide a full assortment of "higher-end" features such as *spot meter*s and adjustable ISOs. (Figure 5.3)

FIGURE   *Single-megapixel cameras typically follow the design and features of 35mm point-*
5.3   *and-shoot cameras.*

These cameras are good options for the user who doesn't need to print big prints and who wants flexible controls but doesn't have a lot of money to spend.

2-Megapixel Cameras

With resolutions around 1600 x 1200 pixels, the typical 2-megapixel camera (Figure 5.4) can output a high quality 8 x 6" print on a desktop printer and a 4 x 6" print on a typical offset press. If you have any notions of wanting to print slightly larger prints or perform any kind of commercial printing of your images, then you probably need to opt for at least a 2-megapixel camera.

FIGURE *2-megapixel cameras come in a variety of designs ranging from simple point-and-*
5.4 *shoots to unique LCD-only designs to more full-featured cameras with manual controls and through-the-lens (TTL) viewfinders.*

3-Megapixel Cameras

For those of you itching to print out big 8 x 10" digital glossies on your desktop printer, then you'll want to spend the extra money for a 3-megapixel model. (Figure 5.5) Offering resolutions around 2048 x 1536 pixels, these cameras can provide suitable quality for most commercial printing needs. As we'll see in Chapter 15, some printing technologies will facilitate larger printing than other technologies.

Be warned, however, that at 2- and 3-megapixels, you will likely run into the dreaded "purple fringe" problem. This mysterious artifact (that can be seen in the building shown in Color Plate 5) occurs when you shoot high contrast areas (typically shots into bright light) using a wide-angle lens. Typically, purple fringing only occurs in landscape shots, as these types of images usually contain a broad contrast range and are typically shot with the lens at a wide angle.

Purple fringing is often referred to as chromatic aberration. However, true chromatic aberration (which is caused by the inability of the lens to equally focus all wavelengths of light) would occur in all images, not just in wide-angle, bright light shots. Rather than chromatic aberration, the true cause is simply the small pixel sizes found on most consumer-grade CCDs. Some cameras are better able to handle purple fringing, thanks to more sophisticated on-board image processing.

Although the problem only occurs occasionally, (and can be easily avoided as as we'll see in Chapter 8) purple fringing can be annoying and it can corrupt otherwise okay images. If you know you don't want to print larger than 4 x 6" on a desktop inkjet, then you can avoid the trouble altogether by buying a single-megapixel camera.

The easiest way to test a camera for purple fringing is to shoot at wide angles into a backlit situation such as a window, or through some trees. You probably won't be able to see the fringing on the camera's LCD so you'll need to take the images home and examine them in your photo editing software.

In general, if you want the best detail, the sharpest images, and the greatest flexibility in printing, you'll want to go for a 3-megapixel (or greater) camera.

FIGURE
5.5   *In the 3-megapixel category, you can choose from point-and-shoot, higher-end prosumer cameras or full-blown digital SLRs with removable lenses such as this Canon EOS-D30.*

How much bigger is that extra megapixel? *If you're considering spending the extra money for a 3-megapixel camera, it's worth doing a little math. A 50% increase in the number of pixels in a camera adds only 22.5% more print area. This is the difference between an 8 x 10" print and a 10 x 12" print. So, the extra resolution won't give you substantially bigger prints. If your camera and optics are good enough, it can, however, give you better detail.*

Blowing up your images

With modern imaging software you don't have to settle for the resolution provided by your camera. Through interpolation (also called *resampling*) you can use your image editing software to enlarge your pictures. So, when we say that a typical 3-megapixel camera can print an 8 x 10" picture, we mean that it can do that without any post-processing. You can, of course, print much larger than this by blowing up your images.

However, you can only blow up a picture so far before you begin to see interpolation artifacts. (Figure 5.6) Obviously, the more resolution you have to start with, the better your results. So, if you want to be able to print your images bigger than 8 x 10", then you should definitely go with a 3-megapixel (or better) camera.

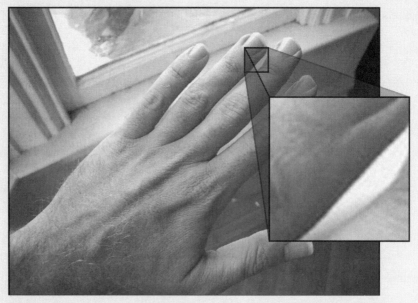

FIGURE *If you interpolate an image up too far, you will begin to see stair-stepping*
5.6   *artifacts, posterization of tones and loss of detail and sharpness.*

Higher Resolution Cameras

If you have the cash, you don't have to settle for a mere 3 million pixels. With super-high resolutions of 6-, 8-, or 10-megapixels, digital camera backs offer digital alternatives to photographers who already have a medium- or large-format camera body. These options are typically very expensive ($10,000-$25,000) and most photographers rent, rather than buy such hardware.

As one would expect, higher resolutions are trickling down to more reasonable prices. The Olympus E10, for example, offers a 4-megapixel CCD in an SLR body for $2,000. For the most part, though, higher-resolution cameras will have a higher price than most users are willing to spend.

Buy some media before shopping. *Because a camera's LCD screen is too small to accurately judge a camera's performance, consider buying your own media card. You can then take the card to your local camera store, use it in a few different cameras, and then examine the results at home. When you do finally buy a camera, you can always re-use the card.*

IMAGE RESOLUTION AND COMPRESSION

Although you may have spent the extra money for a 3.3- or 4-megapixel camera, you may not always want to shoot at full resolution. If your current job is to shoot images for the web (and you're sure you'll never want to print them) then your storage will go a lot farther if you shoot at *VGA* or *XGA* resolution (that is, 640 x 480 pixels or 800 x 600 pixels, respectively) than if you shoot at the camera's full resolution.

For maximum flexibility, you want to be sure that your camera provides a range of switchable resolutions. Most cameras offer at least full-resolution, an intermediate resolution, and two web-quality low resolutions (usually VGA and XGA).

Abandon hope, ye who interpolate here. *Some cameras offer special interpolation modes that produce higher resolutions than the pixel count that their CCDs actually provide. These cameras achieve their results by shooting an image, and then performing an upsample, or interpolation, to produce an image of higher resolution. Unfortunately, these modes all too often produce images with nasty interpolation artifacts. If you want a bigger image than what your camera can provide, it's much better to shoot the cleanest, highest-quality image that your camera can manage, and then sample it up later in an image editor. You'll have more control, will get better results, and your camera's storage will go farther.*

Compression can save a tremendous amount of storage space, but can also adversely affect image quality. Ideally, your camera will offer a range of compression settings from a high-quality JPEG compression, to a really-squeezed, low-quality JPEG compression. For high-quality, you'll want around 3:1 or 4:1 compression.

If image quality is your highest concern, and storage is of little consequence, then you'll want to get a camera that can also store an uncompressed image, usually a TIFF file. While these files are typically huge (9 or more megabytes on a 3-megapixel camera), they will offer none of the compression artifacts of even the best JPEG compression scheme.

Even if you're normally not a stickler for absolutely the best image quality, there are certain conditions that are especially prone to JPEG artifacts. Areas of complex contrast, such as foliage and leaves, as well as areas of broad flat color, such as skies, are often prone to bad artifacting. Having an uncompressed option can be a life-saver if you find yourself shooting under these circumstances.

Finally, when you evaluate a camera's resolution and compression options, pay particular attention to the camera's interface to these features. If you think you will be changing resolutions often, then you'll want to be sure these options are easy to get to, rather than buried beneath a ton of menus.

Some high-end cameras can also store *raw data.* That is, they store the original information that came directly off the CCD. Raw data has several advantages over normal processed data. Remember that your CCD works by taking the data from the pixels on the CCD (which is usually 8, 10, or 12 bits of data per pixel) and interpolating it up to a full 24 bits per pixel. Because raw data has not been interpolated, it's usually significantly smaller than a full, uncompressed TIFF file. For example, a 2048 x 1536 pixel image at 10 bits per pixel comes out to around 3.9mB while a 2048 x 1536 pixel image at 24 bits per pixel comes out to 9.4mB. Some cameras use a *lossless* compressor on their raw data to further reduce its size.

Second, because the raw data hasn't been JPEG compressed, it has no compression artifacts. And finally, raw images are stored *before* the camera performs any internal processing such as color balancing, contrast adjustment, white balance, sharpening, and noise reduction. This frees you to control these processes *after* you've taken the shot, using software provided with the camera. (Figure 5.7)

ASPECT RATIO

The ratio of an image's length to its width is called the *aspect ratio.* Most digital cameras use the same 4:3 aspect ratio that your computer screen and television use, while some higher-end cameras use the 3:2 aspect ratio of 35mm film. (Figure 5.8)

Finally, some cameras, such as the Nikon Coolpix 990, offer a choice of either aspect ratio. (Figure 5.9) However, it's important to note that when you shoot in 3:2 mode, you're simply shooting a cropped version of the camera's native 4:3

FIGURE
5.7 *If your camera provides a Raw data mode, then you can use special software to change parameters such as white balance, sharpening, and contrast after you've shot your image.*

FIGURE
5.8 *Most digital cameras use the same 4:3 aspect ratio as your computer monitor. Other cameras offer the 3:2 aspect ratio of 35mm film.*

ratio. So, when you shoot 3:2, you're shooting lower-resolution images. It's often better to simply shoot 4:3 and crop the image yourself later.

FIGURE **5.9** *Some cameras offer a choice of aspect ratio. Usually, the wider choice is nothing more than a cropped version of the normal 4:3 aspect ratio. Better to shoot full-screen and do the cropping yourself later.*

CAMERA DESIGN

Like any tool, a camera will be of dubious value if it is poorly designed and difficult to use. After you assess your image quality and resolution needs, it's time to start thinking about the camera design that is right for you.

With 150 years of photographic practice behind them, photographers are used to thinking and working in a particular way. However, with the elimination of film – and all of the film-handling mechanics that a film camera requires – it's possible to make a digital camera with a body design and features that film photographers of ten years ago would never have dreamed of. Consequently, camera makers find themselves trying to balance the old against the new. Sometimes the balance works, and sometimes it doesn't.

When you are considering a camera's design, you will be evaluating size, comfort and features. But camera selection also involves trying to find a camera that facilitates your style of shooting. For example, if you're a film photographer, you may be used to SLR viewfinders and so will want a digital SLR. If you're used to the ground glass of a medium format viewfinder, though, you might be biased toward a camera with a good LCD viewfinder. Perhaps you're a sports or nature photographer who needs to be able to shoot at a moment's notice. If so, you'll want to choose a camera that doesn't require a lengthy *boot time* and that offers a good burst mode and a long lens. Or, maybe you take lots of candid "people" shots which will be facilitated by a "split-body" camera that allows for unobtrusive shooting.

Finally, the design of your camera's body influences how easily and quickly you can get to the camera's controls and settings. So, you want a camera whose design makes sense to you and allows you to "feel" your way around without having to take your eye off your subject.

POINT-AND-SHOOT CAMERAS

Many vendors are making digital cameras that follow the design of their 35mm or APS point-and-shoot cameras. Looking little different than their film counterparts, these cameras offer the convenience and familiarity of the point-and-shoot film camera you may already have, and often offer advanced features such as *spot meters* and *macro* functions. (Figure 5.10)

FIGURE *Point-and-shoot digital cameras typically offer the same designs and controls as*
5.10 *point-and-shoot film cameras.*

Point-and-shoot digital cameras range in price from $200-$600 and typically sport *rangefinder* viewfinders. That is, a fixed-focus or zoom lens is used for imaging, while a separate optical viewfinder is used for framing your shot. Most point-and-shoot cameras also offer an LCD screen that can be used as a viewfinder, and most sport reasonably-powered built-in flash units. At the time of this writing, point-and-shoot digital cameras have a maximum resolution of 2.1 megapixels.

The advantage of point-and-shoot cameras is that they're easy to use, while their familiarity makes for quick learning. Point-and-shoot cameras can also be made very small (Canon's S100 Digital Elph is the length and width of a credit card) making them easy to carry anywhere. The downside to these models is that they often lack the features that a serious photographer might want, and their optics are usually not as good as those found in a more expensive camera.

PROSUMER

The more serious photographer will demand more control and better optics than what the typical point-and-shoot camera offers. Although "prosumer" is a loathsome buzzword, it really is the best description of the $500-$2,000 digital cameras that offer advanced features, manual control, and high-quality lenses. (Figure 5.11)

Most prosumer cameras use the same type of rangefinder viewfinders found on point-and-shoot cameras. Vendors typically refer to the rangefinder as the camera's *optical viewfinder*, to distinguish it from the LCD viewfinder that is also usually provided. Because the camera uses separate lenses for the optical viewfinder and for imaging, (Figure 5.12) you will be unable to see the effects of filters and lens extensions when you use an optical viewfinder. In addition, this two-lens arrangement can create *parallax* troubles when you shoot close-up or *macro photography*.

The main drawback to most rangefinder cameras is the generally poor quality of the optical viewfinders provided. We'll discuss viewfinders in more detail later in this chapter.

Prosumer cameras currently offer resolutions from 1.5- to 3.3-megapixels as well as a vast assortment of features ranging from full manual control of shutter speed and aperture to the ability to shoot QuickTime movies. Prosumer camera body designs are incredibly varied, ranging from larger point-and-shoot style bodies to unusual split-body designs that house the lens and CCD in a swiveling compartment that is kept separate from the camera's LCD screen and controls. (Figure 5.13) Such designs can feel very strange to a photographer used to a traditional SLR, but don't rush to discount them. Many of the new, unorthodox designs offer a number of shooting advantages, as we'll see later on.

Mode Selection   Hot Shot

Status Display

Shutter release/
Zoom Control

Flash

Viewfinder
(front)

Focus–assist
Lamp

I/O Ports

Zoom Lens

Viewfinder

Menu Controls

LCD Viewfinder/Screen

Shooting options

FIGURE *At the more-expensive, "prosumer" end, cameras have designs that are similar to*
5.11 *normal point-and-shoot cameras, but that offer many more options such as*
advanced metering and white balance control.

PROSUMER SLR

Some manufacturers offer prosumer *single lens reflex (SLR)* cameras. In an SLR, the viewfinder you look through to frame your shot uses the same lens that your camera uses to make its exposure. (Figure 5.14) Consequently, you can be sure that what you're seeing through the lens is what's going onto the CCD. This approach has several advantages over rangefinder cameras. In addition to a higher-quality viewfinder with better image clarity, you'll also be able to see the effects of any filters you may have placed over the lens. And, when you shoot macro photos, you won't have to worry about the parallax problem found in rangefinder cameras.

FIGURE **5.12** *In a rangefinder camera, the light passing through the camera's lens falls onto the focal plane. The viewfinder uses a completely different light path, meaning that what you're seeing in your viewfinder is not exactly what's landing on the CCD.*

FIGURE **5.13** *Because they don't have to handle film, digital cameras can have very unusual designs, like the split-body of this Sony f505v. Its swiveling LCD viewfinder means you can frame shots from many different angles.*

Most SLRs use a mirror placed in front of the shutter to bounce light up toward the optical viewfinder. When you press the shutter button, the mirror is raised out of the way, the shutter is opened, and the CCD is exposed. The movement of the mirror is what causes your viewfinder to black out when you press the shutter release (with the mirror pulled up, your viewfinder is no longer being fed the light that's coming through the lens). Because digital SLRs have a mirror –

FIGURE **5.14** *In an SLR camera, light passing through the lens is bounced off a mirror and up into the viewfinder. This through-the-lens (TTL) light path ensures that you are seeing the same thing the camera sees. When you press the shutter release, the mirror is flipped up so that the light can pass on to the CCD.*

and, usually, a mechanical rather than electronic shutter – they deliver all of the same visual and audible feedback that a film camera has. In other words, when you press the button, you hear a discernible click, and your viewfinder goes dark for a moment. This can be much more comfortable and familiar than the simple electronic beeps that most rangefinder cameras use to indicate that they have fired.

However, because the light in an SLR is being fed up to the optical viewfinder, you cannot use a digital camera's LCD screen as a viewfinder. As long as the mirror is down, there's simply no light reaching the CCD. (The Olympus E10 gets around this problem by using a *beam-splitter* to feed light to the viewfinder, rather than a pivoting mirror.) SLR cameras are usually more expensive than rangefinder cameras simply because it's more complicated to build a through-the-lens viewfinder. Prosumer SLR models currently run the gamut from $750-$2,000.

LCD-Only Cameras

Eschewing optical viewfinders altogether, LCD-only cameras assume that you would only ever want to use an LCD viewfinder. (Figure 5.15) Available in a range of resolutions and designs, and packing vast arrays of features, these cameras often offer the most radical departures in camera design.

On the downside, because LCD screens tend to hungrily devour batteries, LCD-only cameras are usually great battery hogs. If most of your photography takes you into the wilderness, foreign countries, or other situations where battery charging is difficult or impossible, then an LCD-only camera may not be practical. Also, without an optical viewfinder, you may find shooting in bright daylight to be difficult or impossible with these cameras as direct sunlight can wash out the LCD screen, making it too hard to see images. Finally, many photographers simply never get used to the process of holding a camera at odd angles, or just a few inches from the eye.

FIGURE *Some cameras provide an LCD screen as their only viewfinder.*
5.15

PROFESSIONAL SLR

There are a number of cameras aimed at the higher-end, advanced amateur/professional market. Most of these cameras are built around traditional 35mm film camera bodies, and these units start at around $3,000 for the body. At the time of this writing, the cheapest of these high-end SLR's is Olympus' $2,000 4-megapixel E10 which is a true SLR, but lacks interchangeable lenses.

In addition to superior image quality and the ability to use high-end, professional lenses, these advanced SLRs typically offer other features that the professional photographer needs to have: high frame rates (3-5 frames per second), sturdy body, multiple focus zones, and advanced exposure control. Professional SLRs are also usually much faster than their prosumer counterparts. By accelerating everything from image processing to menu navigation, these cameras are always ready to shoot and are definitely the only viable option for the experienced professional.

"How 'bout using my digital video camera?"

Your digital video (DV) camera probably has a "still" or "picture" mode of some kind. These modes usually record a still image over seven seconds of video-tape or, alternately, record it to a removable flash card. For the user who needs both stills and video, this may seem like an ideal solution.

However, video cameras typically shoot still images that are far inferior to even an inexpensive digital still camera. First off, video has a much lower reso-lution (usually 768 x 540) than a good still camera. Second, the images are usually *interlaced*, meaning they are composed of two alternating, interwoven images (unless your camera has a *progressive scan* mode).Also, if the image is being stored on tape, the image will be compressed using *DV compression*. Third, a video camera is designed and optimized to produce images for the *NTSC* or *PAL* color gamut, color spaces that are more limited than what a dig-ital still camera can produce. Fourth, DV cameras use rectangular pixels so you'll have to correct all of your images to compensate for the change to the square pixels of your computer monitor. Finally, if your camera stores images on tape, you'll face a workflow hassle when you're ready to pull out your im-ages. All in all, it's best to use a video camera for video. Buy a still camera for your still images, unless you're going for a somewhat degraded, video look.

BODY DESIGN AND CONSTRUCTION

Modern cameras can be made out of any number of materials from metal to carbon fiber to aluminum to plastic. (Figure 5.16) Obviously, sturdier materials are more durable (and usually feel better in terms of finish and heft) but even a predominantly plastic body can hold up well.

FIGURE *Although small, Canon's S100 Digital Elph is a very sturdy, all-metal camera.*
5.16

When you are assessing a camera, try to get a feel for the quality of its build. If you lightly squeeze it, does it creak or does it feel solid? A creaky camera might just get creakier – and possibly more fragile – as its screws and joints loosen. If the camera has a split-body, or other unusual design, try to get an idea of the durability of the swiveling mechanism. Will it hold up to normal use, or might it wear out?

Digital cameras can often have strange designs so make sure that your camera sports a finish and moldings that make it comfortable to hold on to and hard to drop. Finger moldings and rubberized components can make an otherwise odd design comfortable to hold.

Doors and port covers can be especially fragile components. Check the battery compartment door and media card door for durability as well as easy access. (Figure 5.17) You'll be using these mechanisms a *lot* so make sure they can stand up to repeated use. And, make sure that you can get to them in a hurry if you need to, as well as when the camera is mounted on a tripod. Rubber or plastic port covers (such as what might go over a battery charging port or a USB port) are often the flimsiest part of a camera. Try to get a feeling for the weaknesses of these covers. Although you won't be able to improve them, they might at least last a bit longer if you are aware of how easily they could be broken off.

FIGURE   *Pay attention to the doors and covers that a cameras uses for its media, batteries,*
5.17   *and ports. You'll be opening and closing these a lot. Make sure they're sturdy and durable.*

Heft is often a concern for more serious photographers. A heavier camera, although a bit of a pain to lug around, is usually easier to shoot with, as extra weight makes for a more stable shot. If you're used to a film camera with a good deal of weight, you may want to look for the same thing in a digital camera.

Finally, try to get an idea as to how much of the camera's body and internal chassis are made of metal. As we'll see in Chapter 9, heat can greatly degrade image quality, and components such as LCD screens and large capacity memory cards can produce a lot of heat. Metal substructures and chassis can serve to dissipate heat that might otherwise affect image quality.

STATUS LCDs

Not to be confused with your camera's full-color viewfinder/playback LCD, is the small status LCD that might be present on the top of the camera. Most modern digital cameras have such a screen for displaying current camera settings and number of shots remaining.

Some cameras skip these displays and assume that you'll simply get this information from the viewfinder LCD. However, if you're in bright sunlight or if your batteries are running low, you may not want to activate your main LCD just to find out if your flash is turned on. And, having a permanent display of camera status makes for faster, more convenient shooting.

Figure 5.18 shows a status LCD from an Olympus C2500, an example of a status display that provides a good amount of information.

FIGURE *You'll want your camera's LCD status display to show at least as many options as this*
5.18 *display from an Olympus C2500.*

HOW TO CHOOSE

In the end, it will most likely be a camera's image quality that wins you over. However, after you've test-driven a few different models, you may find yourself willing to compromise a little bit on quality for the sake of a more comfortable camera.

TRIPOD MOUNT

This may seem like kind of a superfluous item to bring up for discussion (rather like considering what bag you'll choose to carry your camera in) but a poor tripod mount can really ruin your whole day. Any experienced photographer will tell you that there is a difference between a good tripod mount and a bad one. Here's what makes for a goodtripod mount:

- **Metal construction.** A tripod mount is a simple screw socket recessed into the bottom of the camera. (Some tripod mounts also include separate stabilizing holes that can work with higher-end tripods.) If the screw socket is made out of plastic, it can be very easy to strip out the screw threads by forcing the camera in at the wrong angle. Even if you're always very careful, fragile plastic threads can wear out with repeated use. Look for a metal screw mount.
- **Positioned along the lens axis.** Ideally, you want a tripod mount that is positioned so that the camera will pan (rotate) around the axis of its focal plane (Figure 5.19). Such a tripod is required for shooting panoramas.

FIGURE *Ideally, you want a tripod mount that lies on the same axis as the lens.*
5.19

- **Positioned so you can remove the batteries and media.** Typically, once you put a camera on a tripod for a shoot, you want to leave it there. You don't want to have to dismount the camera to change batteries or storage media. Make sure the battery and media doors are unblocked when the camera is mounted.

LENSES

Your camera's lens is where the whole imaging process starts. (Well, actually your light source is where the whole imaging process starts, but let's just forget about that for the moment.) If you have an inferior lens that can't do a good job of focusing light onto the camera's focal plane, then the quality of the camera's CCD and internal processing software won't really matter.

The bad news for digital camera owners is that, because CCDs are so small, the lens on a digital camera has to be of very high quality to effectively focus light onto the small imaging area. The good news is that it's much easier to correct aberrations in small-diameter lenses – which is what most digital cameras have. Consequently, many digital cameras have *very* good lenses.

If you're an experienced photographer who is used to using a 35mm SLR camera with a range of interchangeable lenses you'll probably be disappointed to find that your options for lenses are more limited in the digital camera realm. At the time of this writing, you cannot get a digital camera with interchangeable lenses for less than $3,000. Consequently, unless you've got a lot of money to spend, you'll be looking at cameras with fixed (that is, non-removable) zoom lenses.

As with other features, you should do a little lens testing before you commit to buying a particular camera. The easiest way to test a lens is to shoot some images with it and look for aberrations and image quality troubles. There are a number of different types of lens aberrations ranging from *astigmatism* to *comas* but in a modern, high-quality lens, there are only a few types of aberrations that you need to worry about. When you look for aberrations or image quality issues, be sure to test the lens throughout its zoom range. If the camera offers manual control of aperture, then you'll want to shoot a few more test shots using the biggest and smallest apertures for the lens.

- First, check for general focus and sharpness. How does the lens render fine detail? Does it focus equally from the middle to the edges and corners of the image?
- Chromatic aberrations occur when the camera cannot equally focus all wavelengths of light. Look for slightly blurred or smeared color.
- *Vignetting* is a darkening of the image around the edges, and usually occurs at the extremes of the camera's zoom range. Look for changes in brightness across the image and throughout the zoom range.
- Barrel and pincushion distortion (Figure 5.20) are spatial distortions of your image that work kind of like a fun-house mirror. *Barrel distortion* causes a straight vertical line to be bowed outward toward the edges of the frame, while *pincushion distortion* causes a straight vertical line to be bowed inward toward the middle of the frame. These distortions are more

prevalent at the wide angles of your zoom lens and will definitely occur if you attach a telephoto, wide-angle, or *fisheye* attachment to your lens.

- The contrast produced by a lens may vary when you are using smaller apertures. Try shooting some high-contrast areas using the widest and narrowest apertures of the lens.
- Wider-angle lenses are more prone to lens flares. Zoom the lens to its widest angle and shoot some tests into bright light sources (but never point a camera directly at the sun!) to test for flares.
- Finally, lens quality can also affect color reproduction. If you find that a camera tends to shoot images that are a little "warm" or "cold," the trouble might be in the lens.

FIGURE **5.20** *Although it's slight, this image has a bit of barrel distortion, a slight outward bowing of lines near the edge of the frame. Barrel distortion is usually only visible at the widest angle of a lens.*

It is impossible to eliminate all aberrations in a lens. Your goal in testing a lens is to determine what kind of troubles it has, how bad those troubles are, if you think they will affect the type of shooting that you tend to do, and if you can work around them. For example, all aberrations except for distortions can be reduced by stopping down the lens, and many kinds of distortion can be eliminated using special software.

When you are looking at cameras you'll often see specifications that describe a lens as being *aspherical*. This simply means that the lens is not a perfectly round hemisphere but has some non-spherical elements in it that are designed to eliminate certain aberrations. You might also see that a lens has some sort of *coating* on it which usually serves to reduce reflections and flares.

ZOOM RANGES AND FOCAL LENGTHS

If you have much experience shooting 35mm film, then you probably have a good understanding of the field of view and magnification provided by lenses with particular focal lengths. For example, you're probably used to the idea of a 28mm lens being wide-angle and a 200mm lens being telephoto.

A CCD is much smaller than a piece of 35mm film, and the distance between the lens and the focal plane is usually much shorter. Consequently, the focal length of a lens on a digital camera doesn't yield the same field of view as the same focal length on a 35mm camera. Fortunately, most digital camera vendors are diligent about publishing *35mm equivalencies* when they list focal lengths for their cameras. These equivalencies provide a standard reference point when you compare the lenses of cameras with radically different sizes and body designs. For example, the Olympus C2100 Ultra Zoom has a zoom lens with focal lengths that range from 7 to 70mm. In 35mm equivalencies, though, this equates to 38 to 380mm. Often, vendors will publish a *focal length multiplier* which makes it easy to figure out equivalent focal lengths. For example, the C2100 has a multiplier of roughly 5.4 (70 x 5.4 = 378)

For the photographer who's used to working with super-wide 18 or 28mm lenses, 38mm may not seem very wide. Unfortunately, making a high-quality wide-angle lens of the typically small diameter found on a digital camera is very difficult. So, if you're holding out for a camera with a really wide-angle lens, know that you may have to wait a while. Fortunately, several manufacturers and third-party vendors offer wide-angle and fisheye attachments that clip or screw onto the front of the lens. Although not as high-quality as a dedicated lens, these attachments do provide a workable solution. Similarly, users longing for a powerful telephoto lens can usually find telephoto extenders and adapters for select cameras.

Unfortunately, digital camera makers have adopted a convention started by the camcorder industry wherein zoom lenses are measured using a multiplication factor, rather than by focal range. So, you'll see lenses labeled as "3x" zooms. The problem with this convention is that it doesn't tell you anything about where that 3x range begins and ends. A little research will usually yield the focal length range in both millimeters and 35mm equivalencies.

Finally, some cameras have a fixed focal length, fixed focus lens. Such lenses usually have a wide field of view and a very small aperture, ensuring that everything in the image will be in focus. The advantage to such cameras is that they're easy to use – you don't really even need to look through the viewfinder – and they are usually inexpensive. The downside is that they offer very limited creative control.

"I want my interchangeable lenses!"

It can be difficult for the experienced 35mm photographer to get used to the idea of being stuck with a camera that has only a fixed lens. Yes, this is a limitation – you won't be able to upgrade to higher quality lenses or use lenses you may already have. In addition, the fixed lenses on most digital cameras don't allow for very shallow depth of field. However, despite these caveats, things aren't nearly as bad as they seem.

First, as discussed above, the zoom lenses on most respectable digital cameras (even ones as cheap as $500) are *very* good. In fact, depending on how much money you've spent on your 35mm lenses, the lens on a digital camera might be *better* than what you're used to, thanks to the engineering advantages of making small lenses.

Second, digital cameras that do have interchangeable lenses usually also have image sensors that are a little smaller than a piece of 35mm film. Consequently, because your image area is smaller, you'll need higher-quality (thus "more expensive") lenses than what you would need if you were shooting film. In other words, the lenses you already have may suffer some when they are attached to a digital SLR. And, because of the smaller imaging size, the focal lengths of all lenses will be subject to a focal length multiplier. For example, you have to multiply the focal length of lenses attached to the Canon D30 by 1.6 to determine their 35mm equivalency. All your existing lenses will become more telephoto.

Finally, you might not actually want a detachable lens on a digital camera. Because CCDs are smaller than 35mm film, they are much more susceptible to dust and dirt. By taking the lens off the camera, you expose the CCD to dust particles that can appear in your final image as dark smudges, black marks, or rings. Typically, dust particles are only visible at small apertures, but if you've just spent $5,000 on a Nikon D1, having to avoid small apertures is not an enticing thought.

Because CCDs are charged with electricity, they can develop a static field that makes them attract even more dust. Some theorize that because CMOS chips don't require such a powerful charge, cameras that are CMOS-based are less dust-prone. Only time will tell.

Although you may think "big deal, I'll just be careful when I change lenses" be warned that there are many users who claim that it is impossible to keep dust off the CCD. And, since vendors do not recommend using compressed air inside the camera, cleaning the CCD can be very difficult.

If you've been waiting around for less expensive digital cameras with interchangeable lenses, you might have to wait quite a while. Why not take a more serious look at the quality of the fixed zoom lenses that are already available.

LENS FEATURES

Different camera vendors take different approaches to lens design and it's worth considering a few lens-related points when you evaluate a camera:

- **Does the lens have threads?** A *threaded lens* allows you to add filters, which can be essential for achieving certain types of effects. Some cameras require a special adapter for attaching threaded components. If you're considering such a camera, be sure to add in the cost of the extra adapter and try to determine how easy it is to attach and remove the adapter. Also, find out if you have to remove your attachments before you can remove the adapter, as these actions will make the camera a bit more difficult to use.

- **Are there lens extensions and attachments available?** The lenses on some prosumer cameras can be fitted with special lens attachments that make the lens more telephoto, more wide angle, or even fisheye. (Figure 5.21) If the lens on a camera doesn't offer the focal lengths you want, see if any manufacturer or third-party attachments are available.

- **Does the lens extend and retract?** For the sake of miniaturization, some vendors make lenses that extend and retract when the camera is powered on. Although this is most prevalent in tiny point-and-shoot cameras, there are a number of prosumer cameras, such as the Olympus C3030 and the Canon G1, that also offer extending lenses. Although such lenses allow for a smaller camera, they also make for longer boot and shutdown times, a little bit of battery drain, and require you to remove any filters or lens attachments before you shut down.

FIGURE *Some cameras support special telephoto, wide-angle, or fisheye lens attachments.*
5.21

- **Does the lens come with a lens cap?** Believe it or not, some vendors still don't provide lens caps with their cameras. The theory goes that digital camera lenses are so small that any scratches or abrasions will be tiny enough that the lens will simply focus past them. Although this may be true, the idea of scratching the lens on a $1,000 camera is enough to make most people's teeth itch. If the camera doesn't include a lens cap, make sure you can get a third-party cap that will fit.
- **If the camera has a zoom lens, is its zoom control proportional?** A *proportional zoom control* varies zoom speed depending on how far you push the zoom lens. So, if you push the zoom control just a little way "in" then the lens zooms in slowly. If you press it a long way "in" then the lens zooms in quickly. Proportional zoom controls make it easier to make fine adjustments and to quickly get the lens zoomed to the area you're looking for.

DIGITAL ZOOM

Loosely related to lenses are the *digital zooms* provided by most cameras. Evaluating a digital zoom feature is a very simple two-step process:

Step 1: Turn off the digital zoom feature.
Step 2: Don't ever turn it on again.

That's it! You're done and can now go on to consider other features.

The fact is that most digital zoom features do a terrible job of acting like a zoom lens. Obviously, the camera cannot digitally increase its focal length, so these features work by cropping the image to a smaller area, and then scaling that area up to the full size of the frame. The problem with most digital zooms is that they use bad interpolation algorithms when they scale up, and so they tend to produce jagged, blocky images. Consequently, rather than using a digital zoom, it's much better to shoot the image with your camera's maximum optical zoom, and then crop and enlarge it yourself using Photoshop. This will provide a better form of interpolation as well as give you a good degree of control.

There are two occasions when digital zoom might be useful:

- If you don't have any image editing software that is capable of cropping and upsampling.
- If you don't want to magnify the JPEG artifacts in your image. Because the camera enlarges your image *before* compressing, digital zooms don't worsen any JPEG artifacts. Enlarging in an image editor will.
- If you're shooting at one of the camera's lower resolutions. Most of the time, when you shoot at a lower resolution, the camera simply shoots at full res and then downsamples. Because there's more resolution ot start with, using a digital zoom on a lower-res image often produces fine results.

If you must use a digital zoom feature, you ideally want to have one that offers good interpolation, and one that provides a continuous range of zooming rather than fixed zoom ratios.

FOCUS

Most point-and-shoot cameras and all prosumer cameras offer autofocus lenses. From the user's perspective, these features all work the same way. Using the camera's viewfinder, you place the focusing target (usually the middle of the viewfinder) on the object in your scene that you want to have in focus. When you press the shutter release button halfway, the camera will measure the distance to that object and *lock the focus*; pressing the rest of the way will take the picture.

We'll discuss all of the concerns and practices of using an autofocus system in Chapter 7. When you choose a camera, though, there are a few simple things to look for.

- **Passive vs. Active Autofocus.** Autofocus systems that use a passive *TTL* (*through the lens*) system determine focus by looking through the lens. *Active autofocus* mechanisms employ a separate sensor outside the lens to measure distance; focus is then set accordingly. *Passive autofocus* systems are usually more accurate and have the advantage of working with lens extensions and attachments.
- **Focus assist lamp.** The downside to most passive TTL autofocus mechanisms is that they don't work very well (or at all) in low-contrast situations. A *focus assist lamp* (sometimes called an *autofocus assist lamp*) (Figure 5.22) is a white or red light that the camera automatically shines into your scene when there isn't enough contrast to lock focus. Look for a focus assist lamp that can be deactivated for more distinct shooting.

Focus–assist light

FIGURE   *A focus assist light shines a white or red light into low-contrast scenes to help the*
5.22   *camera's autofocus mechanism.*

- **Number of autofocus steps.** With more autofocus steps, there are more locations that a lens can set itself to in order to get focused. However, as we'll see in Chapter 7, this doesn't necessarily mean the camera will do a better job of focusing.

Continuous Autofocus

Some cameras offer a *continuous autofocus* that constantly refocuses as you move the camera around. The advantage to this mechanism is that when you're finally ready to shoot, the camera might already be in focus. If you're considering a camera with a continuous autofocus feature, make sure it's possible to disable the feature as you may need to occasionally turn it off to save your battery.

Manual focus

Manual focus can be a boon for times when your camera's auto focus mechanism can't lock focus, or when you want to force the camera to focus on something in particular. Unfortunately, because of their designs, most digital cameras don't have an old-fashioned, lens-mounted manual focus ring. Instead, most cameras use a special menu option that requires you to dial in the distance to your subject, or use buttons on your camera to manually focus the lens. Although these controls are okay, the lack of high-quality viewfinders on most cameras can make manual focusing difficult.

At the very least, try to get a camera that has a manual infinity focus lock. This will allow you to lock the focus on infinity, which can be a real time and battery saver when you know you'll only be shooting objects that are far away.

Only recently - with the release of Olympus' E10 - has a camera with a real, manual focus ring (with distance markings) become available for less than $3,000. Hopefully, more vendors will follow Olympus' lead.

SHUTTERS AND IRISES

Your camera's shutter and iris controls allow you to change your camera's exposure to control the depth of field, contrast, and color saturation in your image. While film cameras have mechanical irises and shutters—actual metal, cloth or plastic mechanisms that open and close – digital cameras often use different methods, such as electronic shutters, for exposing the CCD. Rather than having a mechanism that opens and closes in front of the CCD, a camera with an electronic shutter simply turns its CCD on and off for the appropriate length of time. One shutter mechanism is not necessarily better than another, as long as the camera offers the shutter speed control that you need to take the kind of shots you want.

All digital cameras offer an *automatic exposure* feature, which will automatically calculate the appropriate shutter speed and aperture at the time you take a picture. Some cameras, though, also offer manual controls for shutter speed and aperture. When you are assessing a camera's manual overrides, make sure that the camera offers a good range of shutter speeds – ideally ranging from a few seconds to at least 1/500th of a second. It's also nice to have a *bulb mode,* which makes the camera leave the shutter open for as long as you hold down the shutter release button.

As in a film camera, the aperture in a digital camera is controlled by an iris, an interlocking set of metal blades, whose opening can expand or contract to make a bigger or smaller aperture. Many digital cameras, however, only have two apertures, usually f2.8 and f5.6 or f8 and f11. These cameras make up for their lack of aperture options by varying shutter speed. While this configuration doesn't limit the conditions under which you can shoot, it does possibly hobble your creative possibilities. Ideally, you want a camera with more aperture options.

Some cameras, such as the Canon G1, use their iris as a shutter, simply snapping it open and closed to make an exposure. The downside to this scheme is that at higher shutter speeds, the camera may require you to use smaller apertures – f8 on the Canon G1 – since a wider aperture would take too long to close and would prevent the camera from achieving the desired shutter speed. Again, if you want maximum creative flexibility, this sort of mechanism may be too limiting.

VIEWFINDERS

One of the most important features on a camera is the viewfinder. Most point-and-shoot and rangefinder cameras provide both an optical viewfinder – that is, a glass or plastic viewfinder like you'd find on a typical film camera – as well as an LCD screen that can be used as a viewfinder. LCD-only cameras have, obviously, only an LCD viewfinder, while SLR cameras typically have only an optical viewfinder. There are advantages to each type of viewfinder and trying to choose just one can be difficult.

LCD VIEWFINDERS

One of the great advantages of a digital camera, of course, is the built-in LCD screen that can be used to review your images as soon as you've taken them. Most cameras also let you use their LCDs as a viewfinder, displaying a real-time, continuously updated image of what the camera is pointed at.

LCD viewfinders have a number of advantages over optical viewfinders. Because the image on the LCD is coming directly off of the camera's CCD, you get to see a very close approximation of your final image. It's not an exact image because your camera will do some processing (color correction, sharpening, noise reduction, etc.) of the image data before saving. If you're using any lens filters, or lens attachments, though, you'll be able to see their effects on the LCD.

The downside to LCD viewfinders is that images in them can be difficult, if not impossible, to see in direct sunlight. Also troublesome is that LCD screens are very battery-hungry. Most digital cameras use a *thin film transistor (TFT)* LCD screen. When you evaluate a camera's LCD viewfinder, consider the following:

- **How big is the LCD**? Simply put, when it comes to an LCD viewfinder, bigger is better. Most LCDs range between 1.5 and 2 inches (measured diagonally).
- **How bright is the LCD**? Brighter is better as it will make the screen easier to read in direct sunlight. Also, find out if the camera offers a brightness control.
- **How good is the refresh rate**? The frequency with which the camera updates its LCD viewfinder is referred to as the *refresh rate*. A camera with a low refresh rate will deliver a stuttery image in the viewfinder. Low refresh rate can also cause smeared color artifacts and lower resolution. Simply put: an LCD with a slow refresh rate can make it difficult to see and frame the shot you want.
- **How does the LCD viewfinder perform in low light**? If you plan on doing a lot of night shooting, you'll probably need a camera with both an LCD and an optical viewfinder, as there's a good chance that images in your LCD screen will simply appear black in low-light situations. Some cameras such as the Agfa ePhoto 1680 offer a special "high gain" mode on their LCDs that make images visible — although noisy — in low-light.
- **How good is the coverage on the LCD**? Most LCD viewfinders show an image that is 95-98% of the image that will actually be shot. Any less than this should be considered a liability.
- **Does the LCD have an anti-reflective coating**? These can make a big difference when you are shooting in bright sunlight, as they'll greatly cut down on glare on the LCD.

At the time of this writing, the best LCD viewfinder belongs to the Canon G1. In addition to its excellent quality and glare-reduction coating, the G1 features a great swivel design that lets you flip the LCD out away from the camera. The LCD can be quickly and easily rotated to just about any viewing angle, and then safely stored against the camera's body (Figure 5.23). In this regard, the G1 viewfinder is very similar in flexibility to a swiveling design such as the Nikon Coolpix 990. Such a swivel makes it possible to shoot self-portraits, over-the-head shots, and low angles without having to twist, crouch, or crawl on your stomach. For these reasons, swiveling LCDs are ideal for *macro photography*.

FIGURE *The LCD screen on the Canon G1 can tilt and swivel into many positions, making it*
5.23 *easier to shoot with the camera at different angles.*

Viewfinder hoods. *Although the quality of LCD viewfinders has
greatly improved, images in them can still be difficult to see in
bright sunlight. Special hoods that fit over the LCD screen, such as
the Hoodman (www.completedigitalphotography.com/hoodman)
offer a simple, portable solution for reducing glare in direct sunlight.*

OPTICAL VIEWFINDERS

Most point-and-shoot and rangefinder cameras include some sort of optical
viewfinder. Unfortunately, most vendors don't choose to put much effort into
their optical viewfinders so you won't have a lot of options when you shop
around. When you are testing an optical viewfinder, check for simple issues
such as clarity and distortion. Does the viewfinder provide an image that is clear
and easy to see? Most cameras also include one or two status lights within their
optical viewfinders – one to tell you that the camera has focused, and another to
tell you that the flash is ready. Make sure that these lights are easy to see within
the viewfinder and that they are visible in bright daylight.

You'll also want to be sure that the viewfinder provides some kind of focusing target such as *crosshairs*, and if you'll be doing a lot of macro photography,
then you'll probably want some parallax guides (Figure 5.24).

Unfortunately, the rather cheap optical viewfinders on most cameras don't
provide very good coverage. That is, they don't show you the same field of view
that the camera's lens is seeing. On average, an optical viewfinder will display
about 85% of the final image, although some can go as low as 65% or 70%!

FIGURE **5.24** *When you shoot at close range, what you see through a rangefinder's viewfinder is not what your camera will actually shoot. Parallax guides give you an indication of where the real edges of the image are. The image on the left in Figure 5.24 shows the view through the viewfinder while the image on the right shows the resulting picture. Notice that the parallax lines allow us to frame the left side of the image, even though we can't see the right side (because we're too close to our subject). If a camera's viewfinder is above the lens, rather than next to it, then the camera will exhibit parallax shift vertically, rather than horizontally.*

(Figure 5.25) By comparison, the LCD viewfinder in a typical high-quality SLR film camera delivers about 95% coverage.

85% Coverage
(Typical optical viewfinder)   **95% Coverage**
                                          (Typical LCD viewfinder)

FIGURE **5.25** *The LCD viewfinders on most digital cameras offer an almost complete view of the image that will be captured. The optical viewfinders on most point-and-shoot and prosumer cameras offer much lower coverage.*

Because they're displaying a smaller-than-actualsize image, you don't have to worry about accidentally cropping something out of your frame, but you will have to crop your image later. Also, since you have limited resolution in your camera, optical viewfinders can be frustrating in that they don't allow you to make the best use of the pixels at your disposal.

Finally, if you wear glasses, look for a *diopter* adjustment next to the optical viewfinder. (Figure 5.26) This is a small wheel that allows you to adjust the optical viewfinder to keep it in focus.

Diopter Control

FIGURE *A diopter wheel lets you adjust your optical viewfinder to compensate for your own*
5.26 *vision.*

LCD OPTICAL VIEWFINDER

Just to complicate things even further, some vendors are now including optical viewfinders that aren't really optical. Rather, they use a tiny LCD screen just like you'd find in the viewfinder on a video camera. Sometimes called *electronic TTL viewfinders*, these mechanisms have the advantage of showing you the exact same thing that you'd see on a larger LCD viewfinder. So, in addition to better coverage than you'd get from a typical optical viewfinder, you also get the status and menu displays that you'd see on a large LCD viewfinder. Because you look at them through an eyepiece, though, they're easily visible in bright daylight. However, their grainy displays make it difficult to see small detail and nearly impossible to manually focus. Although better than the optical viewfinders found on most digital cameras, they're no substitute for a true, high-quality, optical TTL viewfinder.

SLR VIEWFINDERS

As you saw earlier, the advantage to an SLR viewfinder is that, while a rangefinder uses separate lenses for framing and shooting, an SLR lets you look through the same lens that is being used to shoot the actual image. For this reason, SLR viewfinders are sometimes referred to as through-the-lens or TTL viewfinders. Another advantage of the TTL approach is that you end up with an optical viewfinder that shows a very accurate view of what the final image will look like. In addition to providing better coverage (sometimes as high as 95%) than a rangefinder, SLR viewfinders let you see your image through any filters or lens attachments you may have installed. SLR viewfinders also feel very familiar if you've spent a lot of time with a film-based SLR because they provide the same visual and audible feedback.

SLR viewfinders are most prevalent in the $2,000 and up range of cameras, where you find digital cameras based on professional film-camera bodies. In the under-$2,000 price range, the SLR pickings are slimmer, but there are still a number of good cameras to be found, such as Olympus' E10 and C2500 models.

When you are assessing the quality of an SLR viewfinder, you want to examine the same image and optical qualities that you would look for in any other type of viewfinder. In addition, pay attention to the readouts and displays that are present. Ideally, you want a viewfinder that displays all of the camera's salient settings. (Figure 5.27) After all, when you're framing a shot, you don't want to have to move your eye from the viewfinder to find out whether your flash is turned on. Figure 5.27 shows items you should see in a viewfinder display.

The Frame-Up

The type of viewfinder that you choose will have a substantial impact on your photographic experience. If you're used to a traditional SLR, then you're probably accustomed to holding the camera up to your eye, blocking out the rest of the world, and concentrating on your image. Consequently, using an LCD viewfinder – where you typically hold the camera away from your eye – may take some getting used to. However, if you're a long-time user of medium format cameras that provide ground glass viewfinders on the top of the camera, then an LCD screen might feel very familiar.

These are two very different approaches to framing an image and it's important to consider how you like to work. Ideally, it would be nice to have both high-quality optical and LCD viewfinders. Unfortunately, we have yet to see a camera that delivers both of these options for less than $2,000.

Shooting mode   Aperture   Shutter speed   **Exposure Compensation**

P F2.8 1/320 +0.3

Zoom level   Images remaining   Focus target

FIGURE *Ideally, you want the viewfinder of an SLR to display all of the camera's exposure*
5.27 *settings. This image shows the viewfinder from an Olympus C2100 UltraZoom.*

EXPOSURE CONTROL

Exposure, that combination of shutter speed, aperture size, and your ISO settings, not only determines whether an image will be bright or dark, but is how you control everything from which parts of the image are in focus, to how saturated the colors are and how much detail is present. Of all the features on a camera, good exposure controls are the most important. Consequently, it's essential to take a good look at them before you buy.

WHITE BALANCE

White balance is not actually part of the exposure process. However, because it's a parameter that you'll want to consider right before you shoot, we're going to discuss it alongside exposure controls. The sooner you get in the habit of remembering white balance, the better off you'll be.

White balancing is the process of calibrating your camera so that it can correctly interpret colors under the type of light in which you're shooting. We'll discuss white balance in great detail in Chapter 7. When you are assessing a camera, though, there are some simple things you'll want to consider.

- In addition to an automatic white balance control, does the camera offer separate settings for daylight, fluorescent, and tungsten? Some systems provide white balance presets that are measured in degrees Kelvin (5500°K, for example). This is fine as long as you know which *color temperatures* relate to which kinds of light.
- For maximum flexibility, you'll want a manual white balance control that lets you set white balance for your particular situation by focusing the white balance system onto a white object. Make sure these controls are easy to get to, as you'll be using them often.
- Does the camera use a TTL white balance system or an external white balance sensor? Ideally, you want a TTL white balance system for better accuracy.

Finally, you'll want to take a look at the quality of the camera's white balance. Take some sample pictures using the appropriate white balance settings and check for odd color casts. Chapter 7 will give you a better idea of what to expect when white balance goes wrong.

METERING

Whether you're shooting on full automatic, or calculating your exposures by hand, if you don't have a decent light meter, you'll end up with the wrong exposure. The modern light meter is an incredibly sophisticated device and many camera vendors have not scrimped on adding high-caliber, state-of-the-art metering systems to their digital cameras.

Arguing which company's metering software is better is a discussion that is far too technical for this book. Fortunately, metering systems from companies such as Nikon and Olympus come with years of refinements and redesigns. However, you'll probably find that metering systems from different companies have different characteristics and tendencies. Some may consistently meter shadows well while others may excel at mid-tones or highlights. The good news is that a meter's tendencies will usually be consistent, meaning that over time you will come to learn how your meter will handle specific situations.

Most higher-quality cameras include a selection of different metering modes. These typically break down into variations of the following categories:

- **Matrix (sometimes called Multi-Segment).** A *multi-segment (matrix) metering* system divides the imaging area into a grid, or matrix and meters the light coming from each cell. These readings are then analyzed and averaged to calculate the ideal exposure for the shot.
- **Center-weighted metering** A variation of matrix metering, *center-weighted metering* also divides the image area into a grid, but lends more "weight" to the readings from the middle of the image.

- **Spot metering** A *spot meter* reads only a single area in your image, usually the center. Spot meters allow you to do everything from simple backlight compensations to complex *zone system* metering.

As with white balance sensors, you want a camera that uses TTL metering rather than a meter that's external to the lens. With an external meter, your camera will not be able to accurately account for any filters or lens attachments that you may be using.

There is no one "right" metering system. Fortunately, most cameras include some mix of the three systems described above. To test them, try shooting in complex lighting situations (dark foreground with a bright background and vice versa; darkly shadowed areas; and areas with lots of bright highlights) and see how the camera chooses to meter. Does it preserve shadows? Does it blow out highlights? And, most important, does it do these things consistently? Before testing a metering system, it would be a good idea to read the metering and exposure sections of Chapter 7.

EXPOSURE COMPENSATION

To quickly sum up: exposure compensation controls let you force the camera to over- or underexpose by a certain number of stops (or fractions of stops) without having to worry about actual apertures and shutter speeds. Tell the camera to underexpose by half a stop and it will find a way to do it. These controls are powerful and will often be the only exposure controls you'll need to use.

When you are evaluating a camera, take a quick look to see how these controls are implemented. You'll be using them a lot, so make sure they're easy to use. Second, make sure they allow for at least two stops of adjustment in both directions. Most controls let you adjust in 1/3-stop increments.

ISO CONTROL

One of the great advantages of a film camera over a digital camera is that you can change your recording medium (the film). Although ripping out your digital camera's CCD and replacing it with a more sensitive chip is hardly practical, many cameras do offer an option to change the "speed" or sensitivity of their CCD using the same ISO measure that film photographers use.

Most digital cameras have a standard ISO rating somewhere between 80 and 110. These cameras have a light sensitivity that is roughly equivalent to film rated at 100 ISO. Some digital cameras allow you to increase their ISO rating, typically offering a choice of 100, 200, or 400. The Canon G1 and Pro90 offer a slower ISO 50 speed, while some higher-end cameras can go as high as 1600 ISO! These faster, more sensitive modes allow you to shoot in lower light without using a flash (which is ideal for concerts or other situations where a flash is inappropriate) and allow you to use faster shutter speeds and smaller apertures in bright daylight. However, just as faster film produces grainier images, higher ISO settings in a digital camera produce images with a lot more noise.

The ideal camera is one that provides an automatic ISO mechanism (that is, it automatically selects a faster ISO feature when there is not enough light) as well as allowing manual selection of ISO. Be sure to look at images shot with different ISOs to get a sense of how noisy the camera becomes at higher speeds.

EXPOSURE LOCKS AND PANORAMAS

Panoramic shooting is a great way of shooting broad vistas without having to spring for a fancy wide-angle adapter. Although you may have experimented with shooting panoramas with your film camera, your digital camera is a much better tool for creating collaged (panoramic) images, thanks to powerful stitching software that you can use to process your images.

We'll discuss panoramic shooting in more detail in Chapter 9. When you buy a camera, it's worth trying to get a camera that has a *panoramic* or *exposure lock* mode. Exposure lock simply means that, after you take the first image, the camera locks its exposure and shoots the rest of your panoramic series using those same settings to ensure even exposure across the whole image.

Some cameras, such as the Canon S100 Digital Elph, offer a special *stitch assist* mode that provides excellent visual cues to ease panoramic shooting. These modes often work with special software that can automatically stitch an image as it's transferred to your computer. Although such automation is nice, it's not required for high-quality panoramic shooting.

Exposure lock can also be handy in normal shooting situations when you want to spot meter off of one part of an image, and then reframe your shot. Although most cameras can do this just by pressing the shutter button, they will lock focus as well as exposure. A dedicated exposure lock lets you independently control exposure and focus.

PRESET EXPOSURE MODES

A number of cameras include special preset exposure modes designed for shooting under specific conditions. These modes don't do any kind of magic processing or anything; they simply favor – or lock the camera into – particular apertures and shutter speeds that are appropriate to certain situations. Most cameras with this feature include variations on the following modes:

- **Landscape.** Cancels the flash, locks focus on infinity, and typically uses as small an aperture as possible, for maximum depth of field.
- **Portrait.** Favors wider apertures to produce a more blurred background.
- **Pan-focus.** Intended for times when you need really fast shooting. Focal length is locked on full wide, focus is locked on infinity. Essentially turns your camera into a speedy, fixed-focus camera.

- **Fast shutter.** (Sometimes called "sports"). Forces a large aperture to facilitate a fast shutter speed.
- **Night.** (Sometimes called "slow sync"). Uses slow shutter speeds for dimly-lit scenes and typically fires the flash to provide some foreground illumination. Many cameras let you choose whether to fire the flash at the beginning or end of the exposure.

If you're already used to thinking in terms of appropriate aperture and shutter, then you'll probably just use your camera's manual functions to achieve the exposure effects you need. If your camera doesn't have manual controls, though, preset exposure modes may be the only manual choices you'll have.

SHOOTING MODES

In the old days (circa 20 years ago) of film cameras, you had to pay a lot of extra money to get a camera that offered completely automatic operation. Now, every digital camera offers complete automation and you tend to have to pay a lot of money instead for a camera that offers any manual controls.

PRIORITY MODES

Since it's a given fact that a digital camera will have a fully automatic mode, you'll want to spend a little time investigating a camera's other shooting modes. For maximum creative control, you'll want to have at least one of the following shooting modes in addition to the camera's automatic mode.

- **Aperture priority.** *Aperture priority mode* lets you select the aperture you want to use, leaving the selection of an appropriate shutter speed up to the camera. When you are looking at a camera's aperture priority mode, pay particular attention to the range of f-stops available. You want an aperture priority control that will let you pick any of the camera's possible apertures.
- **Shutter priority.** *Shutter priority mode* is just the opposite of aperture priority mode. Pick a shutter speed and the camera will automatically select the right aperture.
- **Manual.** In true *manual mode*, you get to set both the aperture and shutter speed, giving you full control over the camera's exposure. When you are checking out the manual mode on a camera, be sure that the controls for both aperture and shutter speed are easy to use and convenient. You don't want to miss a shot because you couldn't figure out how to change the camera's aperture, or because it took too long to set the shutter speed. Also, make sure the camera displays some sort of meter reading while you're changing your settings; otherwise, it will be impossible to know if you're over- or underexposing.

Fortunately, most higher-end prosumer cameras, and all higher-end professional cameras, offer all four shooting modes so you probably won't have to skimp on these features. Just make sure the controls are implemented to your liking.

IMAGE BUFFERING

As you'll recall from Chapter 3, after a digital camera exposes its CCD, the image data is passed to a special on-board computer for processing. After it is interpolated for color, white balanced, sharpened, and de-noised (among other things) the data is compressed and then stored on the camera's storage device. All this processing can take a lot of time, which means that your camera can be too busy to take any more pictures. Digital cameras of just a few years ago often required 5-10 seconds between shots to allow the processor time to do its job.

Fortunately, most higher-end cameras now include special memory buffers (and sometimes separate processors) to handle the processing of an image, which frees up the camera to shoot again immediately. When you evaluate a camera, make sure that the *image buffer* can hold at least five or six full-resolution shots. Odds are you won't be shooting more than that in quick succession, but if you are, you'll need to use a special "continuous" shooting mode.

CONTINUOUS SHOOTING

Most higher-end prosumer cameras offer special modes for shooting a rapid series of images. With speeds varying from a single frame to 2.5-3 frames per second, these features are ideal for shooting sports, fast moving objects, or any subject where you want to record a simple motion.

Referred to as *burst, continuous* or *drive mode*, continuous shooting modes usually work just like an autowinder on a film camera. Just press the shutter button, hold it down, and the camera will shoot as quickly as it can. (Figure 5.28)

Note that some cameras can only achieve their full burst speed when they are shooting at a lower resolution. If you want full print quality from your burst images, make sure your camera's continuous mode supports the full resolution of your camera. Note, too, that some cameras can only shoot up to a certain number of shots before they have to stop and flush the series of images out to storage. Be sure to investigate the maximum number of burst shots that can be taken at once.

FIGURE *If your camera has a drive mode, then you can shoot a sequence of shots in rapid*
5.28 *succession. Not all cameras support burst shooting at full resolution.*

Continuous flash shots. *Most cameras can't use a flash when shooting in continuous mode, as there isn't enough time for the flash to recharge. At the time of this writing there is one camera, the Canon G1, that can manage a frame per second in continuous mode while it is firing the flash. If you have a job that needs continuous flash shots, this may be the camera for you.*

MOVIE MODE

Starting with the 3-megapixel generation, many digital cameras now offer the ability to shoot little QuickTime movies. And when we say little, we mean little – both in area (320 x 240 pixels) and duration (sometimes a maximum of 20 seconds).

Most movie modes work the same way: you simply press the shutter button and the camera begins recording; press it again and recording stops. With resolutions limited to 320 x 240 pixels, such movies are really only good for web posting or just playing around.

Because movies – even 320 x 240 movies – quickly generate a lot of data, your camera can't shoot, compress, and store a movie on the fly. So, most digital cameras record video by storing the video frames in the camera's internal memory buffer (the one that buffers full-resolution images to increase shooting speed). When the buffer is full, the movie is dumped to the camera's storage card. Consequently, the length of individual movies is not determined by the size of your media, but by the size of the camera's internal buffer. Most cameras can shoot movies of 20 to 30 seconds.

Note that it can take a while to flush the buffer out to the card – sometimes 30 or 40 seconds – so you can't just keep hitting the button after each movie to immediately start another one.

When you are assessing a camera's movie mode, your main concerns are the maximum duration of an individual movie and whether or not the camera can record sound. Although these movie modes can be fun, they chew up storage like crazy and produce low-resolution, short movies. The fact is, if your video needs are at all serious, you'll need to buy a video camera.

BLACK AND WHITE

Many digital cameras offer special black and white modes for shooting grayscale images. Because you can use your image editing program to convert a color image to grayscale, you might wonder why you would want to shoot in black and white? After all, isn't it better to shoot in color and have the *option* of black and white later?

The advantage of a dedicated black and white mode is that the camera skips the color interpolation process that it would normally go through. In other words, instead of having to make up a bunch of data (as we saw in Chapter 3), a black and white image can use the full, un-interpolated resolution of your camera's CCD.

A black and white mode is essential if you want to perform zone system black and white photography using your digital camera. We'll discuss black and white photography and color to black and white conversion in more detail in Chapter 9.

SELF-TIMERS AND REMOTE CONTROLS

At some point, you've probably owned a film camera that had a self-timer on it. You know: you set the timer and then run as fast as you can to try to get in the shot and look natural in the five seconds or so that you have before the camera fires. Most digital cameras have the same sort of feature.

Some cameras also offer a wireless remote control that provides zoom and shutter controls. These remotes not only facilitate self-portraits, but also serve as a shutter release for long-exposure images. If remote operation is important to you, consider the following:

- What's the range of the remote? Make sure it's long enough for your typical remote shooting jobs.
- Ideally, you'll want to have an infrared sensor on both the front and back of your camera.
- If you will be using your camera to run slide shows (through its video out port) then you'll want remote playback control as well as shooting control.

FIGURE   *A wireless remote control lets you shoot hands-free, just as you would with a cable*
5.29   *release on a film camera.*

CAMERA PERFORMANCE

Great image quality doesn't do you any good if your camera is too slow to get the shots you need. Because a digital camera must do so much calculating and processing to create an image, it's easy for it to get bogged down in ways that film cameras can't. You'll *definitely* want to consider the speed and performance of a camera before you buy one. In addition to the speed of the menuing system, be sure to consider and measure the following:

- **Boot time.** How long does it take the camera to boot itself up. Ideally, you'll want a camera that doesn't need more than three or four seconds of preparation from the time you switch it on. More than this, and you may miss a shot. Check to see if the camera offers a low-power sleep mode, and test how long it takes the camera to wake up. Leaving your camera in sleep mode will help ensure that it's always ready to shoot, although sleep mode can drain your batteries. One of the downsides to cameras with an extensible lens is that they take a while to boot up. In addition, you may not feel comfortable walking around with the camera in sleep mode, as the lens will still be extended. However, if you shut the camera down to retract the lens, you'll be forced to wait through a boot cycle when you're ready to shoot again.

- **Prefocus time.** When you press your camera's shutter release halfway down, the camera will perform all of its autofocusing as well as its metering and white balancing (we'll discuss this *prefocusing* step more in Chapter 7). When you test a camera, try to get a sense of how quickly it can perform these prefocusing steps.

- **Shutter lag.** Some digital cameras still have a noticeable lag between the time you press the shutter release and the time the camera actually takes a picture, even if you've already prefocused. If the *shutter lag* is long enough, you might miss that moment you were trying to capture. This is probably the most important performance characteristic to assess before you buy.

- **Recycling.** Be sure to check how long it takes the camera to *recycle* itself after you get a shot. Ideally, you'll want to be able to shoot again immediately. Most modern cameras can recycle right away by storing the previous image in a memory buffer. When the buffer is full, you'll have to wait for it to flush out to the storage card. Be sure to test the camera's performance both before and after the buffer has filled.

FLASH

No matter what level of camera you're considering, most units will have a built-in flash. Obviously, bigger cameras will have a larger, more powerful flash unit, but even small cameras can offer good flash hardware.

Flash photography is one of the most difficult things for any camera to handle and digital cameras are no exception. Consequently, it's important to carefully evaluate a camera's flash system before you buy.

There are a few simple issues to clarify right off the bat:

- **What is the range of the flash?** Because of their small size, most built-in flashes only have a range of around 10-15 feet. Although this is fine for most snapshot situations, for more serious work you'll need additional lighting.
- **Does the flash have a hot shoe or external flash sync connection?** For maximum flash flexibility and control, you want a *hot shoe* for connecting an external flash. (Figure 5-30) These standard connections are usually designed to work with specific flash units made by the manufacturer. Make sure that the camera offers TTL metering with the hot shoe. If the camera doesn't have an actual hot shoe (or is too small to have one) then look for a connection for an *external flash sync*. This will allow you to connect an external flash (again, usually a specific model) to the camera using a small cable. You'll usually need to buy some kind of bracket to hold the flash.

FIGURE **5.30** *For serious flash work, you'll want a camera with a hot shoe or external flash sync connector.*

- **Where is the internal flash positioned?** Ideally, you want a flash that is as far from the lens as possible. If the flash is too close to the lens, the camera will be far more susceptible to the red-eye effect. We'll discuss this in more detail in Chapter 13.

- **What flash modes does the camera offer?** Look for a camera that offers a completely automatic mode – wherein the camera decides when to use the flash – a *force flash* or *fill flash* mode, which allows you to force the flash to fire to provide a slight fill light, and a *red-eye reduction* mode which reduces the chance of red eye in your image by first firing a short flash to close down the irises in the eyes of your subject. Many cameras also offer a *slow sync* mode which lets you combine flash photography with long shutter speeds to create cool motion blur effects. Be sure the camera lets you specify whether the flash fires at the beginning or end of the exposure. And, of course, you want the ability to turn the flash off altogether.

- **Does the camera offer control over flash intensity?** Many cameras let you control how strong the flash will be by specifying more or less power, usually measured in f-stops, or fractions of a stop. Given the difficulty that many cameras have with flash metering, this manual override can be essential to getting good flash photos.

In addition to the physical specifications of the camera's flash, you'll also want to assess how well the camera meters and white balances when you use the flash. The best test of a flash's performance is to shoot pictures of people's faces indoors under a slight mix of lighting. Because the human eye is so accustomed to flesh tones, it's very easy to spot when a camera is doing a poor job of reproducing them.

Look at the overall exposure of your image. A poor flash system will overexpose the highlights, resulting in bright white smears instead of smoothly-gradated highlights. Skin tones will often go pale or wash out when they are shot with a less-capable flash system. A flash that is too bright will also cast harsh shadows across and behind your subject.

Look at the overall color tone of the image. Is there a color cast of some kind? If you're in a room with strong lights (usually incandescent, or tungsten, lights) your camera may choose to favor those lights when it white balances, resulting in an image with slightly blue highlights. If your image ends up with a slight yellow cast to its highlights, then it probably favored the on-board flash when it was white balancing.

If your camera has a special manual white balance setting for use with a flash, be sure to switch to that setting and try a few shots. You may find that it corrects any color casts that occur with automatic white balance.

PLAYBACK OPTIONS

You'll be spending a lot of time reviewing images using your camera's playback options, especially when you're in the field. Consequently, it's worth taking a little time to explore a camera's playback features. Are they easy-to-use? How quickly can you switch from record to playback mode?

In addition to general usability, look for the following features:

- A *thumbnail* view that lets you view multiple images on-screen at once. This can greatly speed navigation of a large media card (Figure 5.31)

FIGURE **5.31**   *A thumbnail view lets you quickly see the contents of your media card. Some cameras also allow you to zoom in to an image, making it easier to check focus and depth of field.*

- Zoom features that let you zoom in on an image and *pan* around. A good zoom feature can be a great way of ensuring that a shot was in focus. Most cameras include a number of preset zoom levels (2x, 4x, etc.) as well as the ability to zoom out to different numbers of thumbnails. For panning about an image, a smooth pan is much better than a camera that restricts you to looking at specific "quadrants" of an image.
- Easy deleting and locking are a must. In other words, you need a simple, quick interface for deleting single or multiple images. When you have to free up space on a card, you don't want to miss a shot because your camera's interface was too complex.

Some cameras also offer features that automatically rotate the image so that it's upright, no matter whether you shot it vertically or horizontally. This is clever technology, but rotating your camera usually isn't too hard. Other cameras feature printing commands that let you print to special printers designed to work with your camera. Such features can turn your digital camera into kind of a "Polaroid" camera, but for serious work, you'll want more image editing and printing control.

STORAGE AND INPUT/OUTPUT

A digital camera isn't much good if you can't get your pictures out of it. Fortunately, most cameras come equipped with a number of interfaces for moving your pictures into another device.

TRANSFERRING AND VIEWING IMAGES

Early generations of cameras typically sported serial ports. These were usually implemented using a simple mini-plug and a special cable that attached to the standard serial port on your computer. As *RS-232* and *RS-432 ports* have been replaced by *USB* and *Firewire* ports, most vendors have been diligent about updating their camera designs.

Today, almost all cameras come equipped with a USB connector of some kind, along with a cable to connect the camera's USB port to the standard USB port on your computer. USB is a good, speedy interface that makes for quick transfer of images. Some cameras also provide remote camera control through the USB port. If you need a computer-operated camera (either for time-lapse, or other automated operations) then be sure your camera's software supports remote operation.

Transfer Software

Your camera will come bundled with software for transferring images to and from your camera. Some units come with a simple *TWAIN driver* that can be used from within your editing package, while others offer stand-alone applications that allow for *media cataloging*, simple editing, and printing.

Because transferring via cable can take a while (and drain your camera batteries in the process) and because you'll usually want more editing power than what is provided by most bundled software, you don't need to worry too much about the capabilities of a camera's software.

Nevertheless, here are some things that make for a stand-out camera application:

- Drag and drop transfer of images to and from the camera.
- Automatic panoramic stitching (this is not usually included in the main application itself, but in some bundled software)

Of course, if your camera supports a raw data format, you'll want software that allows you to manipulate the raw data.

Epson software. One of the great things about Epson cameras is that their bundled software interfaces smoothly with Epson's excellent color printers. So, you can simply click a button in their software and your computer will immediately grab the images off your Epson camera (via USB) and print them on your Epson printer. For smooth workflow, it's hard to find anything better.

Video Input/Output

Most cameras provide a special video output that lets you connect your camera to a television to view your images. Although televisions don't provide nearly enough *dynamic range* to view your images in all their glory, they do seem to be everywhere, making for a convenient way to review images when you are traveling. A video connection can also make for a convenient way to present a slide show of images and most cameras offer some sort of automatic slide-show feature that allows you to step through all of the images on your camera.

Because not all countries use the same video standard, make sure you get a camera that supports the appropriate standard. Most cameras come in either NTSC or PAL versions.

STORAGE

Film is a very clever invention because it can both capture and store an image. A CCD, on the other hand, can only capture an image. So, once your camera is done *sampling* and processing the image you've shot, it needs a place to put it.

Today, most cameras use some form of *flash memory* card. These are small wafer-like cards that house a type of RAM that doesn't require a constant stream of power (that is, it is *non-volatile*). So, after your camera has recorded an image, you can shut off the power without worrying about what has been stored on the memory card.

Flash memory cards (or just, "flash cards") are a great solution to the digital camera storage problem. They're small, they can hold huge amounts of data (up to 384MB in some cases) and they can be easily swapped with other cards, just like a roll of film.

Currently, there are three major competing flash memory standards. Each standard has its strengths and weaknesses, but the different technologies are so close in price and performance that you won't need to base your buying decision on a camera's storage device.

CompactFlash

Developed by SanDisk, *CompactFlash* cards are small rigid plastic cards with a row of socket holes that protect the contacts of the cards. (Figure 5.32) CompactFlash cards are very durable and currently come in capacities up to 384MB. Inserting a CompactFlash card is very simple since the card can only fit in a CompactFlash slot in the correct way.

Although CompactFlash cards are very durable, they are thin enough that you don't have to apply much pressure to snap one in two. Nevertheless, normal use (including the occasional drop) seems to have no effect on the cards. In addition, many vendors offer lifetime guarantees.

FIGURE *CompactFlash cards provide high capacities and better compatibility than other*
5.32 *formats.*

One advantage that CompactFlash cards have over some technologies (such as SmartMedia) is that the controller (the circuitry that the camera uses to interface with the card) is built into the card itself. This means that camera vendors don't have to do anything different with their cameras when a higher-capacity card becomes available, meaning you can use newer cards in an older camera.

Some vendors tout their cards as being faster than other vendors' cards and, in tests, this can be proven to be true. However, you may not be able to feel a difference between one type of card and another. They all seem much faster than using film, and much slower than the instantaneous times that we'd all love to see from our computers.

CompactFlash cards come in two sizes:

- Type I CompactFlash cards are the standard-size cards used in most cameras. Note that Lexar (a company made up of former SanDisk engineers) manufactures a variation of the Type I card that includes a USB port. If your camera only has a serial port, using a Lexar SmartMedia card can provide you with USB access to your camera's images.
- Type II CompactFlash cards are twice as thick as Type I cards, meaning they can hold twice as much memory. Currently, the most successful use of the Type II format is IBM's series of Type II-sized *MicroDrives*, tiny hard drives with capacities up to 1 gigabyte. Seemingly the ideal storage solution, there are some MicroDrive caveats to be aware of. Early users complained of the drive's fragility. In some cases, dropping the cards could cause a head crash that required reformatting the whole drive. MicroDrives also tend to produce a lot of heat. Consequently, in addition to having a Type II CompactFlash slot, a camera really needs to be designed to manage the extra heat produced by a MicroDrive. Because of their high capacities, MicroDrives present something of an "all your eggs in one basket" risk. Should your MicroDrive crash, you'll lose a *lot* of images. On the plus side, all that space is great for long shoots, and MicroDrives are typically much faster than flash memory cards, which take longer to write because they must first erase the area they are going to write onto.

SmartMedia

Even thinner than a CompactFlash card, *SmartMedia cards* are barely thicker than a piece of paper. Between their size and their exposed plane of electrical contacts, SmartMedia cards feel very fragile. However, in regular use, they don't seem to be any less durable than a CompactFlash card.

The main downside to SmartMedia technology is that the controller circuitry is not included in the card; it must be built into the camera. So, if a company comes up with some breakthrough that allows for twice as much storage on a SmartMedia card, you won't be able to use it in your older camera. Many vendors provide upgrades to their SmartMedia-based cameras, but these require sending your camera back to the factory to have its guts altered, a time-consuming process that most people are hesitant to do.

SmartMedia currently has a much lower maximum capacity than Compact-Flash (at the time of this writing, SmartMedia has a maximum of 128mb) although their prices are very competitive.

SmartMedia cards (Figure 5.33) come in two variations, 3.3v and 5v cards. The variants are not interchangeable and you can tell which is which by looking at the corners of your card. It is possible to incorrectly insert a card, but this doesn't seem to damage the card.

FIGURE   *SmartMedia cards are small and surprisingly sturdy.*
5.33

Memory Stick

A proprietary format developed by Sony for use in their digital cameras, camcorders, and MP3 players, the *Memory Stick* is a small, rectangular flash card with shielded contacts on one end. No better or worse than any of the other formats, the main drawback to Memory Sticks is that the technology is totally controlled by Sony. (Just think "Beta videotape" and you'll understand why this is a problem). Consequently, without 3rd-party development, Memory Stick capacities lag behind other technologies and Memory Sticks are often pricier.

PC Cards

Larger cameras such as large format digital backs and some older SLR bodies use PC Card (also known as PCMCIA) flash memory. These cards are the size of the standard Type I PC Card that you might use in your laptop computer and are typically more expensive than the smaller format flash cards, simply because they're not as popular. More and more, vendors are switching to the smaller formats for all of their cameras.

Floppy Disks

Sony's Mavica line of cameras are well known for their ability to store images on standard 3.5" 1.2MB floppy disks. Given that the average JPEG compressed 3-megapixel image takes up around 800K, the only way to fit images on floppy disks is to compress them like crazy and use a low-resolution CCD. Consequently, these cameras usually produce lousy images. Floppy drives are also somewhat power-hungry and slow.

3" CDs

As of this writing, one or two vendors have announced cameras that record images onto a tiny, 3" CD writer built into the back of the camera. On the positive side, a 3" CD can hold up to 150MB and, in theory, could be very inexpensive in quantity. On the downside, the big drives make for big cameras and it remains to be seen if this technology will stick around. Also, you can't delete images from CDs as you can from flash media, making them far less flexible than electronic storage.

PocketZip (Clik!)

Formerly known as the Clik! disk, the Iomega PocketZip drive uses tiny 40MB cartridges. Speedy, durable, and reliable, the PocketZip's best feature is its cheap media price: only $10 for each 40MB disk. However, only Agfa is currently building PocketZips into their cameras, and they are only producing a few PocketZip-equipped models. Also, Iomega has yet to release a Mac disk reader. Although it is a cool technology, odds are it won't gain much market share against CompactFlash and SmartMedia.

Does Any of This Matter?

Although there are people who will make arguments for one format over another, there's really not much difference. They are all equally reliable, equally speedy, and (mostly) equivalently-priced. CompactFlash is the most popular of the three and, consequently, may have the greatest longevity.

How Much Do You Need?

How much storage you need depends largely on your shooting conditions, how many pictures you typically take, how big your camera's images are, and what level of compression you're using. Obviously, if you're shooting in a computer-equipped studio, then storage is less of a concern as you can dump your pictures to disk as you shoot. Similarly, if you're in the field with your laptop, you'll be able to clear off your camera's storage as it fills. But, if you're planning a 3-month trip through the Amazon, (or even a 3-hour trip to the zoo, and you tend to be shutter-happy) then storage might be a bit of a concern.

If you're like most people, when you shoot film you probably take 36 exposures and get back three or four shots that you like. Maybe. Digital cameras are no different. For every 40 or so images that you shoot, you'll maybe want to keep a third of them. However, with a digital camera, you don't have to wait until you've shot all 40 before you decide which ones you want to keep. Rather, you can delete the bad pictures as soon as you've taken them. Consequently, digital camera storage goes a little farther than an equivalent number of film exposures because you'll be more selective along the way.

Unfortunately, experience is the only way to find out what your storage needs are. It's safe to assume that on a typical 2- or 3-megapixel camera, a 32MB card will get you a couple dozen high-quality images. Start with this estimate and try to get an idea for what this translates into in terms of "keeper" images. Then, make sure you have an appropriate amount of storage before embarking on an important shoot.

Media Tips

There are a few quick things you should know about removable media. Obviously, these cards are fragile, so treat them with care. Go out and eat a box of Altoids, wash out the box, and use it to carry your cards. Then go brush your teeth. Here are some more things to consider:

- The number of images a card can hold depends on the resolution and compression settings that you're currently shooting with. These vary greatly from camera to camera, so you'll need to dig through a camera's manual to find these statistics.
- The bigger the card's capacity, the more power it takes to keep it running. Consequently, in theory, smaller cards use less battery. Although it's difficult to tell if this has any bearing in the real world, switching to a smaller capacity card when your batteries run low may garner you a few extra shots.
- Larger capacity cards generate more heat. If you're using a really tiny camera - such as the Canon S100 Digital Elph – which tends to get hot simply because of its design, it might be worth sticking to smaller-capacity cards.
- If something goes wrong with a larger-capacity card, you'll lose more images than you would if you had been using a smaller-capacity card. So, it might be worth buying a number of smaller cards instead of one big one, just to ensure that not all of your eggs are in the same basket.
- X-rays don't seem to matter, so feel free to take your camera with you to the airport, dentist, or thoracic surgeon.

Media drives

The best way to get images transferred to your computer is through a drive that supports the same media that your camera uses. These USB devices work just like any other drive on your computer. Insert your media card into the drive and it will show up on your desktop. You can then copy files to and from the card. Priced anywhere between $40 and $100, these drives are the fastest and easiest way to transfer images to your computer, and they don't require you to drain your camera batteries.

If you have a laptop computer with a PC Card slot, then you might consider getting a *PC card adapter* for your camera's media. These are special PC cards into which you insert your camera's media. Put the card into your laptop's PC slot and it will appear on your desktop like any other drive.

WHAT'S IN THE BOX

When you buy a camera you'll want to consider everything you're getting for your money, so take some time to assess what else is bundled with your camera. (Figure 5.34)

Don't expect to get a huge media card with your camera. Most vendors ship 8MB cards with their 1- and 2-megapixel cameras, and 16MB cards with their 3-megapixel cameras. If these seem small, that's because they are. Unfortunately, because of the economies of scale, adding a bigger card would usually raise the price of the camera by more than it would cost you to just buy a bigger card on your own. So, you should plan to buy some additional media along with your camera.

Also, don't count on getting rechargeable batteries. As with media, most manufacturers can't compete with third-party offerings, so they skip the rechargeable batteries to keep the camera's price down.

BATTERIES

What with the CCD, the LCD screen, the media drive, the flash, and the motorized zoom lens, the typical digital camera demands a *lot* of power. Because most cameras can really tear through batteries, power management is an important concern, particularly if you'll be shooting in the field for extended periods.

Digital cameras offer two battery options: either a proprietary, (custom) battery, or support for batteries of standard size (usually AA-size). The following describes battery options.

Camera (with strap)

Software

Manuals

Media Card

Battery charger and set of batteries

Cables (video & USB)

FIGURE *Ideally, you want a camera package that includes these components.*
5.34

- **Proprietary batteries.** Canon and Sony consistently use special *propri-etary (custom) battery* packs in their cameras. The advantage to these batteries is that they usually include special controllers that can provide very accurate charge estimates (Sony InfoLithium batteries are particularly accurate in their estimation of remaining charge) and special power-saving operations. They also tend to last a loooong time. On the downside, custom batteries require custom chargers and if your battery dies in the field, you can't just run down to the corner store and buy another.
- **Standard-size rechargeable batteries.** Offering the same battery technology as a proprietary battery, standard-size rechargeable batteries offer the advantage of universality. As better battery technology comes along (as long as it comes along in the same size) you can drop these batteries into your camera. Standard-size rechargeables are much cheaper than propri-etary designs, are readily available, and in a pinch can always be replaced by normal alkaline batteries. (Figure 5.35)

FIGURE *Rechargeable batteries come in special proprietary formats or standard AA sizes.*
5.35

In addition to sizes, there are a number of different battery technologies available.

- **Alkaline batteries.** Alkaline batteries are really not good for much when it comes to a digital camera. In some cases, you'll be hard-pressed to get half a dozen shots out of a set of alkalines before they are too low to be used. Digital cameras have very specific power requirements and as soon as a set of alkalines drops below those levels, the camera will register them as dead. You can usually continue to use them for a while in a lower-power device such as a Walkman. In general, use alkalines only when you absolutely have to. The cost, waste, and environmental impact just isn't worth it.

- **NiCAD (Nickel Cadmium) batteries.** *NiCAD batteries* were, until recently, the most popular rechargeable technology. NiCADs don't deliver a lot of power, though, and they need to be drained completely before you recharge them or they will develop a "memory" that will prevent them from being completely recharged.

- **NiMH (Nickel-Metal-Hydride) batteries.** *NiMH batteries* are relatively inexpensive (usually $25-$30 for a set of four, plus another $35 or $40 for a charger), powerful, quick to recharge, and lack a memory. In addition, NiMH batteries are more environmentally friendly than either NiCADs or Alkalines.. NiMH batteries are the ideal choice for the digital camera owner. In fact, buy a few sets - one for your camera, an extra set to go in your pocket, and a set to go in your recharger.

- **L-Ion (Lithium Ion) batteries.** *L-ion batteries* are also a good choice, although not as prevalent, and they are sometimes more expensive. You can often find chargers that will charge both NiMH and L-ion batteries.
- **Lithium batteries.** Lithium batteries are not rechargeable but offer a lot of power for a long time. Roughly the shape of two AA-size batteries stuck together, you'll need to be sure your camera can use Lithium batteries. Although strong and long-lasting, they're still disposable, and are usually kind of pricey.

When you shop for a recharger, you might want to consider the strength of the charger. Some chargers can recharge faster than others, although they will all take several hours. In general, any recharger will probably serve you jus t fine. We'll discuss battery use, management, and performance in more detail in Chapter 7.

Solar recharger. If you want to take your digital camera camping, hiking or boating, then you might consider buying a solar-powered battery charge. A solar recharger is able to recharge a set of 4 AA-size batteries in 12 hours of direct sunlight exposure and can solve most of your power requirements when you're literally "in the field." Check them out at www.completedigitalphotography.com/solar.

SPECIAL FEATURES

On top of the gobs of features that we just discussed, many vendors pack their cameras with special, unique features that can be a boon or a burden to the digital photographer. With their on-board computers and automatic functions, digital cameras can perform a lot of tricks that film cameras can't. Listed below are some of the more unique features that you may encounter in your camera shopping. Some of these features are cool, others are kind of silly.

- **Time-lapse.** A scant few cameras offer a time-lapse feature which lets you program the camera to automatically shoot a picture at a predefined interval. A good time-lapse feature will let you specify an interval ranging from a few seconds to a few days. For documenting slow processes, creating animations, or producing high-quality time-lapse video, a time-lapse feature is essential.
- **Remote computer control.** Some cameras include software that let you control your camera from your computer via the same serial or USB link that the camera uses to download images. If you need to take pictures in

harsh, industrial conditions, or want to leave your camera unattended, this feature might be the answer.

- **Auto-bracketing.** As we'll see in Chapter 8, *bracketing* is the process of shooting the same image with slightly different exposure settings to help ensure that you get your shot. Many cameras now feature an *auto-bracketing* feature that will automatically shoot four or five images with slightly different exposures each time you press the shutter release.

- **Voice annotation.** Although the ability to record and store small voice annotations (comments) with each image is not a tremendously useful feature, some applications – real estate photography, for example – can benefit from it. If you're trying to take images with as much quality as your camera can muster, then you won't really want to use up extra storage on voice recording.

- **Best shot selection.** Some of Nikon's digital cameras include a unique "best shot selector" which automatically shoots a series of images when you press the shutter button, analyzes them to determine which one is best, saves that one and throws out the rest. This feature is best used in tricky macro situations where it can be difficult to hold the camera steady enough to get a clear shot. (Best shot selection seems to work by simply selecting the largest file as the best. Since the sharpest image will compress the least, the file with the largest size is most likely the sharpest.)

- **In-camera effects.** Many cameras offer special effects features that can automatically *solarize*, tint, or turn your images into negatives. These are, of course, all tasks that can be performed in your computer with a great deal more control. It's almost always better to skip these features and shoot the cleanest, best-looking image you can.

- **Noise reduction.** Some cameras include special noise reduction modes that kick in automatically during longer exposures. Such schemes can often greatly improve the quality of low-light shots.

"ENOUGH ALREADY! WHAT SHOULD I BUY?!"

As you've seen, choosing a digital camera involves balancing and compromising on a number of different features and technical considerations. In the end, though, there are baseline features that you should absolutely demand from a camera. If you want the simplest buying advice possible, then you'll want to pick a camera that provides the following:

- Satisfactory (or better) image quality. Always defer to image quality as the ultimate arbiter of camera value because after the shooting's over (no matter how easy or difficult it was) if you don't have a decent image, then you've wasted your time.
- Controls and body design that you find comfortable and that you feel will facilitate the way you like to shoot. This includes not only the shape and feel of the camera, but the quality and coverage of the unit's viewfinder(s) as well as the focal length of the lens (in other words, does the lens provide the wide angles or telephoto qualities you want to shoot with), the right type of storage and connectivity, and support for any external flash units you might want to use.
- Resolution that's appropriate for your intended output medium. Although it's simple to follow the "more is better" approach to choosing a resolution, this isn't always the case. If you're not sure about the resolution needs of your intended output medium, check out Chapter 15.
- *Exposure compensation controls* that are easy to access.
- For maximum creative flexibility, look for manual exposure and priority modes.
- Manual white balance control is a must for ensuring color quality.
- Adjustable ISOs guarantee that you'll be able to shoot under different lighting conditions.
- At the very least, your camera should have two metering modes: a matrix metering mode and a spot meter.

Obviously, your needs might go far beyond this, but these items will help to ensure that you can get the shots you need when you need them.

CHAPTER

Building a Workstation

IN THIS CHAPTER

- Choosing an Operating System
- Building your System
- Software
- Accessories

Ask any experienced film photographer and they'll tell you that shooting the picture is only half the work of taking a photograph. The other half occurs in the darkroom where you exercise precise control of developing and printing techniques to achieve the results you imagined when you were shooting. Digital photography is no different, but of course there's no darkroom involved. Rather than a darkroom equipped with enlargers, plumbing, and photographic chemicals, you need nothing more than a decent computer, a lot of storage, some image processing software, and a printer.

In this chapter you'll learn the issues and questions that you need to resolve when you construct a workstation for processing your digital images. Although computer hardware and image editing software will be covered in this chapter, printers and other output devices will be covered separately in Chapter 15.

Your first step in assembling a workstation is one you may have already taken, and that is to select an operating system.

CHOOSING AN OPERATING SYSTEM

Odds are, if you're interested in digital photography, you already own a computer and have, thus, already chosen an operating system. If you haven't, though, or if you're thinking of upgrading, or if you simply don't like your operating system, then it's time to make a choice. Since the operating system (OS) you choose will affect all your other buying decisions, it's the first issue to consider.

As far as digital photography is concerned, OS choice is really a matter of preference. Whether you choose the Mac or Windows, you'll get pretty much the same capability and spend about the same amount of money. The main differences between them are in their interfaces, but a discussion of the strengths and weakness of each system is way beyond the scope of this book. So, rather than engage in yet another "which OS is better" argument, this chapter will simply cover the issues that are relevant to digital photographers.

MACINTOSH

The Macintosh is where mainstream digital image editing began. Photoshop and its first competitors were originally written for the Mac OS between 1988 and 1990, providing Apple and its developers with ten years of tweaking and refining. As a result, the Mac OS has a slight advantages over Windows when it comes to software. Apple's *color matching software*, ColorSync, is several years ahead of its Windows competition, and ColorSync is supported by a huge range of vendors, from software developers to scanner and printer manufacturers. However, it takes a little work to use color matching software. If you don't really think you'll bother with the necessary practices (see Chapter 10, then ColorSync doesn't really matter.

On the hardware side, Apple's thorough integration of Firewire and USB into all of their latest hardware makes for systems – both desktop and laptop – that are well-prepared for connecting to digital cameras. In addition, all Macs include built-in video hardware that allows for *Video LUT animation* - a feature that greatly eases many image editing tasks (see the topic "Monitors" later in this chapter).

The Mac OS's best "feature," though, may be its future. By the time you read this, Apple will most likely have shipped OS X, their fully rewritten "modern" operating system. OS X is Apple's implementation of UNIX (the BSD variety) making it a rock solid, time-tested OS. OS X's UNIX foundation provides one main advantage to the digital photographer: memory management. Digital photos tend to take up a lot of memory, and memory management is one of UNIX's primary advantages. Consequently, OS X offers the possibility of much better performance when you handle large files than what current operating systems can provide.

OS X offers another advantage in the form of Aqua, Apple's new user inter-face. Built in to Aqua is a new display technology called Quartz. Based on Adobe's *PDF* technology, Quartz provides incredibly sophisticated compositing technology at the OS level. As such, Quartz offers the promise of new compositing applications and improved printing workflow.

Finally, with OS X will come a number of long-awaited software packages that may be of interest if you are interested in more sophisticated graphics. Three-dimensional (3D) packages such as Maya have already been announced for OS X, as have other powerful graphics programs.

WINDOWS

The main advantage of Windows over the Mac OS is that it is ubiquitous. Consequently, you probably won't ever have trouble finding a service bureau that can handle your Windows-based files. Similarly, repair shops and new equipment are often easier to find and less expensive because the Windows realm is more competitive.

Windows also has a slight software advantage, as there are a number of graphics applications that currently run only on Windows. If you hope to go be-yond image editing and into animation, compositing, and 3D work, you may have more options available under the Windows OS.

The main disadvantage to a Windows-based computer is that it is more diffi-cult to maintain. With more complicated hardware and software setups, you may spend a lot more time fiddling you're your computer than you will fiddling with your images.

For the type of work covered in this book, your only real concern is the ability to run a capable image editing program, so either Mac or Windows should work just fine for your digital darkroom forays.

BUILDING YOUR SYSTEM

Once you've picked an OS you're ready to pick out a computer. No matter what OS you've chosen, your hardware concerns are mostly the same. When you select a computer, you'll want to pay particular attention to:

* RAM
* Processor Speed
* Storage
* Monitors
* Input/Output/Options

Of course, you'll probably be using your computer for more than just processing images, so if you have other concerns (perhaps you'll also be using it for editing video, making music, checking e-mail,), then you'll need to factor in the particular requirements of those tasks as well.

RAM

Although a fast processor is essential for good performance when you use an image editing program, of greater concern is the amount of random access memory (RAM) in your computer. High-resolution digital photos can be very memory hungry, and if you start performing complex effects, your memory needs will go even higher. As such, the amount of RAM installed in your computer will have a huge effect on image editing performance.

Adobe recommends a RAM size equal to two to three times the size of your typical image. Although your image may only be 4 MB, by the time you've added three or four more layers, your image's RAM requirements will have quadrupled. Things get even more complicated when you factor in the RAM requirements of Photoshop's History palette or if you plan on using filters that need to load your entire image into RAM. For maximum performance, you'll want a RAM level closer to 20 times the size of your file. Also, remember that your OS and other applications will also need some memory, so don't base your RAM needs on Photoshop alone.

In the end, if you're on a budget, you may want to consider paying for a slightly slower, less-expensive processor and putting the money you save into more RAM. (Figure 6.1)

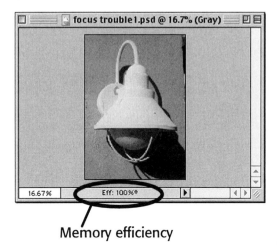

Memory efficiency

FIGURE **6.1** *Photoshop provides a couple of RAM displays that make it easy to determine if your computer would benefit from more RAM.*

PROCESSOR SPEED

These days, even the slowest processors available are plenty fast for most Photoshop work. If you're in a high-pressure production environment where you need to crank out images in a hurry, then it's worth investing a little more for a faster CPU. For most work, however, you can get by with a fairly average (by today's standards) processor.

Many people think that a higher clock rate means an inherently faster processor. So, when they see 700MHz, they immediately assume that the processor must be faster than a 500MHz unit. If the processors in question are the type of processor, then that assumption is correct. However, a 500MHz G4 will perform much faster than a 500MHz Pentium III. So, it's important to look at more than just the clock speed of a chip when you assess processor speed. Unfortunately, many computer salespeople simply push higher clock speeds because it's the easiest way to make a sale. Do a little research before you buy.

In the end, if you're having trouble deciding between a 500MHz and 750MHz processor, go for the 500MHz computer and spend the extra money into RAM. More RAM will make a bigger difference to your image editing application than will an extra 200MHz of processor speed.

STORAGE

The bad news is that digital images can take up a lot of space. The good news is that hard disk storage is really cheap. Simply put, the more storage you have, the better. Bear in mind that you'll need space for your OS, your image editing applications, and any other software you plan on using, and that's all *before* you've shot any pictures. A 6-10GB drive is a good starting point, but 20-30GB will keep you editing for a long time. Your main concern when you shop for a computer is to look for simple, inexpensive expansion options.

For Mac users, storage expansion will take the form of external Firewire drives or internal IDE drives (as long as you're using a tower machine that has internal drive bays). For Windows users, extra storage will usually be in the form of inexpensive IDE drives. SCSI drives are also possible for both platforms, but these drives are more expensive, and most digital photography tasks don't require the extra speed that SCSI can provide.

You'll also want some kind of storage both for backing up and for transporting images to service bureaus. Recordable CDs offer the best price per megabyte but they can be rather slow to write to. Zip and Jaz drives are speedy and re-writable, but are too expensive for long-term storage. Ideally it's nice to have both, but if you have to choose just one, go with a recordable CD. Blank CDs are cheap, everyone's got a CD reader, and the CDs have a long shelf-life.

 CDR or CDRW. *Some recordable CD drives can also create re-writeable discs using special, more expensive re-writeable media. CDRWs are great for storing copies of work in progress. Backing up in-progress works to a re-usable CDRW while you're working, and then to a normal CD when you're finished is a great way to prevent the confusion of having multiple-versions of a work-in-progress.*

MONITORS

You're going to be spending a lot of time staring at your computer screen so it's important to choose wisely when you select that screen. In addition to the usual questions of brightness, sharpness, and contrast, as a digital photographer, you should be particularly choosy about color reproduction. How picky you should be depends largely on the final destination of your photos.

If you're shooting for the web, color fidelity is less of a concern as there is no *color calibration* system for the web. That is, even though you may have the color perfect on your screen, there's no telling what type of screen is being used by anyone else who sees your image. So, you can simply choose a monitor that looks good to you, and is comfortable to use.

If print is your final destination, then get ready to spend some additional money. For serious print work (that is, commercial press-ready print work) you're going to want a high-quality monitor that can be hardware calibrated. We'll discuss hardware calibration more in Chapter 10. Typically, a print-quality monitor is going to start at $800 or $900 and go up from there.

Of course, you'll need a video card to feed a signal to your monitor. If your computer doesn't already have a video card, then you'll want to consider the following when you shop:

- **What resolutions does it support?** For most image editing work, you want to be sure you're using a video card that supports 1024 x 768 pixels. Because of the palette-heavy interfaces of most image editing programs, a screen with any less resolution than 1024 x 786 can feel uncomfortably cramped. Higher resolution is fine, but it takes a good monitor to display a very high-resolution image with no visible distortion.

- **What color depth does it support?** Or, how much *video RAM (VRAM)* does it have? The number of colors that a video card can simultaneously display is known as its color depth. *Color depth* is also referred to as *bit depth* since more bits-per-pixel means more simultaneous colors. The amount of video RAM installed on the card determines both the color depth and resolution that the card can display. Make certain that your card can support millions of colors (or *24-bit color*) at your desired resolution.

- **Does it provide any acceleration?** Some video cards include special co-processors for accelerating both two-dimensional (2D) and three-dimensional (3D) performance. 2D acceleration means scrolling and screen redrawing will be much faster while 3D acceleration will greatly improve your computer's performance when you're working in a 3D modeling and animation package.

- **Can it perform video LUT animation?** A look-up table is the full index of colors that a monitor can display. By changing the contents of this look-up table, or LUT, it's possible to immediately change the contents of the screen. Animating the LUT is a quick and easy way of cycling through changes on-screen. If your video card supports *video LUT animation,* then many color correction and editing tasks in Photoshop will be much easier as the program will be able to manipulate the LUT to display color corrections in real-time.

When you shop for a monitor, you'll want to try to assess the monitor's image quality. First, look for overall color quality and sharpness. Check the edges of the screen for any convergence troubles (slight red, green, or blue fringing around pixels) and for distortion problems – slight bulging or pinching of the image. In addition, you'll need to consider these questions:

- **Size.** The physical area of your screen is largely a subjective choice. Do you prefer squinting at a smaller image on a 15" monitor, or bathing in the radiation of a big 22" monitor? Whatever size fits your ocular preference and desktop space is the size that's right for you.

- **Frequency.** The refresh rate – the frequency with which a monitor's screen is redrawn – is measured in hertz (Hz). The higher the number, the more frequently the screen refreshes. The more frequent the refresh, the less flicker a screen will have. Ideally, you want a screen that supports multiple frequencies and different resolutions. Higher frequency is better.
- **Curvature.** The front of a monitor usually has a slight curve to it. If you're willing to pay more money, you can get a monitor with less curve, or even one that's totally flat. Less curve means less distortion at the edges of your image.

LCD MONITORS

If desk space is a concern, or if you're not thrilled about the potential health effects of sitting in front of a cathode ray tube (CRT), then an LCD monitor might be a good choice for you. Just a few years ago, there was no point in even considering an LCD for serious photography work, because the image quality simply wasn't good enough. LCD technology has greatly improved, though, and an LCD monitor is now a viable option for the serious digital photographer and image editor.

However, be warned that LCD monitors often don't offer *contrast ratios* that are as good as what you'll find on a CRT. Lighter shades, for example, will often appear completely white on an LCD, making it difficult to judge the true color balance of an image. As with any monitor, over time you'll probably come to understand how the image you see on your LCD screen will actually look when it is printed. In the meantime, expect to do a lot of printing and adjusting and reprinting to get the colors and contrast ratios that you're looking for.

When you use an LCD screen, be aware that the brightness and contrast of most screens changes depending on your viewing angle. If you're using a big enough screen, then you can be tricked into thinking the edge of the screen is darker than it really is. When you consider an LCD, try moving from side to side, and up and down in front of the screen to see how the brightness and contrast varies over the surface of the image (yes, people will look at you funny, but given the price of the typical LCD monitor, it will be worth the humiliation).

For critical print work, you may want to find a place where you can view your files on a high-quality CRT before printing.

Finally, you'll want to consider size and weight when you shop for a laptop. Remember that you're already going to be lugging a bag of camera gear, so you don't want to weigh yourself down even further with a computer that's too heavy.

What about a laptop?

The ideal computer choice for a digital photographer is a good, high-powered laptop. Because it is portable, a laptop computer not only allows you to edit, retouch, and print your images anywhere, it also makes for a great mass storage device for those extended digital photography expeditions.

For the most part, choosing a laptop computer involves all of the same processor, RAM, and storage considerations as choosing a desktop. Although there are currently no Mac or Windows laptops available that offer all of the computer power that you can find in a desktop, you should have no trouble finding a laptop that delivers all the performance you'll need for digital photography.

In addition to the performance concerns discussed previously, you'll want to look for the following:

- **A very good screen**. An LCD is never as good as a high-dollar monitor, but there are plenty of laptops that offer very good screens that are suitable for image editing. As with a desktop monitor, look for a resolution of 1024 x 768 and check the screen for general image quality and sharpness.
- **A video out port**. The ideal laptop setup is to use your laptop LCD screen in the field, and a high-quality monitor when you're back home. At the very least, a video out port will allow you to take your computer to a service bureau and connect to a monitor there for final proofing. Using a two-monitor system can also make your virtual workspace more comfortable. You can, for example, keep all of your image editor's tool palettes on your laptop's LCD screen and your image on your CRT.
- **USB, Firewire, or serial ports.** Be sure to get a computer that provides the type of port that your camera uses. Currently, most cameras connect through a USB port, but some higher-end cameras use Firewire, while most older cameras use a normal serial connection.
- **A PC Card slot.** A PC Card slot provides a simple, quick way to transfer images to your computer. Using an adapter like the one shown in Figure 6.2, you can simply insert the media from your camera directly into your laptop. The media will show up on your desktop just as a floppy disk or CD would. You can then drag and drop files from the card to your computer's hard drive. PC Card adapters are currently available for CompactFlash, SmartMedia and Memory Sticks.

FIGURE *With a PC Card adapter, you can insert your camera's media directly into your*
6.2 *laptop.*

SOFTWARE

When it comes to editing, correcting, manipulating, and adjusting your digital images, you'll probably spend most of your time in a single image editing application. However, there may be times when you also move your images into special programs designed for panoramic stitching, animation, video production, or compression.

IMAGE EDITING APPLICATIONS

In case you haven't noticed already, this book was written by a Photoshop chauvinist. Yes, there are other good image editing applications out there, and yes, some of them have features that Photoshop needs. In the end, though, the combination of features, interface, third-party and user support, and

Photoshop's excellent color fidelity and printer support make it difficult to recommend something else.

Beginning users may find Photoshop to be very complicated because it is a complex, powerful program. However, with just a little bit of explanation, even beginning users can quickly learn the Photoshop basics. In this book, all examples and tutorials will be Photoshop-based, and a demonstration version is included on the Complete Digital Photography CD-ROM.

ON THE CD

If, for some reason, you decide to use something other than Photoshop, make sure it has the following features.

LEVELS AND CURVES CONTROLS

There's no better, easier way to adjust contrast, color, and saturation than with Levels and Curves controls. Although your program's interface may vary somewhat, make sure that it includes the controls and adjustments that are highlighted in Figure 6.3a and Figure 6.3b.

An Eyedropper tool with an information readout

For more refined image analysis, it's essential to have an Eyedropper tool and some sort of Information window or palette. With these tools, you can find out exactly what the color values are in a particular part of an image. Such information can be very handy when you make tone and color adjustments.

Good Paintbrush and Clone tools

For retouching, you've got to have a good set of paintbrushes. Make sure your program supports pressure-sensitive tablets for more natural looking brush strokes. A *Clone* (sometimes called Rubber Stamp) tool is absolutely essential for everything from erasing artifacts to touching up images. Although nowadays this shouldn't be too much of a concern, make sure your program's paint brushes are anti-*aliased* (that is, have soft edges).

Access to individual color channels

You'll perform a lot of corrections and adjustments by working on specific color channels. (Figure 6.4) Make sure your image editor lets you view and edit specific color channels directly.

Support for multiple color spaces

Although your camera and desktop printer both operate in RGB color space, you may need other color spaces for specific tasks. Commercial printers usually require documents to be in CMYK color, while some corrections and adjustments are easier to perform in L*A*B color. If you do a lot of black and white work, you'll probably want the ability to make *duotones, tritones*, and *quadtones*.

Load & Save controls
for storing custom
curves

Eyedropper controls
for setting white and
black points

Shadow, gamma, and   Separate controls
whitepoint sliders   for output levels

Figure 6.3a

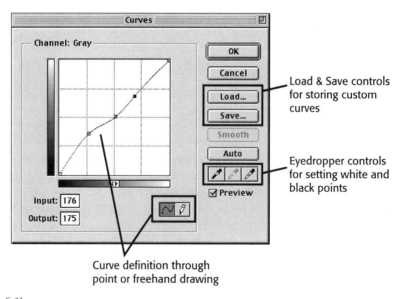

Load & Save controls
for storing custom
curves

Eyedropper controls
for setting white and
black points

Curve definition through
point or freehand drawing

Figure 6.3b

FIGURE *If you're not going to use Photoshop for your image editing tasks, be sure that the*
6.3 *program you choose offers Levels and Curves dialog boxes similar to the ones shown here. You will learn more about shadow, gamma, and whitepoint later in this book.*

FIGURE *The image editor you choose should have support for editing and viewing individual*
6.4   *color channels.*

Support for Photoshop plug-ins

You can expand and extend Photoshop's features through the use of special
plug-ins, small bits of code that can be added to Photoshop. Photoshop plug-ins
(sometimes referred to as *filters*) allow you to do everything from blurring an
image, to adding 3D objects. Many digital cameras interface with your computer
through a Photoshop *Acquire Plug-in,* a special piece of software that lets
Photoshop communicate with your camera through a serial, USB, or Firewire
cable. If your camera requires the use of such a plug-in, then you'll definitely
need an image editor that supports it.

Unsharp Mask, Blur, and Noise filters

You'll use these three basic filters for a lot of everyday editing chores, so make
sure your application provides some equivalent.

File format support

TIFF, JPEG, GIF, BMP, and ideally Photoshop are the bare minimum file formats
that your application should support. Obviously, if your job requires specific file
formats, you'll want to be sure your application supports those as well.

The tutorials and examples included in this book will use all of the features
discussed here. Your program might have other approaches or equivalent features to the items listed above , but you should still be able to follow along with
the tutorials and examples.

PANORAMIC SOFTWARE

In Chapter 9 we'll discuss panoramic shooting, the process of shooting a series of image "tiles" that can be *stitched* together to create a seamless panorama. If your camera didn't ship with stitching software, then you'll need to buy some.

WAVELET COMPRESSION

Utilizing new *wavelet compression* technologies, products like AltaMira's Genuine Fractals PrintPro do an extraordinary job of both losslessly compressing your image and enlarging it to huge dimensions with little or no artifacting. If you want to blow your images up to larger sizes, Genuine Fractals, a set of Photoshop Import and Export plug-ins, is the only way to go.

How big can you enlarge images? In November of 2000, Nikon took a photograph from a Coolpix 990 and used GenuineFractals to blow it up to 65 x 43 feet (that's right *feet!*). The resulting 6-story high image was printed on vinyl and hung on the side of a building in New York City's Times Square.

IMAGE CATALOGING SOFTWARE

One of the great things about a digital camera is that you can shoot and shoot and shoot. Unfortunately, one result of all this shooting is that you'll end up with a drive filled with zillions of files, each with a weird name like P000394.jpg. An image cataloging program not only provides a way of keeping your images organized, sortable, and searchable, it can also provide a quick and easy way of viewing a disk full of images at the end of the day. Think of it as a giant digital light table. Although there are a number of applications out there, check out Extensis' Portfolio. (Figure 6.5) Offering good speed, powerful features and decent networking, it's a good choice for the typical digital photographer.

ACCESSORIES

Finally, there are one or two accessory items that can make your life with your digital camera easier, the main one being a media drive that supports the type of media used by your camera. (Figure 6.6) These drives typically connect through your computer's USB port. Insert your camera's media into the drive's slot, just as you would insert a floppy into a floppy drive, and it will appear on your desktop as another volume, allowing you to drag and drop images onto your computer's hard drive.

If your camera uses a USB cable to connect to your computer, and if you've already got a number of USB devices installed, then you may need to get a *USB hub*. Offering multiple USB ports, USB hubs make it possible to connect multiple USB devices simultaneously.

FIGURE **6.5** *An image cataloging program such as Extensis Portfolio is a must-have for managing the huge number of images that you can quickly produce with a digital camera.*

FIGURE **6.6** *A CompactFlash or SmartMedia drive provides a simple, quick way of getting your images into your computer. In addition to saving time, you'll save camera battery power.*

Finally, you will, of course, want a printer of some kind. Printing is a huge topic, however, and Chapter 15 is devoted entirely to choosing and using any number of different types and brands of printers.

READY! AIM!

If you've read and considered the last two chapters, and made all of the relevant purchases, then you've got everything you need to start shooting! The next section of the book (Chapters 7 through 9) deals exclusively with shooting and, for the most part, won't involve your computer very much. Don't worry, though, you'll get plenty of mouse time when you start working with Photoshop in Chapter 10.

CHAPTER

7

Shooting

IN THIS CHAPTER

- Initial Camera Settings
- Framing and Focusing
- Metering
- Automatic Exposure
- Simple Flash Photography
- Power and Storage Management

Supposedly, when she was shooting, famed photographer Margaret Bourke-White used to simply set her camera on 1/100th of a second and then shoot the same image over and over using every aperture that her camera could manage. This, combined with her gift for composition, ensured that at least one of her images would come out looking good.

If you're like most people, you probably find yourself shooting whole rolls of film hoping that one or two of the images will be "keepers." Unfortunately, no camera technology can guarantee that you'll always shoot great images, but there are a number of things you can do to improve your chances of getting images you like, and digital cameras offer a number of creative advantages that make it easier to take good shots.

Because you don't have to worry about film and processing, digital cameras actually make it very easy to take Bourke-White's approach to photography. A much better philosophy, though, is to spend some time learning how to intelligently use the tools and features found on your camera.

Although there is plenty of room for artistry in the photographic process, when it finally comes down to pressing that shutter button, you have to make a *lot of* simple mechanical decisions, ranging from lens choice to exposure options. As we discussed earlier, this book is going to leave the discussion of photographic artistry to the photographic artists. Composition, perception, and other more "artistic" topics are well-covered in any number of books, and a list of recommendations is included in Appendix A.

Once you have a vision of how you want a particular image to look, you need to know how to use the controls and settings on your camera to achieve that vision. In this chapter you'll learn about the framing *controls* and automatic exposure options that your camera provides. In the next chapter, we'll delve more deeply into the complex processes of light metering and selecting an exposure.

INITIAL CAMERA SETTINGS

Before you start to shoot a picture, you'll need to configure your camera based on your current shooting conditions, and on the type of output that you want. For example, you'll need to set the camera's resolution and compression settings differently if your images will be used on the web rather than print. Preparing your camera to shoot begins with selecting a shooting mode.

CHOOSING A MODE

Most likely, your digital camera has a number of shooting modes that dictate what exposure decisions the camera will make, and what decisions will be left up to you. Your first task when you approach a shot, therefore, is to choose the appropriate shooting mode. Often, shooting on full automatic will be all you need to do (and don't worry, shooting on automatic doesn't mean you're a wimpy photographer). In other cases, you may have a lighting situation that's just tricky enough, or a compositional vision that's just unusual enough that you need to throw the camera into a mode that will provide you with the appropriate manual overrides. Every photographic situation is unique, of course, but there are some general guidelines for determining when you should use each shooting modes. As you learn more about digital photography, and your camera in general, you'll get a better idea of which mode to choose.

Full Automatic

Most automatic modes take care of everything. They select a white balance, ISO, shutter speed and aperture, and choose whether or not to use the flash. Most automatic modes also let you select a metering mode, if your camera offers a choice. Some automatic modes will let you override white balance and ISO settings, while other cameras require you to switch to a special Program mode if you want to change these settings. For the most part, the automatic mode on your camera will do a good job in just about any situation. If you're in a hurry to catch a fleeting action, this may be your best bet. Or, if you're simply tired of thinking about your camera all the time, and just want to take a picture, go with automatic mode.

Shutter Priority and Aperture Priority Modes

Automatic modes can be really great, but they tend to take pictures that are "correct." That is, everything in the scene will be in focus, well-lit and sharp. There will be times, however, when you'll want to shoot an image "incorrectly." Perhaps you want to use a slow shutter speed to make a fast-moving object look blurry, for example. Or maybe you want to try to render some parts of your image out-of-focus to bring attention to other parts.

Shutter priority mode lets you select the shutter speed you'd like to use. The camera then selects an aperture that can be used with that shutter speed to create a proper exposure. Shutter priority is ideal for times when you have to freeze motion, such as capturing action at a sporting event.

Aperture priority mode works the same way, but allows you to select an aperture, and leaves the choice of shutter speed up to the camera. Aperture priority modes give you control over the *depth of field* in your image, allowing you to control how much of the image is in focus (Figure 7.1).

FIGURE *By controlling the camera's aperture, we can control the depth of field in an image.*
7.1 *Note the difference in background between these two images. The upper image has a much deeper depth of field, resulting in a sharply focused background, while the lower image has a very shallow depth of field, resulting in a blurry background.*

Most shutter and aperture priority modes also yield control of ISO and white balance. In Chapter 8, you'll learn much more about how to use these modes.

Manual Mode

As you would expect, full manual mode gives you control of everything. Although this may seem like the ultimate "power user" mode, you may find that you often only need control of one exposure parameter or the other, and so you will use a priority mode. However, full manual mode is a must for maximum creative freedom and for handling difficult lighting situations.

Special Shooting Modes

Some cameras offer special shooting modes for specific situations. In these modes, certain features are preset. For example, Landscape modes typically fix the focus on infinity and select the smallest possible aperture to ensure maximum focus and depth of field. Sometimes, these special modes are the only way to gain access to certain features such as slow-sync flash (which we'll discuss later). Before you use any of these modes, though, spend some time with your camera's manual and be sure that you understand *all* of the settings that might be affected.

As you learn more about the decisions you'll make when you shoot, choosing a mode will become more obvious. Because this book won't cover how to use the controls of specific cameras, it's important for you to spend some time learning how the various modes on your camera work.

IMAGE SIZE AND COMPRESSION

Your camera probably allows you to select from a number of different sizes and compression settings so, before you shoot, you want to be sure that you've chosen settings that are right for the type of output that you'll be using, and that make the best use of your available storage space.

Image size is simply the dimensions, in pixels, of the image the camera will create. A 3-megapixel camera, for instance, typically offers a maximum resolution of roughly 2048 x 1536 pixels, along with options for shooting in XGA resolution (1024 x 768 pixels) and VGA resolution (640 x 480 pixels). Some cameras offer additional resolutions, such as the Coolpix 990's 2048 x 1360 pixels, an image size that's a slightly lower resolution than the camera's highest setting, but that offers the same 3:2 aspect ratio as 35mm film.

Which size is the "correct" size depends on how you will be outputting your images. If your images are destined for the web, then you might be able to get away with 640 x 480 resolution. The correct image size for print depends on the type of printer to which you'll be outputting, as well as the final print size of your image. We'll discuss these issues in detail in Chapters 10 and 15.

In general, it's best to shoot at the highest resolution your camera provides. This will yield the greatest image detail and best print quality, as well as providing you with the most flexibility when you output. Although you may be shooting images that are destined for the web, if you end up getting a particularly great shot, you might find that you'd like to re-use the image for a print job. Shooting at maximum resolution allows you to use your images for a different purpose at a later date.

Higher resolutions also make it possible to enlarge sections of an image, allowing you to blow up a single element in a picture, or to crop and enlarge an image to create a new framing.

Similarly, it's best to always shoot with the lowest level (highest quality) of compression, particularly if you're shooting images that don't fare well under JPEG compression (see Chapter 3). JPEG artifacts are difficult, if not impossible, to remove later so it's best to avoid them altogether.

Obviously, choosing the largest image size with the lowest compression setting means you won't be able to fit as many images onto your storage medium. If storage becomes an issue when you're in the field, then you might want to switch to different image size and compression settings. If your destination is the web, then you can afford to lower the camera's resolution (and hope that you never want to print any of your images). On the other hand, if your final destination is print you'll want to keep your resolution the same, but increase your compression (and hope that the artifacting isn't too bad).

 Money can buy photographic happiness. *Storage is one of those few problems that you can easily solve by spending additional money. If you want to be sure that you can always shoot at the highest quality your camera allows, then you'll need to invest in more storage.*

Most cameras will remember the last resolution and compression settings you used, even after the camera has been shut off. If your camera doesn't remember its settings, and if it doesn't default to the settings you'd like, then you'll need to get into the habit of configuring these settings every time you turn on your camera.

WHITE BALANCE

Different types of lights shine at different temperatures, or colors. Direct sunlight, for example, has a color temperature of 5500°K (light is always measured in degrees Kelvin) while fluorescent lights have a color temperature of 4500°K. One of the amazing characteristics of your eyeballs is that they can adjust automatically to all of these different temperatures, and can even understand mixed temperatures – sunlight shining through a window into a fluorescent-lit room, for example.

Film and digital cameras are not so sophisticated. Film has to be specially formulated for a specific type of light, or it won't be able to accurately represent color. So, you end up with "daylight" film that understands how to record color in daylight, or "tungsten" film that is capable of accurately recording color under tungsten lighting. Use either film in the wrong kind of light, and your colors will be off (using daylight film indoors will produce images that are very gold or reddish, while using tungsten film outdoors will produce images with a blueish cast).

CCDs have the same trouble. Fortunately, though, a digital camera's understanding of color is entirely dependent on how the data coming off the CCD is processed by the camera's internal computer. So, by telling the camera what kind of light you're shooting in, you can make sure that the camera interprets its color data correctly.

White balancing is the process of getting a camera to accurately represent white. Because white light contains every other color, (remember Maxwell's experiment) if a camera can accurately reproduce white, then it can accurately render every other color. Color Plate 4 shows the same scene shot several times, each with a different white balance setting.

Setting white balance

Each time you take your camera into a new lighting situation, you need to consider how to best white balance it for the available light. Proper white balance is essential to getting accurate color, and it's a step that has no equivalent in the film world. Consequently, even if you're an experienced film photographer, *you must learn to start thinking about white balance!*

All cameras have an automatic white balance feature and, depending on the quality of your camera, this may be all you need to use. The simplest automatic white balance mechanisms look for the brightest point in your shot, assume that that point is white, and then balance accordingly. More sophisticated automatic white balancers perform a complex analysis of many different areas in your image. Both mechanisms are surprisingly effective, but sometimes you have to second-guess them.

Let's say, for example, that you're shooting a marching band on a dreary, foggy day, and the brightest thing in the scene is the gold sheen of a tuba. Your camera could very well assume that the bright gold tuba was white, and throw off the color balance of your whole image. Or let's say you're shooting the Irish golf team on a well-watered golf course during St. Patrick's Day. Because the dominant color in the scene would be green, the camera could easily get confused about how to balance for white. Auto white balance works best outdoors in bright sunlight. Even a few clouds can confuse an auto white balance mechanism, and shift the colors in your image toward blue.

Fortunately, any high-quality camera will offer preset configurations for different lighting conditions. For example, most cameras offer preset modes for Daylight, Tungsten, Fluorescent, and possibly a Cloudy or Overcast setting. (Tungsten is sometimes called "Incandescent" or "Indoors".) Because there are two different temperatures of fluorescent lights – "cool white" and "warm white" — some cameras offer separate settings for each fluorescent color.

Other cameras will actually specify manual white balance settings in degrees Kelvin. So, you'll want to be sure you understand which setting corresponds to which type of light (Figure 7.2).

These white balance presets are usually more accurate than automatic white balance in the situations for which they're designed. However, you can't always be sure that your lighting situation is exactly the color temperature that your camera's preset is expecting. For example, partial cloud cover may change the daylight temperature in your scene just enough that your camera's Daylight

White Balance in K°
3000°K – White Tungsten
3700°K – Yellow Tungsten
4000°K – Fluorescent
4500°K – Fluorescent
5500°K – Sunlight
6500°K – Cloudy
7500°K – Shade

FIGURE *Some cameras use manual white balance controls that are measured in degrees*
7.2 *Kelvin. If your camera simply presents a list of temperatures, here are the types of lights they correspond to.*

preset will no longer be accurate. So, some cameras offer white balance "fine tuning" which allows you to alter a preset white balance to be warmer or cooler.

For the absolute best results under any lighting situation – and especially under mixed lighting – you'll want to use your camera's manual white balance. To use a manual white balance control, you hold a white object – such as a piece of paper – in front of the camera, and then press the camera's manual white balance button. The camera will calculate a white balance based on the light in your scene.

TIP

Measure the right light with the right white. *When you manually white balance, be sure to hold your white card in the light that is hitting your subject. If you hold the card directly in front of the camera's lens, the camera may not measure the light in your scene. This is particularly critical in a studio situation where your camera might be sitting in very different light from your subject.*

Also, don't use a super bright white paper like you may use in your inkjet printer. A normal piece of 20-lb copier paper is just the right level of white for a good white balance and can be easily glued onto the back of your gray card.

When you first get your camera, it's worth taking some test pictures to learn more about your camera's white balance peculiarities. You may, for example, learn that your camera's automatic white balance does a much better job outside than it does indoors. You'll probably also get a feel for the accuracy of your camera's white balance presets.

You should also dig through your camera's manual to determine if your camera has a *TTL* white balance system, or a white balance sensor that's outside of the camera's lens. External sensors can sometimes pick up color casts from objects that are outside the picture. A bright red car sitting just outside of the frame of your image might be all it takes to throw the camera's white balance a little out of whack. Some experimentation will help you understand how sensitive your camera's external white balance sensor is.

Bad White Balance! Bad!

A lot of people assume that they can simply use their image editor to correct images with bad white balance. This is true, but it can take a lot of work to correct a bad white balance. The color shifts that occur from incorrect white balance don't affect all of the colors in an image equally. For example, the highlights in an image might be shifted more than the shadows. So, you won't be able to do a simple "remove a certain amount of blue from the image" sort of correction. Also, by the time you're done correcting the white balance, you may have used up enough of your image's dynamic range that further corrections and adjustments will be difficult. In the end, it's best to shoot with the most accurate white balance that your camera can manage.

Virtual Color Filters. You can also choose to white balance your camera incorrectly with the goal of getting stylized or moody images. An incorrect white balance can often produce results similar to shooting through a colored filter. Check out www.completedigitalphotography.com/virtualfilters for more info.

White balance and the Raw mode. If your camera offers a Raw mode, then you can choose to set the white balance of your image later. Although Raw images take up more space and can be a bit of a hassle to work with, if you aren't sure of a correct white balance setting for a particular lighting situation, and if you don't have a white object that you can use for a manual white balance, then shoot with the Raw mode and adjust the white balance of the image later.

White Balance and Interchangeable Lenses

If you have a digital SLR with interchangeable lenses, be aware that your camera's white balance presets may work better with some lenses than with others. Different lenses have different color qualities – some are warmer or cooler than others. Your camera's white balance presets, unfortunately, might not be calibrated correctly for the color qualities of some of your lenses. Only experimentation can tell you whether a particular lens works properly with, let's say, the daylight white balance on your camera. If you find it doesn't (for example, perhaps Daylight white balance always produces images that are too warm when it is used with a particular lens) then you'll need to use auto or full manual white balance when you shoot with that lens.

Similarly, fitting your lens with a filter can mess up your camera's automatic or preset white balances as they can shift the color of the light passing through your lens. Be sure to test any filters before using them to shoot critical images.

METERING

You're going to be reading a lot about metering, both later in this chapter, and in Chapter 8. For now, simply be aware that your camera has different metering choices. It probably defaults to some form of matrix metering, which will be the best option for most shooting situations. However, like other settings, your camera might remember its meter setting even after you've turned it off. So, it's a good idea to get in the habit of making a quick check that your meter is set to the appropriate mode before you shoot.

SHARPNESS, SATURATION OR CONTRAST

Many cameras offer different levels of sharpness, color saturation, contrast, or even all three. Only you can decide which settings suit your taste, so you'll need to try a lot of test shots with these different settings. Be aware, however, that as you increase sharpness, you will also increase contrast. Your goal when you configure these settings is to allow the camera to capture the most dynamic range and detail possible. If you set contrast or sharpness too high, you may lose color information that you need later (you'll learn more about these issues in Chapter 11).

For example, consider the images in Figure 7.3

ISOs

As you saw in Chapter 4, a digital camera's sensitivity to light is measured using the same ISO scale that is used by film cameras. The higher the rating, the more light-sensitive the camera, and a more light-sensitive camera offers different creative possibilities. In addition to allowing you to shoot using less light, a higher ISO rating allows you to shoot in bright light, but with smaller apertures and higher shutter speeds. Unfortunately, there's no magic way to simply make your camera's CCD more sensitive to light. However, your camera's ISO controls can do a pretty good job of pulling more detail out of a dark image, effectively emulating a change in sensitivity.

In Chapter 3, you saw that when data is dumped from the camera's CCD, it is passed through an amplifier and then to an analog to digital converter. By increasing the amount of amplification between the CCD and the analog to digital converter, a camera becomes more sensitive to light (Figure 3.1). Simply put, your camera's ISO settings do nothing more than amplify the signal coming from the CCD.

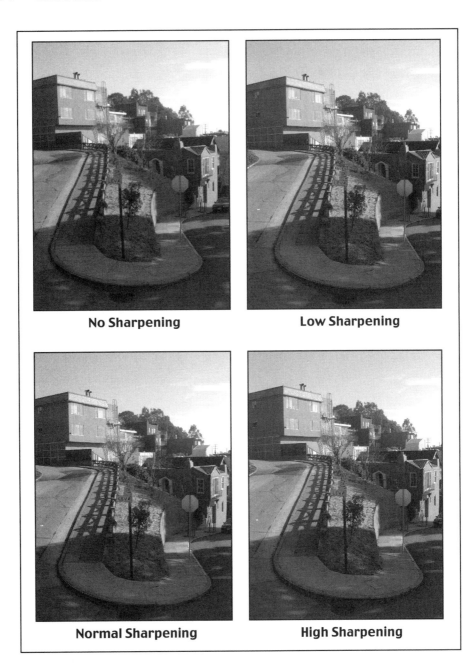

No Sharpening   Low Sharpening

Normal Sharpening   High Sharpening

FIGURE
7.3 *Some cameras allow you to change the amount of in-camera sharpening they perform. (These images have been shrunk to fit on this page, a process which tends to sharpen images.) The relative differences should be the same, but to see what the images originally looked like, check out the full color versions on the Complete Digital Photography CD-ROM.*

ON THE CD

Although the most common ISO speeds are 100, 200, and 400, higher-end models can go as high as 1600 ISO, while cameras such as the Canon G1 offer a super slow ISO 50.

There is a price to pay for this increased sensitivity, though. As you amplify the CCD's signal, you also increase any noise that the CCD has picked up. Consequently, higher-ISO images tend to be fairly noisy. (Figure 7.4)

FIGURE   *Although using higher ISOs affords greater shooting flexibility, it also increases the*
7.4   *amount of noise in your image.*

Some cameras handle this extra noise better than others, producing low-contrast noise that almost looks like the increased grain that you'd find in a film with a faster ISO rating. Other cameras produce increased noise that is quite ugly (Figure 7.5).

ON THE CD

FIGURE **7.5**   *All noise is bad, but some noise is worse than others. When shooting at high ISO, the Canon G1 produces very speckly noise with bright color artifacts, as can be seen in this image. Check out the color image on the Complete Digital Photogaphy CD-ROM.*

In Chapter 13 we'll look at some methods for trying to remove noise from your images.

TIP

Keep an eye on your ISO. *Most cameras remember your last ISO setting, even after you've turned the camera off. So, if you spent a long night shooting at ISO 400, don't forget to check your ISO setting the next day, before you go out shooting in bright day-light. Although your camera will be able to shoot in daylight at ISO 400, there a chance your images will be overexposed, they will certainly be noisier than at a slower speed, and your depth of field will be deeper.*

FRAMING AND FOCUSING

After you configure your camera settings as described in the last section, you're ready to start framing and focusing your shot. As we said at the beginning of this chapter, composition and other areas of photographic "artistry" are beyond the scope of this book. However, there are a number of technical concerns that will immediately improve the composition of your images, no matter what your artistic or journalistic intent might be.

FOCAL LENGTH

The great thing about a zoom lens is that it provides great flexibility when you frame a shot. Without changing your position, you can quickly zoom into a subject to get a tighter view and a different framing. However, it's essential that you pay attention to the other elements of your image that change when you zoom in and out.

It's easy to think of your zoom lens as a big magnifying glass and, to a degree, it is. As you zoom in, your subject appears larger and larger. This is why digital camera manufacturers label their lenses with a magnification factor – 2x, 3x, etc. However, a few other things happen to your image when you zoom.

As you go to a longer focal length, (zoom in) your field of view gets narrower. The human eye has a field of view of about 50 to 55°. This is considered a "normal" field of view and any lens that produces a 50 to 55° viewing angle is said to be a "*normal lens.*"

More important, though, is to pay attention to the way that a lens magnifies different parts of your image and how it compresses depth overall as you zoom in and out.

Consider the images in Figure 7.6.

Both of these images were shot from the same location. The only thing that changed between shots was the focal length of the lens. However, as you can see, with a shorter focal length (wider angle) the background appears much farther away – the image is deeper. Now look at the two images in Figure 7.7.

In these two images, the subject remained in the same place, but the photographer moved further away and used a different focal length to keep the image framed the same as the first image. Notice how much closer the trees look in the second image. As the photographer moved back and zoomed in, the depth in the image compressed, and the trees appeared to move closer.

As you can see, field of view is a function of the position of your camera and the focal length that you choose to use. When you shoot with a wide-angle lens, objects that are closer to the lens get magnified more than objects that are farther away, while a telephoto lens magnifies near and far images by the same amount. Because all objects, no matter how far away they are, are magnified equally, a telephoto lens compresses the depth in your scene.

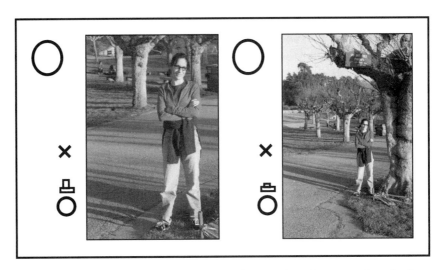

FIGURE **7.6** *In these two images, neither the photographer nor the subject moved. In the first image, a slightly telephoto focal length was used, while in the second image, a very wide focal length was used. Notice how much farther away the background trees appear in the second image.*

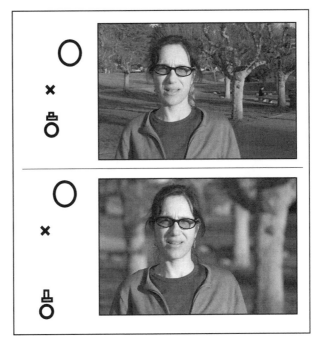

FIGURE **7.7** *Although these two images are framed the same, notice how different the backgrounds are. In addition to the lower image being blurrier, the trees in the background seem much closer, even though the subject didn't move.*

At some point, you've probably looked at a photograph of yourself and thought "that doesn't really look like me." One reason for the poor result might be that the photographer was using a wide-angle lens. Shooting a portrait with a wide-angle lens is problematic because some parts of your subject's face are closer to the lens than others. Consequently, those parts will be magnified more than the parts that are farther away. Check out the pictures in Figure 7.8. The image on the left was shot with a slightly telephoto lens and really does look like the actual person. The image on the right, although good for a laugh, is not a very good likeness. The nose is too big and the ears have been rendered too small. In addition, the distance between the nose and ears – the depth of the picture – is too long.

FIGURE **7.8** *A change in focal length can make a huge difference in the appearance of your subject. The image on the left was shot with a long focal length. Next we zoomed out and moved closer to our subject to produce the weirdly distorted image on the right.*

Typically, portrait photographers use a slightly telephoto lens. Some even use special "portrait" lenses that have some spherical aberration designed into the lens. These aberrations tend to soften the detail in the image to improve skin tones.

Your choice of focal length – and the corresponding position of your camera – will have a lot to do with the sense of space and depth in your image. As you saw in Figure 7.8, the difference in results when you shoot at close proximity with a wide-angle lens and when you shoot from far away with a telephoto lens can be quite dramatic. So, just because you can zoom in to the framing that you want for a particular shot doesn't mean that it's the right choice for the shot.

Your subject might be better served by repositioning the camera, and choosing a different focal length.

Geometric distortion

It's important to pay attention to any potential distortion cause by inferior optics in your lens. Most zoom lenses exhibit some form of barrel or pincushion distortion when the lenses are zoomed to either of their extremes. These distortions will show up as curves and warps around the edges and corners of your image (you can see an example in Figure 5.20).

When you find yourself at the limits of your zoom range, be sure to check the edges of your image for distortion. If you can live with it, then by all means, take the shot. If it bothers you, then you might need to reposition your camera and select a new focal length. If the distortion isn't too bad, you may be able to remove it with your image editing software, as we'll see in Chapter 10.

One way to avoid embarrassment. *If you're using a rangefinder camera with an optical viewfinder, note that, because you aren't looking through the camera's imaging lens, it is actually possible to shoot with the lens cap on! Some cameras are smart enough to warn you, others will let you blithely go along shooting black frames. Be sure to double-check!*

TIP

FOCUSING

Although your digital camera invariably has an automatic focus, that doesn't mean that you don't have to give some thought to focusing. One downside to the typical digital camera is that it can be difficult to tell whether your autofocus mechanism has really worked. LCD screens are usually too small to be an accurate gauge of focus while the typical optical viewfinder is usually just plain lousy. Consequently, it's a good idea to understand some of the workings of your camera's autofocus system so that you can learn when you might be facing a troublesome focusing situation.

Using Autofocus

No matter what kind of system your camera uses for determining focus, the process of focusing the camera is probably the same. You simply frame your shot and press the shutter button down halfway. The camera will calculate and lock focus (as well as exposure and auto white balance) and then beep, or show a light to indicate that it's ready. Pressing the button the rest of the way will take the picture using the focus, exposure, and white balance settings that the camera has calculated.

Although this system is simple to use, photographers who are new to autofocus cameras can be quickly frustrated by what seems to be an extreme lag between the time they push the button and the time the camera actually takes this picture. This *shutter lag* is usually because the photographer is simply pressing the button down all the way when they're ready to take the picture, rather than pressing the button down halfway and giving the camera a chance to prefocus. By pressing the button all the way down, you're asking the camera to focus, calculate exposure and figure out white balance all in the instant that you want to take the picture.

Although this prefocusing step may sound like an inconvenience, it's really no more trouble than what you'd have to do with a manually focused camera except that, instead of focusing manually, the camera is focusing for you.

 Shutter lag even with prefocusing. *Some older cameras (and, unfortunately, a few newer ones) have a bit of a shutter lag even if you've already pressed the shutter release halfway down to go through the prefocusing step. Unfortunately, there's really nothing you can do to work around this problem except to learn how long the lag is so that you can try to anticipate when you need to press the shutter to capture the action you want.*

Your camera might also have a continuous autofocus mechanism which automatically focuses every time you move or zoom the camera. With continuous autofocus, your camera stands a much better chance of being ready to shoot at any time. However, it can also drain your battery and can sometimes be distracting, as you will constantly hear the lens working. If your camera has a speedy autofocus, you may find little advantage to a continuous mechanism.

Some higher-end cameras such as the Nikon D1 and the Canon D30 also feature a *focus tracking* or *servo tracking* feature which can automatically track a moving object and keep it in focus for as long as you hold the shutter button halfway down. For sports photography, this feature can help to ensure that you're always ready to get the shot.

Most digital cameras employ one of two different autofocus mechanisms, each with its own strengths and weaknesses.

Active Autofocus

Although less popular than it used to be, some lower-end cameras still provide *active autofocus* mechanisms because they're typically the cheapest autofocus mechanism to implement. An active autofocus mechanism works by using an infrared beam to measure the distance to your subject; your camera then sets the focus accordingly. It's called an "active" system because the camera is actively emitting a signal in an effort to measure distance.

The easiest way to tell if your camera uses an active system is to look at the technical specifications included in your camera's manual. You can also simply look at the front of the camera and see if you can identify anything that looks like an infrared emitter (it will look something like the little window on the front of a TV remote control).

Although active infrared autofocus mechanisms work fairly well, they have a number of limitations.

- You must have a clear line of sight between you and your subject. Bars in a zoo, fence posts, or other obstructions can keep the camera from accurately measuring distance.
- Because the infrared beam is not originating from the lens, the camera may not correctly calculate focus if you're using any kind of lens attachment such as a wide-angle or telephoto adapter. Consequently, most cameras with active autofocus mechanisms don't provide for such attachments.
- If you're standing close to another strong infrared source – such as a very hot campfire, or the birthday cake of a really old person – then the heat from that source can confuse the camera's autofocus mechanism.
- On the positive side, active autofocus systems work just fine in the dark.

Passive Autofocus

Most higher-end prosumer cameras use a *passive autofocus* system, sometimes called a *contrast detection* system. You should be able to find out what kind of system your camera uses by simply looking at the specifications table in your camera's manual. For example, the Olympus C2100 specifies its autofocus system as a "*TTL* contrast detection autofocus."

As you might have guessed, contrast detecting autofocus systems work by focusing the lens until the image has as much contrast as possible. The idea is that a low-contrast image is a blurry image. So, by increasing contrast, you're increasing sharpness. The top image in Figure 7.9 shows an out-of-focus image. Look at the individual pixels up close and you'll see that there is very little change from one pixel to the next. That is, the pixels have little contrast between them. In the lower image in Figure 7.9, a sharp image, you can see that individual pixels have a more dramatic change in contrast from pixel to pixel.

When you press the shutter release halfway, your camera takes an initial reading of the contrast in your shot. It then focuses the lens closer and checks the contrast again. If contrast has increased, then the camera continues focusing inward until the contrast decreases. With a decrease in focus, the camera knows it has gone too far and can step back to zero in on the correct focus. Obviously, there are a lot of variables that can affect this process, such as the camera's ability to detect contrast, the precision with which it can move its lens, and the speed with which it can go through this whole process. Theoretically, a camera

FIGURE **7.9** *If you look closely at the pixels in the upper, blurry image, you'll see that there is very little change in tone from one to the next. That is, there is very little contrast between them. In the lower image, there is a big contrast change from pixel to pixel. This is why searching for high contrast is a good way of detecting focus.*

with more autofocus steps can achieve a more precise focus position and, therefore, achieve better focus. However, digital cameras typically have *very* deep depths of field so tiny changes in focus usually aren't that important. Also, most of the steps in an autofocus system are centered around very close (macro) ranges where they tend to be needed, and where depth of field offers less compensation.

Contrast detection is largely a function of the available light in your scene. If the area in which you're pointing your camera is too dark, or is uniformly colored, then your camera won't be able to detect any contrast and will be unable to determine focus. Today, most cameras include an automatic *focus assist lamp* (also known as an an autofocus assist lamp) which simply shines a light onto your scene if the camera can't detect focus. By lighting up the scene, your camera's autofocus mechanism can simply "see" better. Some cameras use a normal white light focus assist lamp, while others use a less intrusive red lamp.

A passive autofocus mechanism has many advantages:

- Because they look through the camera's lens, passive autofocus systems work with any filters or lens attachments you may be using and you can be sure that what they're focusing on is actually in the camera's field of view.
- Because they're simply analyzing what the camera is seeing, they can work through windows, water, or other transparent materials.
- They have no distance limitation, although your camera's autofocus assist lamp will have some sort of limiting distance.

On the downside, passive systems do require light in your scene and a subject that has enough detail to produce contrast. However, these limitations are minor and, as you'll see later, you can usually work around them using one of several techniques.

Autofocus and wide-angle lenses. *If you're using a digital SLR with interchangeable lenses, be aware that very wide-angle lenses (14-18mm) can confuse autofocus mechanisms. For example, although the camera's autofocus may think that it's focused at infinity, it might actually be focused much closer. When you use such lenses, you may get much better results by focusing manually.*

Focus Spots

Obviously, you want your autofocusing system to only worry about focusing on the subject of your image, not the entire scene. So, your camera has a *focusing zone* or *spot* that determines which part of the image will be analyzed for focus. Most cameras simply use a small area in the middle of the frame as the focus target, and sometimes they even mark the area with crosshairs in the camera's optical viewfinder.

However, if your subject isn't in the middle of the frame, then there's a good chance that your camera is going to focus on the background of your image, leaving the foreground soft or outright blurry. You can get around this problem by taking advantage of the fact that when you press your camera's shutter button down halfway, the camera calculates focus and then locks it until you either let go, or take the picture.

So, if you want to focus on something on the right side of the frame, you can simply point the camera's focusing target (usually the middle of the frame) at that object, press your shutter button halfway, hold it down, *and then reframe your shot,* to your desired framing. When you press the button the rest of the way, the camera will take the picture using the focus that it initially calculated. Figure 7.10 shows an example.

FIGURE *To keep the camera from focusing on the sky, the camera's focusing target was*
7.10 *pointed at the lamp post and the shutter release was pressed halfway down to lock focus. The image was reframed, and the picture was shot with correct focus.*

Be aware, though, that there are some potential pitfalls to this technique.

In addition to calculating focus, when you do a half-press of your shutter button, your camera also calculates exposure and white balance (if you're using automatic white balance). If the lighting in your frame is substantially different after you reframe than it was from when you locked focus, your camera's exposure could be off.

As we explained earlier, automatic white balance mechanisms can be confused when they are presented with a preponderance of similar colors. When you perform your initial focus, make sure there are no fields of color that might confuse your camera's white balance. For example, if your subject is standing against a dull gray wall when you lock focus, and then you reframe so that only a bit of that wall is showing, your white balance could be out of whack.

Camera manufacturers have come up with two solutions for these problems. The first is a separate *exposure lock* button that allows you to separately lock your camera's exposure and focus (Figure 7.11). Different exposure lock features work in different ways, but most allow you to do something like this: frame your shot as you want to shoot it; measure and lock the exposure; move your camera and lock focus on your subject; and then return to your final framing with everything ready to go. As we'll see later, exposure lock is also necessary for taking good panoramic shots.

FIGURE *The exposure lock button on the Canon G1 allows you to lock focus and exposure*
7.11 *independent of each other.*

Other cameras include multiple focus zones, usually three, sometimes as many as seven. A camera with multiple focus spots looks at several different points in your image to try to determine where your subject might be. Once it has decided, it analyzes the focus spot closest to your subject to determine when the image is in focus.

Multiple autofocus spots (Figure 7.12) allow you to frame your image as you like without having to worry about your subject being in the middle of the frame. However, it's important to pay attention to where the camera is focusing, as it will often pick the wrong subject. Consequently, some cameras let you manually select a focus point to ensure that your autofocus mechanism analyzes the right area. Most cameras with multi-spot autofocus mechanisms also allow you to put the camera into a single, *center-spot focusing* mode (sometimes called *spot focus*) which forces the camera to behave like a normal single-spot autofocus camera.

FIGURE *Multiple focus zones let you control where the camera's auto-focus mechanism will*
7.12 *look when it determines focus.*

If your camera uses a TTL contrast detection focusing system, the center
focusing spot (no matter how many focus zones the camera has) is usually a
dual-axis zone. That is, it examines contrast along both a horizontal and vertical
axis. If the camera has multiple zones, there's a good chance that the other
zones are *single-axis zones* which only measure contrast (and therefore, focus)
along a horizontal axis. For locking focus on horizontal subjects, such as hori-
zons, a single-axis zone can be problematic. For these situations, you may want
to force the camera to use its center, dual-axis zone.

If there's any one rule to using an autofocus camera – whether a single-spot,
or multi-spot focusing system – it's simply to pay attention. Don't just assume
that the camera will be able to calculate everything accurately. If your camera
has a single-spot focusing system that sometimes requires you to lock focus and
reframe, then be sure to look for any potential metering and white balance troubles before you shoot. If your camera has a multi-spot focusing system, then be
certain that it has chosen the correct subject and focusing zone.

What to do if Your Autofocus Won't Lock Focus

If you're using a contrast detection autofocus system, there will be times when it
won't be able to lock focus. If you're shooting in low light, contrast can be low
enough to foil your camera's autofocus system. Hopefully, the camera has an

automatic focus assist lamp that will activate to light the scene. If the focus assist lamp lights up and the camera still can't focus, try moving the camera slightly. You may illuminate something contrasty enough that the camera will be able to focus – but be sure that it doesn't focus on something at the wrong distance.

Autofocus mechanisms can even get confused in bright daylight if your camera is pointed at something low-contrast. In Figure 7.13 you can see that the middle of the frame is filled with something that is a solid color (the lamp). The lack of contrast in the lamp's color can confuse a contrast detecting autofocus as shown in the image on the left. By tilting the camera up so that its focusing target is sitting on top of a more contrasty subject at the same distance, the autofocus can get a lock as shown in the image on the right.

FIGURE   *Because this white lamp is a solid color, there's little contrast for a camera's contrast*
7.13   *detecting autofocus mechanism to detect. So, to get the camera to lock focus, you must*
            frame the shot at a point where there is some contrast, lock focus, and then reframe
            (be sure you lock on a point that's the same distance away as is your subject).

Advanced Autofocus Mechanisms

If you've got a higher-end digital SLR such as the Nikon D1, then your camera probably uses a more advanced form of autofocus called phase difference or phase detection. Phase detection autofocus is a TTL metering system that uses a complex arrangement of prisms and two tiny CCD arrays that are placed next to the focal plane. Both CCDs see the same part of the image, but one CCD looks through the left edge of the lens while the other looks through the right edge.

When the lens is focused too close, the image in the left-looking CCD will be slightly to the left of the right-looking CCD. When the lens is focused too far, the opposite occurs. By analyzing the two images and determining the difference in shift between them, the camera can calculate which way to move the lens, and how far it needs to go.

As with other autofocus systems, the quality of a phase difference system depends on its ability to quickly and accurately control the lens motor, as well as its ability to detect what area needs to be in focus.

Phase difference systems are incredibly accurate and generally very speedy. In addition, many of these systems are capable of focusing in near darkness. On the downside, some phase difference autofocus mechanisms become less reliable at apertures below f5.6. As the aperture gets smaller, the CCDs lose their line of sight out of the lens and the lens can become confused. In general, though, these systems, whether single- or multi-spot, are by far the most accurate, quickest autofocus mechanisms available.

Manual Focus

Your camera's autofocus mechanism is probably all that you'll ever need. However, if you run into a situation where your camera can't autofocus, and you can't work around it, or if you have a particularly "creative" shot that you want to compose, you might need to resort to your camera's manual focus. (This is all assuming you're using a prosumer-type camera that lacks interchangeable lenses with focus rings. If you're using a professional-level SLR, you'll probably be regularly switching between automatic and manual focus.)

Unfortunately, manual focus features on digital cameras leave a *lot* to be desired. Between poorly designed controls and viewfinders that lack focusing aids, getting an accurate manual focus out of your camera can be difficult. A few years ago, most digital cameras simply offered you a choice of distances. So, in addition to having to try to estimate the distance to your subject, you had to hope that the camera provided a preset focus distance that was close to what you needed.

Many digital cameras still work this way, but a number of vendors now include a more robust control that lets you smoothly move throughout the focus range of your camera. However, determining when you've achieved focus will be difficult as neither your camera's LCD screen or optical viewfinder may be good enough to let you see focus.

Fortunately, digital cameras typically use very small apertures and, as we'll see, small apertures create such deep depth of field that you often don't have to worry about your focus being dead on. You can further improve your chances of getting good focus by using your camera's manual controls to set as small an aperture as possible when you're using manual focus.

Even if your camera doesn't have a full manual focus control, it probably has a preset control for locking focus at infinity. This can be a handy feature for landscape photography or other times when your subject is far away. Lock your camera camera's focus at infinity and it will not only perform faster (since it won't be having to try to autofocus) but your batteries may last a little longer (since the camera won't be moving the lens around).

METERING

When you press your camera's shutter release, you expose the camera's CCD to light. By adjusting the camera's shutter speed and aperture size, you can control how much light will reach the CCD, but how do you know how much is enough? By using your camera's light meter.

At the simplest level, a light meter helps ensure that your pictures are not too bright or too dark, so that you can actually see the subjects in your image. With a little thought and planning, though, your light meter – and the associated exposure controls – becomes the most powerful creative tool on your camera. In this section you'll learn the basics of metering, and take a look at what exposure options you have when you shoot with your camera in automatic mode. Manual controls and advanced exposure topics will be covered in Chapter 8.

WHAT YOUR LIGHT METER TELLS YOU

To really know how to get the most from your camera's built-in light meter, it's almost as important to understand what it *cannot* do, as it is to understand what it *can* do. The light meter on a typical prosumer, point-and-shoot, or even slightly higher-end camera, cannot tell you anything about the colors in your scene, how much contrast there is, or how to preserve all of the detail that's present. In other words, your light meter doesn't tell you (or your camera) the *best* exposure for the scene you are shooting. Rather, your light meter simply tells you an *adequate* exposure for the scene you are shooting – that is, one that will not grossly over- or underexpose your image. Ideally, you will take your meter's reading as a starting point, and build from there into the best exposure.

Really, all your light meter does is measure the *luminance* of the light reflected by your subject. Whether it measures the luminance of the entire scene or just a part of the scene depends on the type of meter you are using.

Figure 7.14 shows a grid with an equal number of black and white squares. If you were to measure it with a light meter, you would find that Figure 7.14 is reflecting 18% of the light that is striking it. Most of the time, the tones in a typical scene will average out in about the same way, meaning the scene will reflect 18% of the light that hits it. Since this is only a measure of luminance (not color) you can also think of this 18% reflectance as a shade of gray. This particular gray shade is known to photographers as *18% gray* or *middle gray.*

FIGURE *Although each of these squares is black or white, the entire field of squares meters as*
7.14 *middle gray.*

The *most important* thing to know about your camera's light meter is that *it always assumes that it is pointed at something that is 18% gray.* In other words, your light meter is generating an exposure recommendation that will accurately reproduce middle gray using the current lighting. Obviously, if the lighting in your scene suddenly changes, the readings will no longer be accurate, (even if the scene is still reflecting 18% of that light) and you'll have to re-meter.

To get the best results from your light meter, then, you'll want to meter off of something that is middle gray, such as an 18% gray card. Readily available at any photo supply store, you can simply place this card in your scene and use it as the subject for your metering. There will be situations, of course, where you won't have time, or won't be able to place a gray card in your scene. Fortunately, since the typical scene usually works out to be middle gray, your meter's middle gray assumption is usually safe.

The problem, of course, is that many of the objects in your scene will be brighter or darker than middle gray. Take a look at the penguin in Figure 7.15. Notice that in the first shot, his black feathers are not completely black and his white feathers aren't completely white. The camera metered to produce gray (an accurate assumption given the average tones in this image) and so nothing is really black or white.

The second image was overexposed by one stop. Notice that now his white feathers really do look white, although they have lost some detail. The black feathers are now even grayer. The third image was intentionally underexposed by one stop. Now the black feathers are truly black, although the whites have been dulled.

FIGURE **7.15**   *When left to its own devices, your camera will assume that this penguin is gray and will meter incorrectly for both his white and black feathers. With some overexposure we can restore the white to his feathers, or we can underexpose to darken up his black feathers.*

Now take a look at Color Plate 7. The left-hand image was shot with the camera's recommended metering while the right-hand image was underexposed by half a stop because the orange color of the car was a bit darker than 18% gray. As you can see, colors have a luminance – or tone – just as black and white images do and, therefore, need the same type of compensation for accurate reproduction. Simply put, by overexposing your images your colors will become lighter, while underexposing will make your colors darker. Such adjustments allow you to either restore the right color to the objects in your scene, or to intentionally boost or decrease the saturation of objects within your scene.

As stated earlier, your camera's light meter generates exposure settings that create an adequate picture. In general, your camera's meter will yield images with good color and proper exposure throughout the shadows and highlights. However, because of your light meter's assumptions, your picture may come out looking a little flat, as darker or lighter tones will all be rendered as middle tones. However, with some adjustments you can turn these images from adequate to exceptional by changing your exposure to improve color accuracy, contrast, and saturation (or tonal accuracy and contrast if you're shooting black and white).

THE RIGHT METER FOR THE JOB

Your camera probably offers a choice of different metering modes. These are usually selected from a button on the camera's body, or from a menu within the camera's menuing system. Shooting a well-exposed image begins with your selection of the metering mode that's right for your scene.

Matrix Metering

A *matrix meter* (sometimes called a *multi-segment* meter) divides your image into a grid and takes a separate meter reading for each cell in the grid. These cells are then analyzed to determine an exposure setting.

Matrix metering is the best choice for most situations and is certainly the best option when you're simply trying to get a quick shot using your camera's automatic features. However, there are some situations that are particularly difficult for a matrix metering system. Learning to identify such situations will make it easier to understand when you should switch to a different metering system.

In general, if you are facing a scene that has both bright highlights and dark shadows, there's a good chance your meter will get confused. Different meters respond to these sorts of situations in different ways and only experience with your camera will help you predict how your meter might respond to the lighting situation shown in Figure 7.16.

Your main concern when you use a matrix meter is to understand how it will preserve shadow and highlight areas. Try to find some tricky situations and spend some time experimenting with your camera's ability to preserve shadow information. Then try to determine how far it can be pushed before it blows out bright areas such as skies. This information will inform the exposure adjustment decisions you'll be making later.

Shooting the same scene with two different cameras can produce very different results, as you can see in Figure 7.16. This street scene presents a difficult lighting situation as the street-level details are dark and shadowy while up at the top of the building things are bright and sunny. Notice how the Nikon chose a metering that revealed lots of street-level detail while the Olympus chose to provide more extreme contrast between the daylight and shadowy areas.

Center-Weighted Metering

A variation of matrix metering, *center-weight metering* also divides your image into a grid of cells, but when analyzing the readings, a center-weighted metering system gives preference to the cells in the middle of the image. Typically, the middle 80% of the cells are considered more important than the outlying regions. Center-weighted metering is designed for those times when your subject is in the middle of your frame and your background contains bright lights, dark shadows, or other extreme lighting situations that might throw off the metering in the center of your image.

FIGURE **7.16** *The left image was shot with a Nikon Coolpix 990 while the right-hand image was shot with an Olympus C-2500. Both cameras were set for matrix metering and were on full automatic. Notice how differently they chose to meter.*

Spot Metering

A *spot meter* measures only a small area of your image, usually the center. The metering from this area is the only information used to calculate an exposure. The most common use for your spot meter is for dealing with extremely backlit situations – a person standing in front of a window, for example – that would normally cause your camera to underexpose your foreground. Spot meters, though, can also be handy with dark backgrounds, such as the one shown in Figure 7.17. In the upper image, the background is deeply shadowed and has lost detail. By activating the camera's spot meter and metering off of the shadowy background, the camera produces an image with much better shadow detail. Fortunately, the foreground detail was not washed out in the process.

Spot meters are also used for complex *zone system* metering, as we'll see in the next chapter. However, such metering usually requires a spot meter with a very small – 1° or so — metering circle. The spot meters in most cameras use a much bigger sample area. To get an idea of how big your camera's spot is, try shooting a series of images like the one shown in Figure 7.17, but from greater and greater distances. Eventually, your spot will be larger than your subject and your metering will fail. At this point, you can get a rough idea of the size of your camera's metering spot.

FIGURE   *Switching from the matrix meter to the spot meter made it possible to reveal more*
7.17   *detail in the shadowy background area.*

AUTOMATIC EXPOSURE

If you're shooting using your camera's automatic mode, then it will automatically meter and select an exposure whenever you press the shutter release halfway. As you saw earlier, the camera's meter makes a number of assumptions about the contents of your scene, the main one being that your scene has an average reflectance of 18%. This is great for most scenes, but if you head into a bright white, highly reflective field of snow, then your meter will be dead wrong.

When you shoot a scene that's brighter or darker than middle gray, you'll want to over- or underexpose your shot. In the old days, if you were using a manual film camera, you would over or underexpose by adjusting your camera's aperture and shutter speed controls. If you're using your digital camera in its automatic mode, or if your digital camera doesn't have manual shutter speed and aperture controls, you'll have to use other tricks to force a change in exposure.

Fortunately, almost all digital cameras these days offer exposure compensation features – simple controls that let you easily over- or underexpose by up to two stops, usually in 1/3-stop increments. If you think your scene needs to be overexposed by a stop, you simply press the + exposure button three times. Exposure compensation controls are the quickest and easiest way (and, on some cameras, the only way) to make exposure adjustments.

When you shoot in automatic mode, most cameras will opt for a high shutter speed to help ensure a sharp image – slower speeds can result in a blurry image if you're not holding the camera steady. When you use exposure compensation, most cameras try to achieve the requested change in exposure by changing shutter speed. When this isn't possible, either because the camera's shutter can't go any faster, or because slowing the shutter speed would risk blurring the image, then the camera will make changes to aperture. Sometimes, the camera will make slight changes to both shutter speed and aperture. Fortunately, these changes are usually minor enough that you won't see any change in the camera's ability to freeze motion, or in the image's depth of field.

 Controlling exposure with your spot meter. *If your camera has a spot meter, you can force an over- or underexposure by pointing the camera at something darker or lighter. Meter off of a darker subject, and your camera will overexpose. Meter off of a lighter subject, and you'll get an underexposure. However, because your camera will probably lock focus at the same time as exposure, you'll need to be certain that you are metering off of something that is at the same distance as the image you would like to have in focus.*

Automatic metering and exposure compensation can be summed up very simply:

- If your scene is very bright, then your meter will underexpose, and the bright objects in your scene will appear gray. Correct this by using your exposure compensation controls to overexpose.
- Conversely, if your scene is dark, then your meter will overexpose, and the darker objects in your scene will appear gray. Correct this by using your exposure compensation controls to underexpose.

Exposure compensation controls are powerful tools and you will continue to use them even after you've learned some of the more advanced techniques that will be covered in the next chapter. Get comfortable with your camera's exposure compensation controls, learn how to use them quickly, and begin learning how to recognize how much compensation is necessary for different situations. Because there are no hard and fast rules for over- or underexposing, you've just got to go out and practice!

SIMPLE FLASH PHOTOGRAPHY

Using your camera's built-in flash is pretty simple: just turn it on and let the camera worry about when and how much to fire it. Using your camera's built-in flash well is a bit more difficult. Unfortunately, the small flash units provided by most cameras are pretty low-powered and, because they are usually positioned so close to the camera's lens, they don't often produce very flattering light. However, your camera's built-in flash does have its uses, and with a little know-how, you can get it to yield good results.

FLASH MODES

Most digital cameras provide several different flash modes. If you're shooting in a fully automatic mode, then your camera is probably using its automatic flash mode which tries to determine, on-the-fly, whether or not the flash is needed. If the camera decides the flash is needed, it fires it for the appropriate time. In addition to this mode, your camera probably provides the following:

- *Fill (or force flash)*. This mode forces the flash to fire and is an ideal way of creating fill lighting in brightly-lit situations.
- *Red-eye reduction*. The "red-eye" effect is caused by the light from your flash bouncing off the retinas of your subject's eyes as they look into the lens. If the flash on your camera is placed very close to the lens, there's a much better chance of getting red-eye, because it's easier for the light to bounce straight back into the lens. Red-eye reduction modes work by firing a flash (or the camera's autofocus assist lamp) to close the subject's iris. When you use these modes, be sure to inform your subjects that there will be two flashes. Otherwise, they might move or close their eyes after the first firing. Whether you're shooting with or without a red-eye reduction flash, moving slightly to one side before you shoot can prevent your subjects from looking directly into the camera's lens. You can also try turning on all the lights in the room in an attempt to narrow everyone's pupils.
- *Cancel*. This simply de-activates the flash. This isn't exactly a mode, but it is an important feature for times when you're shooting in an area where a flash is not appropriate.

Spend some time with the different flash modes on your camera to learn their characteristics. In particular, determine if the flash consistently over- or under-exposes, and if it tends to produce odd colorcasts. If so, then you might want to adjust its settings as described below.

Ol' Blue — er — Red eyes... *Generally, people with lighter-colored eyes are more susceptible to red-eye in photographs than people with darker-colored eyes. Probably the worst red-eye situation is shooting a blue-eyed person in a dark room. When you shoot lighter-eyed people, it's a good idea to take the time to review your images on your camera's LCD. If your camera has a zoom feature in its playback mode, zoom in and check out the eyes. You may find you need to re-shoot.*

When you shoot a picture using your flash, a lot of things happen in a very short amount of time. First, the camera opens its shutter and begins exposing the image sensor according to the settings defined by you or your camera's light meter. Then, the camera turns on the lamp in its flash unit. With the lamp on, the camera begins measuring the flash illumination that is bouncing off the subject and returning to the camera. In this way, the camera can meter the flash's light in while it's flashing. When it has decided that the flash has cast enough illumination, it shuts off the flash, finishes the exposure, and closes the shutter.

After the flash is finished firing, any left-over charge is saved for the next firing. Consequently, your flash's recycle time can vary depending on how much it had to fire. In other words, you'll get faster recycle times when you use your flash in brighter light, since the flash won't have to fire for as long and, hence, won't have to recharge as much.

One problem with on-board flashes is that they're really not positioned to provide very flattering light. Our eyes are used to a strong overhead light source, so placing a light source directly in front of a subject usually produces a somewhat weird lighting perspective. In addition, a poor flash exposure can result in harsh lighting with overblown highlights and hard-edged black shadows if the flash fired too much, or an underexposed image if the flash fired too little. (Figure 7.18)

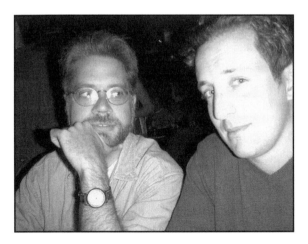

FIGURE *At times, you may find that your camera's on-board flash creates harshly-lit scenes*
7.18 *with blown-out highlights.*

Fortunately, many cameras now offer flash power adjustment controls which let you increase or decrease the power of the flash by one or two stops in either direction. After a test shot, you may find that your camera's flash is too strong. Dialing down the power by a stop or so may be enough to produce a much better exposure. (Figure 7.19)

FIGURE *After dialing a -.3 flash exposure compensation, our slightly overexposed image*
7.19 *becomes much more pleasantly lit.*

Remember that your camera's flash has a limited range, usually no more than 10-15 feet. So, as your focal length increases, your flash's effectiveness decreases. That is, if you zoom in on an object 20 feet away, don't expect your flash to do a great job of illuminating it. Increasing the flash power by a couple of stops may improve your flash performance at these distances.

FLASH WHITE BALANCE

You don't usually use your flash in a room that is completely dark. Rather, you're usually firing your flash in a room that is lit with other lighting, thus creating a complex mixed-lighting situation that requires a special white balance.

Some cameras have a separate white balance setting for flash that can often correct color cast problems, but on most cameras, automatic white balance will yield the best results. In fact, on most cameras, using anything *but* automatic will yield bad results.

To get an idea of your how your camera white balances when you use the flash, take some test flash pictures indoors under normal incandescent (tungsten) lighting using the camera's automatic white balance. If the images come out with a slightly blue cast, or if the highlights are blue, then the camera's white balance chose to favor the room's tungsten lighting. If the images come out a little yellow, or have yellow highlights, then the camera white balanced in favor of the flash.

There's little you can do about these color casts. Sometimes dialing down the flash's power will reduce the effect, or you can try to filter your flash. If you find blue highlights in your flash pictures, buy some yellow filter material at your camera store and simply tape a piece of it over your flash. This will balance your flash for tungsten, making it better match the indoor lighting (which your camera is white balancing for anyway).

Fill Flash

Don't get trapped into thinking that your flash is only for shooting at night, or indoors. Your camera's fill flash mode is a great tool for shooting better pictures in bright sunlight.

When you shoot into backlit situations, you usually have two choices. You can spot-meter off of your foreground subject, which will cause the background to overexpose and wash out completely. Or, you can matrix meter which will properly expose the background, but leave your foreground subject dark and underexposed. A third solution is to activate your camera's fill flash. This will throw enough light on your foreground that the camera will properly expose both the foreground and background (Figure 7.20).

FIGURE **7.20** *In the image on the left, we shot using our camera's matrix meter, which sacrificed some quality in the foreground to better-expose the background. In the image on the right, we used our fill flash to get a better foreground exposure.*

Fill flash is also great for subjects wearing hats, or for subjects that are shaded by overhanging foreground objects. Usually, the bright outdoor light will be so strong that your flash will provide a rather soft fill light, with none of the harsh shadows you might see indoors or in lower light.

POWER AND STORAGE MANAGEMENT

Film cameras do have one marked advantage over digital cameras: they don't *have* to have batteries. With an all-manual film camera, all you need is film (as long as you don't want a light meter) making it simple to go on looooong photographic excursions without carrying batteries, battery chargers, and laptop computers.

Digital cameras are not so efficient. For a simple day's shooting, you probably won't have to worry too much about batteries and storage when you use your digital camera, unless you're very shutter happy, or have a tiny storage card. For long trips, though, you'll want to make some effort to conserve and maximize both batteries and storage.

FEEL THE POWER

The easiest way to allay your power fears is simply to buy lots of batteries. If your camera uses a custom, proprietary battery, then buy an extra. If your camera didn't ship with an external charger (that is, you have to recharge batteries in the camera) then you'll probably want to spring for a charger as well. If your camera uses AA-size batteries, then pick up two sets of NiMH rechargeables and a charger.

NiMH batteries don't usually reach their full level of performance until they've been charged a couple of times, so make sure to give them good strong charges the first few times you recharge them. Unlike *NiCad* batteries, you don't have to drain NiMH batteries before you charge them because they have no memory, so after the second recharging, feel free to "top them off" before you go shooting. Be aware, though, that NiMH batteries will lose their charge over time, whether they're in or out of your camera. A month on the shelf is often enough for them to drain completely, so if you haven't used your batteries in a while, be sure to give them a good charge. Also, once they're fully charged, take them out of the charger. Leaving the batteries in the charger, constantly recharging, can shorten their life.

Obviously, when you travel abroad, you'll need to buy the appropriate adapters and converters to power your charger, as well as any other equipment you may choose to lug along.

Even with a spare set of batteries, though, it's still a good idea to get in the habit of shooting with an eye toward battery conservation. The two systems on your camera that use the most power are the LCD screen and the flash. If your camera only has an LCD viewfinder (or if you prefer using the LCD viewfinder) then you may want to conserve power by limiting the amount of time that you spend reviewing images on the LCD screen.

Your camera probably has a sleep mode that causes it to switch to a low-power setting if you don't use it for a while. Try to get a feel for how long it takes the camera to wake up. You may need to wait an extra 2-5 seconds if your camera has gone into its sleep mode. Most cameras doze off if you don't use them for 30 seconds. This is fine for everyday, snapshot shooting, but it can be a real bother if you're shooting portraits or other studio work that require a long set-up. For these occasions, you may want to change the sleep time to its maximum (15-30 minutes). If you know you're going to be away from the camera for a bit, turn off the LCD screen to conserve power.

Over time, you'll get a better idea of how many pictures you can expect to get from a set of batteries. However, there will still be times when your batteries will wane before you're done shooting. For these instances, you may want to employ some of the following battery-saving measures.

- Switch off your camera's LCD and use the optical viewfinder. If your camera doesn't have an optical viewfinder, then turn the LCD off whenever you're not framing a shot. Also, if your camera's LCD provides a backlight that can be turned off, turn it off!
- Some cameras include a "review" setting that controls how long an image will be displayed on the LCD after you shoot. Turn this review off, or at least lower it to its smallest value.
- Try to avoid flash pictures. If you have to shoot in low light, switch to a higher ISO, or try long exposures from a tripod.
- Switch to a smaller storage card. Higher-capacity cards consume more power so a smaller card can sometimes let you coax one or two more pictures out of your batteries. If you use an IBM Microdrive, try switching to a flash memory card, as they use less power.
- Turning your camera off and on often uses more power than simply letting it sleep (turning it off and on usually causes the camera to zoom the lens a lot). Unless you know it will be a while until your next shot, then simply let your camera sleep.
- If you know that your pictures will all be shot at the same distance (infinity, for example) then lock the camera's focus on infinity. Keeping the camera from autofocusing will save a tiny bit of power.
- If you need to transfer pictures to a computer in the field, don't use your camera's cable connection. Use a media drive or PC card adapter instead.

Finally, be aware that cold temperatures will noticeably shorten battery life. If you're shooting outside in below freezing temperatures, your batteries will probably go quickly. You can often squeeze a little more power out of them by taking them out of the camera and warming them up inside your pocket. This may sound hard to believe, but it's true. A few minutes inside your coat can often get you an additional dozen pictures. Don't put the whole camera in your pocket, as this will most likely fog up your lens (see the cold weather tips in Chapter 9). Lithium batteries (not to be confused with L-ion rechargeables) often stand up much better to cold weather than do NiMH or alkaline batteries.

MEDIA BARON

Earlier in this chapter you read about some image size/compression strategies for saving media. In the end, though, your storage will be finite and you'll be stuck needing more space. The ideal solution is simply to buy more media cards. Given their price per megabyte, though, this may not be an option. Fortunately, there are some alternatives.

Laptop Computers

For extended trips, consider taking a laptop computer. In addition to giving you a place to store images, you'll have a complete darkroom with you. With a laptop and your favorite image editing application, you can assess right away whether your day's shooting was successful, and determine if you need to go re-shoot something. Be sure to bring all necessary power, modem, and cable adapters.

Digital Wallet

If you don't feel like lugging your laptop computer around, consider the Minds@Work *Digital Wallet*. (Figure 7.21) Measuring roughly the same size as a paperback book, the Digital Wallet is nothing more than a 6gB hard drive with a media slot in the side. Stick a PC Card, Compact Flash, SmartMedia Card, or Memory Stick into the slot, and the Digital Wallet will copy the card's contents to its drive. You can then put the card back into your camera, erase it and start shooting again. Once you're back home, you can connect the Digital Wallet's USB port to your computer and copy your images to your workstation.

Iomega Fotoshow

Essentially a portable 250 MB Zip drive with slots for CompactFlash or Smart-Media cards, the Fotoshow also provides a video out port for viewing your images on a TV. The Fotoshow has one advantage over the Digital Wallet. It uses removable storage, making for unlimited storage capacity, and allaying fears that all of your photographic eggs are in the same basket. On the downside, it can't run on batteries, making it unusable in the field, and it's video out is NTSC only. If you're traveling to a country that uses PAL or SECAM video, you won't be able to connect the Fotoshow to a TV.

FIGURE *The Digital Wallet provides six gigabytes of portable, battery-powered storage.*
7.21 *With the right adapter, you can simply insert your camera's media card and dump your images into the Digital Wallet, freeing your card for more shooting.*

Zip disks, cables, and PC adapters

Finally, you can simply lug around some Zip disks and all of your camera's connectivity options. Then, you only need to find a service bureau or a friend with a computer to transfer your camera's images to your Zip disks. Obviously, your service bureau or friend will need a Zip drive and the appropriate port, and you'll need to bring your camera's transfer software....

AND THAT'S JUST THE BEGINNING!

The automatic modes on many digital cameras can do an extraordinary job of metering, white balancing, and shooting. Even the best photographic algorithms can be fooled, however, and none of them really know how to do anything but take "correct" pictures. For tricky lighting situations, or for times when you want to break the rules, you're going to have to take control of your camera.

CHAPTER

8

Manual Exposure

IN THIS CHAPTER

- Motion Control
- Depth of Field
- Shutter Speed and Depth of Field
- Tonal Control
- Adjusting Exposure
- Exposure Practice
- Brackets and Histograms
- Exposing to Avoid Purple Fringing

As you've probably already discovered, your digital camera's automatic shooting features can – and usually do – produce great pictures. Some of today's sophisticated matrix metering systems go far beyond simple light metering and offer a level of sophistication that's roughly akin to having an experienced photographer with a spot meter standing by your side.

However, like all automated systems, the light meters in your camera have to make certain assumptions, and most meters assume that you are wanting to take a "correct" photograph. That is, most cameras will produce images with good tone and contrast and with the subject clearly in focus. There will be times, however, when you may have a different idea of what the subject of your image is. Or, perhaps you have different ideas about focus, contrast, or tone.

For these instances, it's time to throw your camera into manual override and start making some exposure decisions on your own. Manual exposure controls allow you to create images that are very different from what your camera's automatic features may deem "correct." They also allow you to shoot higher-quality images by affording you more control of the color and contrast that your camera will produce.

Your exposure choice determines more than just how bright or dark your image will be. By changing your camera's exposure, you can alter four characteristics of an image: motion control, depth of field, tonality, and detail. Selecting the proper exposure involves balancing these choices against what your camera is capable of under your current lighting. To get the most out of this chapter, you'll need to have an understanding of the reciprocity concepts discussed in Chapter 4.

MOTION CONTROL

Controlling motion in your image – that is, controlling how much your camera freezes motion as opposed to letting it blur – is a very intuitive process. Simply set your shutter speed higher to freeze motion, lower to let things blur. Once you dip below 1/30th of a second, you'll need a tripod to hold the camera steady; otherwise, camera shake will introduce unwanted blur into your image. (Figure 8.1)

Slow shutter speeds are also handy for shooting in very low light. By leaving the shutter open for several seconds, or even minutes, your camera's image sensor can gather enough light to create an image. However, be warned that at longer shutter speeds, your image will get noisier and noisier. (Figure 8.2) The sensors in most consumer digital cameras are designed for exposures of less than one second. At longer shutter speeds, many of the individual pixels in the image may begin to behave strangely, sometimes getting "stuck" so that they appear bright white.

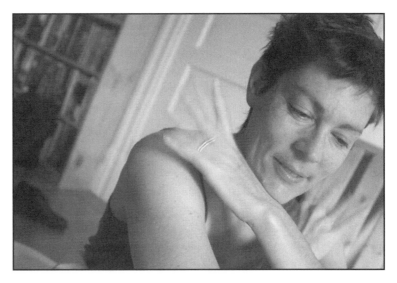

FIGURE **8.1** *A slow shutter speed was used to capture the subject's drumming fingers. Because she was sitting still, no other blur was introduced.*

FIGURE **8.2** *During long exposures, your images will get noisier and noisier.*

Some cameras - such as the Canon G1 and Canon EOS D30 - employ special noise reduction schemes when you shoot at longer than one second. Although Canon's noise reduction process is a secret, most likely these cameras are employing some form of *dark frame subtraction,* a noise reduction process you can perform yourself using your image editing application. To perform a dark frame subtraction, you need two images: your long-exposure image, and a second image shot with the same exposure settings as your first image, *but with your camera's lens cap on.*

Because the exposure is the same, the pixels in the camera's CCD have time to malfunction in exactly the same way that they did in the first image. However, because the lens cap was on, the black frame is essentially a photograph of only the stuck, noisy pixels from the first image. In Photoshop, you can subtract the black frame from the image frame. Chapter 13 will cover the details of performing dark frame subtraction.

Be sure to shoot your dark frame right away to ensure that both images are shot with the camera at the same temperature. A difference of even one or two degrees will result in enough change in noise that the technique won't work.

When you shoot long-exposure images, use a slower ISO speed, as you don't want to introduce any of the extra noise that a higher ISO will produce (unless you want to cut down on the length of the exposure, then switch to a higher ISO to reduce exposure time).

TIP

Shooting outside at night? Cool your camera before you shoot. *The noise that a digital camera produces is directly related to the temperature of the camera's CCD. For every 6-8°C increase in the temperature of the CCD, noise will double! So, if you know you're going to be shooting long exposures outside, take your camera out 20-30 minutes early and let it cool down to the outside temperature. As the camera cools, you should see a marked decrease in noise. Do not try to cool your camera down by putting it in the refrigerator or putting it on ice! Cooling it too quickly can cause damaging condensation to form inside the camera.*

Despite the excellent low-light capabilities of most digital cameras, it will often be too dark to shoot anything but a long-exposure image. If you find yourself in such a circumstance, look for a way to steady your camera, and try shooting some longer exposures, such as the one in Figure 8.3.

If you don't have a tripod handy, try leaning against something, or setting the camera down on a sturdy object. If you must shoot with the camera handheld, switch on the camera's LCD viewfinder, put the camera's neck strap (if it has

FIGURE *There wasn't enough light in this dark venue to get a good shot of this violinist, but*
8.3 *that didn't mean that – with the help of a slow shutter speed there wasn't still an*
interesting picture.

one) around your neck, and pull the camera taut. You may find that the strap offers a good amount of support. Remember to squeeze the shutter gently to prevent shake, and *don't* hold your breath when you shoot. Holding your breath
usually causes your body to tense up, resulting in more shake. Instead, try
shooting while gently exhaling, or take long inhales and exhales and shoot in
the slight pause that occurs between them.

Using longer shutter speed in bright light. *When you shoot*
in daylight, choosing a slower ISO will allow you to use longer,
motion-blurring shutter speeds (since the CCD will be less sensitive
to light, it will be able to withstand longer exposure). If you want
to be sure that you're able to freeze an action, then switch to a
higher ISO (but, as is always the case when you shoot high ISO,
be aware that your images will be
noisier).

DEPTH OF FIELD

Depth of field is the measure of how deep the focused area of your image will be. In an image with deep depth of field, everything will be in focus. A more shallow depth of field will yield blurry backgrounds or foregrounds.

It is important to understand the depth of field in an image is centered around the are onto which you are focusing. In other words, if you currently have a depth of field that is about ten feet deep, that doesn't mean that things farther than ten feet from your lens will be out of focus. Rather, it means that things *within ten feet of the point on which you are focusing* will be in focus.

Figure 8.4 shows the same image shot with varying depths of field.

Depth of field is a function of two parameters: aperture size and focal length. *Smaller apertures and shorter focal lengths yield deeper depths of field.* So, for the greatest depth of field you'll want to choose a high f-stop and zoom *out* as far as possible.

FIGURE *In the second image, our depth of field is much shallower than in the first image.*
8.4 *To vary the depth of field, we moved farther away from our subject, zoomed in, and used a smaller aperture.*

In the first image in Figure 8.4, a small aperture and medium focal length were used. For the second shot, the camera was positioned farther from the subject and zoomed in to increase the focal length, and a very large aperture was selected. Notice that, as discussed earlier, the longer focal length has resulted in an image with somewhat compressed depth. However, because the background is out of focus, this change in depth is not too noticeable. Balancing depth of field against focal length is one of the considerations you'll have to weigh when you shoot.

 Depth of field and field of view. *The rule that a lens with a long focal length produces a shorter depth of field than a lens with a short focal length assumes that both lenses are positioned to produce the same field of view.*

If you've got some experience with 35mm or larger formats, it is important to realize that, because of the tiny focal lengths found on most digital cameras, (which are inherent to the small designs of most models) digital camera depth of field is much deeper than you might be expecting. On a typical digital camera, the depth of field produced by an f5.6 aperture works out to be more like the depth of field produced by an f16 aperture on a 35mm camera. This is great news for users who want really deep depths of field. However, photographers who are used to being able to separate foregrounds from backgrounds using very shallow depths of field may be a bit frustrated.

In general, to get shallow depth of field using a typical prosumer digital camera, you'll need to use the widest aperture possible, zoom in as far as you can, and position the camera close to your subject. (Figure 8.5) If you're much farther than five feet away, don't expect to get shallow depth of field. If you're using a digital SLR with interchangeable lenses, you'll have an easier time. Although the sensor in a digital SLR is still smaller than a piece of 35mm film, the longer focal lengths make for shorter depths of field. In Chapter 14 we'll look at some ways of simulating depth of field in Photoshop.

 Depth of field and focal length multipliers. *If you're using a digital SLR with interchangeable lenses, your camera probably has a focal length multiplier (see Chapter 5). Note that depth of field is not impacted by this multiplier.*

No matter what type of camera you have, it can be difficult to achieve shallow depth of field in bright daylight. Unless your camera provides very fast shutter speeds you will be unable to open your aperture very wide. *Neutral density filters* are special filters that screw on to the end of your lens and serve to cut down the amount of light entering your lens, without altering the light's color.

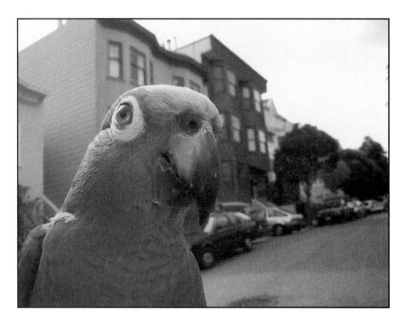

FIGURE *Most digital cameras are not capable of capturing very shallow depth of field. While*
8.5 *this is great for maintaining sharp focus, you may be frustrated if you want to*
intentionally blur out the background. The slight blurring of the background in this
image is about the most you can expect from a small digital camera. This image was
shot using a Nikon Coolpix 990.

With less light, you may find you have some extra room to move around, expo-
sure-wise.

Neutral density filters are usually rated using an ND scale where .1ND equals
1/3rd of a stop. So a .3ND filter will reduce the incoming light by one full stop.
Neutral density filters can be stacked on top of one another to selectively add or
subtract more stops. However, even the best filters are not perfect so it's better
to use as few as possible. In other words, if you want a 1-stop filter, then use a
single .3ND filter instead of three .1ND filters.

Here's a cool neutral density filtering trick: Let's say you want to photograph
a building on a busy street corner at noon, but you don't want to include any of
the people that are pouring into and out of the building. Stack up a few neutral
density filters until you have an 8-10 stop filter. This will increase your exposure
time to ten or fifteen minutes, meaning that anything that's not stationary for at
least that long won't be included in the shot.

SHUTTER SPEED AND DEPTH OF FIELD

Because of the reciprocal nature of apertures and shutter speeds (again, see Chapter 4), you can trade depth of field for more motion stopping power. That is, you can go to a wider aperture (less depth of field) so as to use a higher shutter speed (more motion stopping). Conversely, you can switch to a slower shutter speed (less motion stopping) to use a smaller aperture (more depth of field). As we saw earlier, depth of field is also a function of focal length, so to reduce depth of field even further, you'll want to zoom to a longer focal length and position your camera accordingly.

These are the types of trade-offs and considerations that you need to mull over when you choose an aperture. Because there can be many different aperture/shutter combinations that will work for a given lighting situation, understanding the effects of different combinations will allow you to take better pictures.

TIP

Nearsighted? Try this. *If you are nearsighted enough to need glasses, try this quick little depth of field experiment. Take off your glasses and curl up your index finger against your thumb. You should be able to curl your finger tight enough to create a tiny little hole in the curve of your index finger. If you look through the hole without your glasses you will probably find that everything is in focus. This hole is a very tiny aperture and, therefore, provides very deep depth of field. Deep enough, in fact, that it can correct your vision. On the downside, it doesn't let a lot of light through so, unless you're in bright daylight, you may not be able to see anything well enough to determine if it's in focus. Next time you're confused about how aperture relates to depth of field, remember this test.*

TONAL CONTROL

In addition to motion control and depth of field, the exposure you choose determines how much contrast your image will have, how saturated its colors will be, and how much detail you'll be able to see. As you saw in the last chapter, your light meter generates exposure settings that render the tones in your image as middle gray. By over- or underexposing, you can boost those gray shades to white or black. In the case of color images, your light meter generates exposure settings that render the colors in your image as mid-toned colors. With a change in exposure, you can boost the saturation in the image to produce darker or lighter colors, and stronger contrast.

Figure 8.6 shows two images, both shot with a Canon G1. In the first image, the camera's default metering was used while the second image was intentionally underexposed. Color versions of these same images are shown in Color Plate 7. Notice that, in addition to a more pronounced contrast, the underexposed image has deeper, more saturated colors.

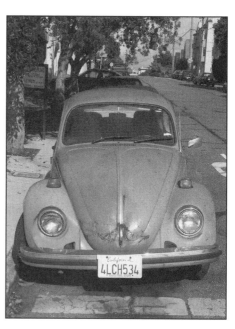

FIGURE *The image on the right was intentionally underexposed by 1/3 of a stop to increase*
8.6 *color saturation and contrast in the image.*

To capture the best tonality and saturation – and to improve your options when you correct and adjust an image – you want to expose your image so as to capture the widest contrast range that you can manage. That is, you want good solid blacks, nice white whites, and everything in between. The trick is to not underexpose an image so far that all of the dark areas turn to solid black or to not overexpose an image so that all of the highlights blow out to complete white (Figure 8.7). If you expose for a wide tonal range, you'll have a broad range of grays between those black and white extremes.

Film photographers often follow the maxim that you should "expose for shadows and print for highlights." In other words: when you shoot, you should underexpose to preserve shadow details, but then adjust your printing exposure to brighten the shadows back up and return the highlights to white. Different

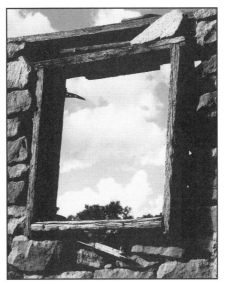

FIGURE **8.7**   *If you overexpose an image too far, you'll lose detail in the bright midtones and highlight areas as colors wash out to complete white. Similarly, if an image is underexposed too far, it will lose shadow detail as those areas darken to complete black.*

films respond differently, of course, but most photographers always underexpose slide film by about half a stop when they shoot in typical outdoor lighting situations. When they shoot indoors under controlled lighting situations, slide photographers typically expose "normally" so as not to oversaturate skin tones.

Why should you be concerned about quaint, old-fashioned, analog technologies such as slide film? Because, for the most part, the sensors in digital cameras behave just like good old Kodachrome slide film. So, if you've got some experience shooting 35mm slide film, you can keep doing just what you've always done, although the workflow in the digital world is a little different and, as you'll see in a minute, your digital camera provides some extra tools to help you calculate exposure.

The downside to both color slide film and the typical digital camera is that neither have very much color *latitude,* so there is very little margin for error. If you underexpose too far, you'll lose both shadow detail and highlights.

Treat your digital camera like slide film. *On most digital cameras, you can simply set your exposure compensation control to -.3 and leave it there. This little compensation will help increase the saturation in most of your images. Obviously, if you're shooting in low light, or shooting bright images that need to be overexposed, then you'll need to change your exposure. For most bright lighting situations, though, you can stick to this simple adjustment.*

DON'T KNOW MUCH ABOUT HISTOGRAMS

A *histogram* is a simple graph of the distribution of all of the tones in your image. Histograms can be easily created by most image editing applications and are a great way of understanding exposure.

Take a look at Figure 8.8 and its accompanying histogram.

Grayscale images can contain up to 256 shades of gray ranging from solid black to solid white. The histogram in Figure 8.12 is simply a bar chart showing how much of each shade of gray is present in the image, with each vertical line representing one shade. Black is at the far left and white is at the far right.

From the histogram, you can see that the image in Figure 8.12 is fairly well-exposed. It has a good range of tones from black to white, which means it has a lot of contrast. Most of the tones are distributed toward the lower end because of the dark grays and shadows in the background. However, even though the background is dark there is still a good range of middle gray tones and lighter tones from the gray of the flamingo.

Notice that the shadow areas do not *clip*. That is, they curve down to nothing by the time the graph reaches the left-side. Also notice that there are a large number of tones overall, an indication that the image has a good dynamic range and, therefore, a lot of editing potential. Although the brighter areas are a little weak, we can correct for this in our image editor.

Now take a look at Figure 8.9.

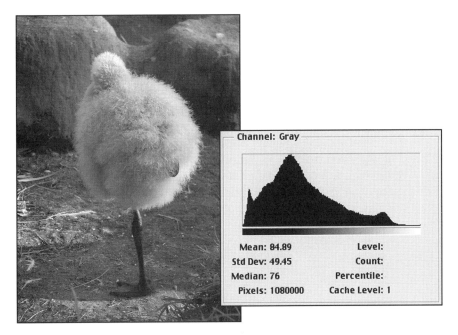

Channel: Gray

Mean: 84.89   Level:
Std Dev: 49.45   Count:
Median: 76   Percentile:
Pixels: 1080000   Cache Level: 1

FIGURE **8.8** *With a histogram, you can analyze your images to determine which type of tonal corrections they might need.*

Channel: Gray

Mean: 65.88   Level: 97
Std Dev: 57.00   Count: 2698
Median: 37   Percentile: 67.46
Pixels: 3145728   Cache Level: 1

FIGURE **8.9** *An underexposed image has a very characteristic histogram.*

You can probably tell by looking at Figure 8.9 that this image is underexposed, but the histogram still provides some interesting information. As you can see, there is no white information in this image at all (nor even any light or medium gray information) and at the lower end, there is a preponderance of solid black. Notice that the shadow areas don't curve down to black as they do in Figure 8.8. Rather, they are "clipped" off the edge of the histogram. In a well-exposed image, the shadow areas would be spread over a large number of darker tones, with only a little solid black. If you look in the shadow areas of the image, you'll see that they look completely black, rather than having any variation or range in their dark tones. In other words, the shadows have lost detail.

An image that is overexposed will exhibit a similar histogram, but weighted on the other end, with tones grouped in the white areas, and clipped highlights.

Now look at Figure 8.10.

Channel: Gray

Mean: 160.60　　　　Level: 158
Std Dev: 65.18　　　　Count: 1945
Median: 200　　　　Percentile: 33.24
Pixels: 1150800　　　Cache Level: 1

FIGURE *In a low-contrast image, the tones will be in the center of the histogram. Notice the*
8.10 *lack of dark black or light gray tones.*

This image was shot using the camera's suggested exposure. It's not a bad image, but it lacks punch. The image is very flat, and lacks contrast. A quick look at the histogram shows why. All of the tones are grouped in the middle of the graph – they don't cover a broad range – and there are no white or black tones.

Just as careful processing and printing is essential to producing good photographic prints, your digital images will need some special adjustments to take advantage of the tonal information that your camera captures. In Chapter 13, you'll see how you can use the tools in your image editing application to adjust and correct an image, so that an underexposed image like the one in Figure 8.10 can be turned into something more like the image shown in Figure 8.11.

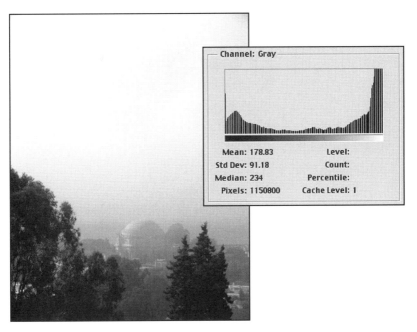

FIGURE *After a simple tonal correction, the image appears punchier and more contrasty.*
8.11

Many digital cameras can show you a histogram of any image you've taken. Figure 8.12 shows a histogram display from a Nikon Coolpix 990. In addition to displaying the histogram, the Coolpix also flashes clipped highlight areas in the small thumbnail above the histogram. If you think you're shooting in a difficult lighting situation, shoot a test shot and then take a quick look at the image's histogram. If you see clipped highlights or shadows, then you'll need to try a different exposure and shoot again.

For color images, the histogram shows a composite of separate red, green, and blue histograms. Most image editing applications can produce separate histograms for each color channel, and these can be useful for identifying some types of problems, as we'll see later. For general exposure analysis, though, the normal RGB composite histogram is fine.

FIGURE *The Nikon Coolpix 990 can display a histogram of any image you've shot. Notice that*
8.12 *the image thumbnail also indicates areas where the highlights have been*
overexposed, or "clipped."

DETAILS DETAILS

Earlier, you learned that some autofocus mechanisms work by detecting contrast within an image. The fact that more contrast means sharper focus – and therefore, more detail – is an important concept to remember when you choose an exposure for an image.

Figure 8.13 shows the same image shot with a range of exposures. Notice how the level of detail and sense of texture changes from exposure to exposure.

When an image is underexposed, the shadow areas lose detail because they go down to solid black. Similarly, when an image is overexposed, the highlight areas wash out to complete white, reducing contrast – and therefore detail – in the highlight areas. In other words, fine texture and detail is often defined by the small highlight and shadow areas on the texture's surface. Consequently, you'll want to expose to reveal these highlights and shadows. In general, to preserve texture you'll want to capture as broad a tonal range as you can.

TIP

Lower your camera's sharpening. Sometimes, in high-contrast situations, you can get better tonal range by setting your camera's contrast or sharpening setting to low (assuming your camera has a contrast or sharpening setting). As you've seen, an image with more sharpness has greater contrast between individual pixels. This can sometimes mean less tonal range because more pixels are represented by high-contrast shades than by a broad range of tones. All cameras are different, of course, so do some experimenting with your camera's sharpness controls. Take some test shots with identical exposure settings, but different sharpness settings, and examine the resulting histograms to learn how each setting affects tonal range.

FIGURE   *This heavily-textured wall was shot with a variety of exposure-compensation settings.*
8.13   *In addition to looking brighter or darker, notice how the level of detail and texture*
changes with different exposure settings.

To sum up, in addition to depth of field and motion control, your goal when you choose an exposure is to pick settings that will produce the broadest tonal range, while preserving shadow and highlight detail. When you use a digital camera in most situations, it's pretty safe to say that if you protect your shadow areas when you shoot, you can always save the highlights later in editing.

ADJUSTING EXPOSURE

As you've seen, there are a lot of creative options to weigh and choices to make when you choose an exposure for an image. For example, you may know that you want a shallow depth of field and so you will select a long focal length and wide aperture. However, perhaps your images include a lot of dark-colored objects that you feel need to be underexposed. At this point, you would probably choose to adopt a shorter shutter speed – rather than a smaller aperture – to preserve your shallow depth of field. Of course, if there are some fast-moving objects in your scene that you were hoping to blur, then you'll have to consider just how much you can slow down your shutter speed. All of these different factors must be weighed and balanced.

Once you've made your decisions, you can begin to use your camera's controls to adjust your exposure accordingly. Fortunately, even if you have a less expensive camera, you probably have enough controls to make some simple adjustments.

In this section, we'll cover all of the ways that you can adjust exposure on your digital camera. Which adjustments to make will depend on your image, of course, and which controls to use to make your adjustment will depend on which exposure characteristics you want to change, and which you want to preserve.

EXPOSURE COMPENSATION

Nowadays, even if they don't include priority or manual exposure modes, most digital cameras provide exposure compensation controls. Whether you access them through buttons on the camera, or through the camera's menuing system, exposure compensation controls give you a quick, easy, and very effective way to adjust the exposure that your camera's light meter has chosen. What's nice about exposure compensation tools is that they let you think in terms of over- or underexposing, without worrying about how to achieve those changes in exposure. In other words, you can simply think "I want to overexpose by one stop" instead of thinking something like "I want to overexpose by one stop but in this mode I don't have control of aperture so I'll have to change the shutter speed; I'm currently at 1/250th so overexposing by one stop would be 1/125th." (Figure 8.14)

Exposure Compensation Display

FIGURE *Most cameras simply indicate exposure compensation with a numeric readout of the*
8.14 *current amount of compensation (in this case, -.3 stops).*

The downside to exposure compensation is that you have no control over *how* the camera achieves its new exposure. In other words, if you tell it to over-expose by two stops, you don't know if this overexposure will come through changes in aperture or shutter speed. Consequently, you can't predict if the compensation will change your image's depth of field (through aperture change) or motion control (through shutter speed change). Because of the tiny focal lengths of the average digital camera, a change of a stop won't make much – if any – difference in depth of field. However, if you're shooting in low light – low enough that an extra stop could push you into a slow shutter speed – then you may want to carefully review your images after shooting. Because small digital cameras have such deep depth of field, changes in aperture won't usually affect your depth of field.

If you throw your camera into automatic mode and watch its exposure choices (assuming your camera displays its selected shutter speed and aperture) while you change exposure compensation settings, you will probably think that there's no seeming logic to whether it adjusts aperture size or shutter speed. Typically, a camera will adjust shutter speed first and only adjust aperture if it runs out of shutter speed options. If your camera only has two or three aper-tures, then adjusting shutter speed might be its only choice.

PRIORITY AND MANUAL MODES

If you're an old-school photographer who isn't used to a camera with exposure compensation controls (or if you're simply not interested in using exposure compensation controls) then you will probably select a priority mode when you want to adjust your exposure. With priority modes, you'll have complete control over how your exposure adjustments are being achieved. (Figure 8.15)

FIGURE *Most cameras offer a simple dial or switch for changing the camera from full*
8.15 *automatic mode to a priority or completely manual mode.*

Typically, you'll select shutter priority when you want to control motion, and aperture priority when you want to control depth of field. You can select either aperture or shutter if you want to change tone and saturation, texture, or detail. Or, you can combine a priority mode with your camera's exposure compensation controls. For example, you might use a shutter priority mode to ensure the motion control that you want, but then use exposure compensation controls to boost saturation or detail.

Using a priority mode is very simple: just select the aperture or shutter speed that's appropriate for what you're trying to achieve, and let the camera do the rest. Most cameras will warn you when they think you've chosen an exposure combination that will result in over- or underexposure. Don't worry, the camera's just trying to tell you that your settings don't conform to its idea of a good picture. Check your manual for details on how your camera indicates a bad exposure combination.

Full manual modes give you control of both aperture and shutter speed and offer more flexibility than any other shooting mode. However, because some digital cameras have manual controls that are cumbersome, you may find it easier to simply use a priority mode.

AUTOMATIC RECIPROCITY

Many cameras allow you to automatically cycle through reciprocal apertures after the camera has metered. The Nikon Coolpix 990, for example, provides a simple wheel that, when turned in automatic mode, cycles through other exposures that yield the same exposure. In this way, you can quickly choose an equivalent exposure with a shutter speed or aperture that is more to your taste. Note that, because these are reciprocal exposure settings, they will still yield the same middle gray exposure as the camera's initial setting. If you want to over- or underexpose, you'll have to perform those adjustments separately, using the exposure compensation controls. An automatic reciprocity feature combined with the camera's exposure compensation controls might be all the manual control you'll ever need, as you can usually achieve any exposure you want using these simple adjustments.

ISO CONTROL

When you put a roll of film in a film camera, you're stuck with that film's ISO rating for the whole roll. That is not true with a digital camera. If your camera has an adjustable ISO feature, you can change the ISO for each picture you take. In the simplest applications, higher ISOs mean you can take pictures in less light. You can, however, also look at ISO adjustments as one more exposure control that you have.

ISO 200 is twice as sensitive to light as ISO 100. And, as you might expect, ISO 400 is twice as sensitive as ISO 200 and four times as sensitive as ISO 100. As you learned in Chapter 4, every doubling of light is measured as a stop. So, when you change from ISO 100 to 200, it's as if you've opened your camera's aperture one more stop. This extra stop can often be what you need to save a shot.

For example, let's say you're shooting at dusk at ISO 100 and you've got your camera's aperture open pretty wide to reduce depth of field. Unfortunately, with your current aperture, your meter has recommended a shutter speed of 1/15th of a second, too slow to be shooting with your camera handheld. Although you left your tripod at home, you don't have to compromise your depth of field choice. Just crank your ISO up to 200 to pick up an extra stop, allowing you to set your shutter to 1/30th.

Or, maybe you're shooting a football game on a somewhat cloudy day and, even with your aperture open all the way, the fastest shutter speed your meter recommends is 1/60th. Crank the ISO up to 200 or 400 and you can shoot as fast as 1/250th for plenty of action-stopping power.

Of course, as you increase ISO rating, you'll be increasing the amount of noise in your image. Different cameras produce different amounts and qualities of noise so you'll want to experiment with your camera to determine if you can accept the noise it produces at higher ISOs.

Even digital cameras do it... *Some cameras that only have a few apertures will make tiny changes to ISO sensitivity to create additional stops, usually without introducing too much noise.*

Just as there is a reciprocal relationship between aperture and shutter speed, when you start manipulating ISO, you must think of reciprocity between all three factors. As you increase ISO, you may need to close your aperture or increase your shutter speed.

EXPOSURE PRACTICE

Over the last few chapters you've read a lot of theory and ideas about how exposure works. Now it's time to actually go out and practice some of it by doing some shooting. However, for your practice to do you much good, you need to take the time to annotate your images. You won't learn much about which exposure calculations work if you can't remember what that exposure was when you get home and look at your image. How will you know whether the exposure was a good or a bad choice, if you can't remember what the choice was?

For each picture you take, you'll want to record all of the camera's exposure settings – shutter speed, aperture, ISO setting – as well as your white balance setting. If you tend to change compression settings while you shoot (to save storage space, for example) then you may want to note this as well, as knowing the compression settings for an image may provide a clue to any annoying artifacts or contrast changes.

You can either choose to make these notations the old fashioned way (that is, to write them down) or you can see if your camera will remember them for you. Many cameras record a number of parameters when an image is stored to disk. Figure 8.16 shows the information screen from a Nikon Coolpix 990.

This information is stored using a standard format called *EXIF* (Exchangeable Image File) that was created by the Japan Electronic Industry Development Association in 1995. If your digital camera is EXIF-compatible (and most are) then all of its files are EXIF files, whether they use JPEG or TIFF compression.

The great thing about EXIF files is that their image data can be read by any program, even if that program isn't specifically EXIF compatible. The EXIF data is simply stored in the header information of the file, so any application that can read JPEG or TIFF files can still read an EXIF-compatible file.

To read the EXIF data, though, you'll need a special application that can decode the header information (Figure 8.17).

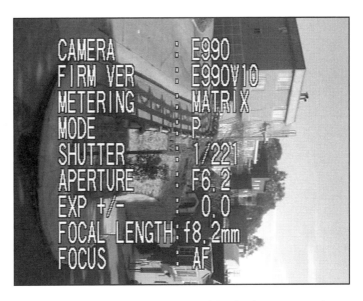

FIGURE *The Nikon Coolpix 990 stores several screenfuls of information and parameters about*
8.16 *each shot. This data is stored with the file and can be read using special software.*

FIGURE *The EXIF display from iView Multimedia, a shareware image cataloger included*
8.17 *on the Complete Digital Photography CD-ROM. Check out*
ON THE CD *www.completedigitalphotography.com/exif for other EXIF readers for Mac and*
Windows.

EXIF is great because it means you don't have to take time away from your shooting to record settings. On the other hand, you do have to use special software to read the settings. If you're a photographer who's already used to making exposure notes, then you may find that writing them down by hand is still the way to go. Many people find that taking the time to write the information by hand also serves to help them remember and understand their choices. If your camera offers a voice annotation feature, you can simply dictate the exposure settings to your camera. This will, of course, use up valuable image space, so use this feature carefully.

In this section, you'll be led through the exposure decisions required to take several photographs.

AN INTENTIONAL UNDEREXPOSURE

The good news is that there is no "right" or "wrong" way to take a picture. There might be "better" or "worse" ways but the only thing that makes an image right, or correct, is whether or not the image serves to reveal what you saw in the scene you were photographing.

You could argue that an image is "right" if it looks like the subject that was being photographed, but the question of what something *actually* looks like is subjective. True, you could get a color meter and a luminance meter and carefully measure everything in a scene to determine what it looks like, but even if you managed to perfectly reproduce that color and luminance, you still wouldn't necessarily have a good picture.

You also wouldn't necessarily have an image that matched what you *saw*. Remember that your eyes have very different sensitivities than does your camera. You may often have to force the camera to see things the way your eyes do.

For example, look at Figure 8.18.

This matrix-metered exposure is probably fairly close to what this street scene actually looked like. The sun was low and there were some dark shadows, but they were not too dark. Because of a slight haze in the air, there were no strong white highlights. In general, it was a fairly medium-toned scene and the medium-oriented light meter in the camera did a good job of recording those tones.

When we were looking at the scene in person, however, there was a marked perception of a dark swath being cut through a lighter area. This was a purely geometric/tonal perception that can be reduced to a very simple illustration as seen in Figure 8.19.

To capture this idea, it was essential to reveal the contrast between the dark street and the brighter houses. The human eye is far more sensitive to luminance and contrast than is the sensor in a digital camera. This, and the fact that the

FIGURE *This street scene was shot with the camera's default metering and is, consequently, a*
8.18 *little "flat" in tone, lacking contrast and good saturation.*

FIGURE *While actually standing at the scene of this photograph, one couldn't help perceiving*
8.19 *large shapes of dark and light.*

camera's light meter assumes that the scene is 18% gray, means it was necessary to underexpose the image to plunge the street into deeper shadow.

Dialing -.3 into the camera's exposure compensation control created just enough underexposure to render the image the way it was envisioned without compromising either shadow or highlight detail. (Figure 8.20) (By the way, a second image was also shot using an exposure compensation of -.7, just in case -.3 wasn't enough, but the second image was too dark.)

FIGURE   *With a simple underexposure, the shadows were plunged into darkness and the*
8.20   *desired contrast was created.*

ANOTHER UNDEREXPOSURE

While I was out walking one afternoon, I looked up to see Sutro Tower – a large radio antenna that sits in the middle of San Francisco – casting shadows into a light haze that had moved in (Figure 8.21). It was obvious that an underexposure was necessary to ensure preservation of the subtle shadows that the tower was causing. Unfortunately, it was very windy, so a fast shutter speed was necessary to freeze the motion of the trees.

The camera, a Canon EOS D30, was switched to shutter priority to allow for manual selection of a fast, tree-freezing shutter speed and the camera's exposure compensation controls were dialed to a -.3 exposure compensation to darken the shadows and increase the saturation of the hazy sky. After shooting the image, a quick check of the camera's information screen showed that the exposure compensation had not altered the desired shutter speed. (The camera's LCD

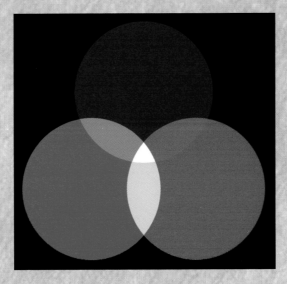

Color Plate 1: Red, Green, and Blue, the three additive primary colors of light can be mixed to create any other colors. As you combine them, the resulting color becomes lighter, eventually becoming white.

Color Plate 2: Noise in a digital photo doesn't always look like simple grain. Often, noise can appear as tiny flecks of red, green, or blue color. Noise is usually worse in darker, shadowy areas.

Color Plate 3: Different digital cameras will often make very different decisions about color. These images were shot with two different cameras, each set on auto mode. Notice how differently they chose to reproduce the colors in the scene.

Color Plate 4: While film photographers need to select a film that is balanced for the type of light in which they'll be shooting, digital photographers need to make certain that their cameras are properly white balanced for the current light. Use the wrong white balance setting, and your images will have strange color casts that can be difficult to remove.

Color Plate 5: Some 2 and 3 megapixel digital cameras suffer from a type of color aberration that causes purple fringing along areas of high contrast in an image. Chapter 8 gives some tips on avoiding purple fringing while chapter 13 provides some tutorials on removing fringing.

Color Plate 6: Though this book presents a number of rules and guidelines, it's important to know that these rules aren't carved in stone. This panoramic image, for example, is out-of-focus, noisy, riddled with stitching seams and poorly exposed. Nevertheless, it's still a pleasing picture.

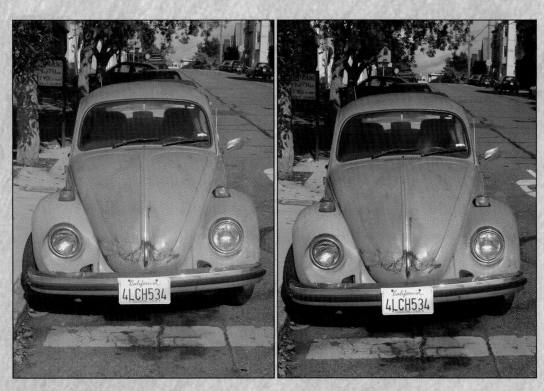

Color Plate 7: Through careful choice of exposure when shooting, you can capture images with better color saturation.

Color Plate 8: With some simple Levels and Curves adjustments (as shown in Chapter 11) we were able to increase the contrast, and improve the detail in this image.

Color Plate 9: To bring more emphasis to the eagle in the foreground, we desaturated the background in this image using a simple Hue/Saturation adjustment, as described in chapter 12.

Color Plate 10: Originally a grayscale image, this figure was colored using the "painting with light opacity" technique discussed in chapter 14.

FIGURE   *One afternoon, Sutro Tower in San Francisco was throwing impressive shadows into*
8.21   *the afternoon haze. To ensure the camera would capture the subtle shadings, shutter*
priority with a fast shutter speed was used.

was too small to check the focus visually – slight motion blurs would not appear. By checking the shutter speed, however, we were able to ensure that the trees were frozen.)

MANUAL OVERRIDE

The rooftop greenhouse shown in Figure 8.22 (and Color Plate 8) presented a few exposure concerns. First, there was the bright white panel on the roof of the greenhouse, which definitely needed to be overexposed, ideally without ruining the nice dark shadows of the foreground roof. Second, because of the position of the camera, a shorter focal length was required. So, to preserve a shallow depth of field and set the greenhouse apart from the background, it was necessary to use a wide aperture.

FIGURE *This image presented a few exposure problems that were easily adjusted while we*
8.22 *were shooting.*

Finally, there was the overall tone of the image. The misty background and white sides of the greenhouse presented a situation with a lot of subtle gray shades. To smoothly render the subtle striations of the mist-shrouded hillside and to preserve the deep yellow of the greenhouse windows (which would lose saturation from the aforementioned overexposure), it was essential to capture as much tonal range as possible.

The light meter read f5.6 at 1/250th of a second. To overexpose by a half stop, the camera's manual controls were used to increase the aperture to f4. After we shot the image, we consulted the camera's histogram (Figure 8.23). As you can see, neither shadows or highlights are clipped, and the image has a broad tonal range. An additional shot was taken at normal exposure. The histogram in Figure 8.23 shows that without the overexposure, the camera captured a much lower range of tones.

OF BRACKETS AND HISTOGRAMS

As you can see from the examples above, there are a number of decisions that go into choosing an exposure. The good news, though, is that you don't necessarily have to be right about your choice, because you can always shoot multi-

FIGURE   *Checking the camera's histogram after taking the shot shows that both highlights and*
8.23   *shadows are okay and that there seems to be a good amount of dynamic range.*

FIGURE   *Checking the histogram of the shot that didn't have our exposure adjustment shows*
8.24   *that, indeed, overexposing produced more dynamic range.*

ple shots, each with a different exposure, just as Margaret Bourke-White did. *Bracketing* is the process of shooting one or two extra exposures above and below your target exposure to provide yourself with a margin of error in your exposure calculation. If you've made a somewhat accurate, educated guess about exposure, one of your bracketed images will most likely be good, even if your original guess was off. Bracketing is a tried-and-true practice of film photographers, but it's a lot easier with a digital camera.

With digital bracketing you don't have to worry about the waste and expense of shooting extra film. Sure, storage may be a concern, but after bracketing, you can quickly check your images on your camera's LCD and throw out the ones that are obviously wrong. So, if you've bracketed two shots on each side (resulting in five pictures) and two of the pictures are obviously bad, you can simply delete them.

Many digital cameras offer *auto-bracketing* features which let the camera take care of bracketing for you. On the Canon EOS D30, for example, you can dial in a bracketing range (Figure 8.25). Then, when you press the shutter, the camera will automatically shoot three exposures, one at your chosen exposure, one stopped down a stop, and a third overexposed by one stop. (The D30 also lets you change the bracketing interval.)

FIGURE *If your camera has an auto-bracketing feature, you can set it to automatically shoot*
8.25 *a series of bracketed exposures.*

Even if you don't have an auto-bracketing feature, however, your camera's exposure compensation controls make it simple to quickly bracket your shots. If your camera's compensation controls are externally-located (rather than buried within a menu) then learn to change them without moving the camera. This will allow you to shoot, make a quick compensation, and then shoot another shot right away. It's best to always perform your brackets in the same order to prevent confusion. Most auto-bracketing features start with the desired exposure, then shoot one interval under, then one interval over, then the next interval under, the next over and so on.

Whether you bracket your shots or not, if your camera provides a histogram then *get into the habit of using it!* After you've bracketed a series of shots, for example, you can quickly go through them, identify the ones that have badly clipped highlights or shadows, and throw them out.

Even if you're not bracketing, if you're facing a difficult shot - or one where you want to ensure that you've captured a wide tonal range (as in the green-house example above) - then shoot a couple of shots and compare their histograms. Similarly, if you're unsure whether or not an image needs to be over- or underexposed, taking a quick test shot and examining its histogram will probably provide you with an answer.

If the meaning and use of the histogram is a bit confusing for you now, don't worry, it will become more clear when you start correcting some images in Chapter 11.

EXPOSING TO AVOID PURPLE FRINGING

ON THE CD

As discussed in Chapters 2 and 5, many 2- and 3-megapixel cameras suffer from a unique digital artifact known as the "purple fringe." Purple fringing is a calculation artifact that is roughly related to *blooming* and occurs in cameras with these higher resolutions because their pixels are packed so closely together. You can see an example of purple fringing in Color Plate 5.

Fortunately, the conditions that produce this artifact are fairly easy to predict and so you can often keep things under control with some simple exposure adjustments.

Purple fringing usually occurs when you shoot into a high-contrast situation using your camera's full wide angle (or close to it). For these reasons, it is usually landscape shots that suffer the most from purple fringing. Skies usually create troublesome contrast situations and landscapes typically prompt you to use a wide angle. Trees are also usually bad subjects as regards purple fringing. Because they also typically have a bright sky behind them, and because they include so many difficult small details, you'll often find that shots taken from beneath a tree, or through a tree (for example, on a horizon) will have bad purple fringing around the small foliage details.

If you find yourself in such a situation, and you know your camera is subject to this problem (not all cameras will be), try the following:

- Zoom in to a longer focal length. In fact, shooting several images at different focal lengths may be your best hedge
- If you can't get a framing you like without shooting at full wide, then try closing down your camera's aperture. You will, of course, have to adjust your shutter speed appropriately. Be careful if you make this adjustment using your camera's exposure compensation controls, as they won't necessarily compensate with an aperture adjustment. It's better to use your camera's manual controls (or automatic reciprocity control, if your camera has one).

- Some cameras seem to only exhibit purple fringing in the edges of their photographs. If this seems to be true of your camera, then try to frame the image so that particularly troublesome subject matter (trees, bright shapes, fine details) are away from the edge of the frame.

If you're using a camera with a very long zoom lens such as the 10x zooms found on the Olympus C2100 or the Canon PowerShot Pro90, then be aware that long zooms sometimes exhibit bad purple fringing at their extreme tele-photo ranges. If you find this to be true, consider backing off from full zoom when you shoot in potential purple fringing situations.

Obviously, no matter how careful you are, you won't always be able to avoid these purple fringing artifacts. As you might expect, though, there are some ways to remove these problems using your image editing program. It's much easier, though, to simply avoid the problem in the first place. You'll learn some purple fringe removal techniques in Chapter 13.

CHAPTER

Special Shooting

IN THIS CHAPTER

- Macro Photography
- Black and White Photography
- Shooting Panoramas
- Shooting for the Web
- Shooting for Video
- Using Filters
- Shooting in Extreme Conditions

At the end of the Apollo 11 moon landing, Neil Armstrong and Buzz Aldrin blasted off from the moon in their tiny lunar module, aiming for a rendezvous with crewmate Michael Collins in the orbiting *Columbia* service module. As the tiny speck of a spaceship rose up from the moon, ground controllers recorded Collins saying "I got the earth coming up behind you – it's fantastic!" Back on earth, after the rocks and spacesuits and Hasselblad cameras were all unloaded, and the film was developed, Armstrong and Aldrin were able to see what he was so excited about: a photograph of the earth rising above the moon, with the lunar lander flying close by in the foreground. In other words, a single picture encompassing all of humanity except for one man: Mike Collins, the photographer.

Like all of the astronauts, in addition to having the "right stuff" Collins had to have a comfortable knowledge of basic photographic principles. A quarter of a million miles from earth, he still had to worry about f-stops, shutter speeds and film stocks in addition to worrying about asphyxiation, burning up on re-entry, and drowning in the ocean.

Hopefully, you won't ever have to face such photographic concerns. However, it is important to realize that certain types of photography require special equipment, techniques, and preparation. In the case of lunar photography, you would need a massive government-funded space program in addition to your digital camera and a decent computer. Web photography, on the other hand, requires a camera with appropriate resolution, and you need a good understanding of how your images will be sized and compressed for delivery.

In this chapter you'll learn about all sorts of special shooting considerations, ranging from shooting in black and white to shooting in extreme weather.

MACRO PHOTOGRAPHY

Although the term "*macro photography*" would seem to describe a process of photographing very large objects, it's actually just the opposite. With your digital camera's macro photography feature, you can take high-quality images of extremely small things.

Digital cameras are particularly well suited to macro photography. Their generally excellent optics make for sharp, clear images while their low-light sensitivity means you can get them into small spaces to capture up-close images. Finally, the macro features of some cameras allow for amazingly close shots – as close as 2cm in some cases! A 35mm film camera would normally require a very expensive, specialized macro lens for such photography, and often needs a lot of extra lighting.

Nevertheless, when you shoot macro with your digital camera, there are some things to remember.

FINDING THE OPTIMAL MACRO FOCAL LENGTH

After you've put your camera into macro mode, the camera's zoom control will still function. However, your macro feature may have been designed to work with a very specific range of focal lengths. Although you'll be able to shoot at any focal length, focal distances in the camera's macro "sweet spot" will produce superior images. And, some cameras simply can't automatically focus in macro mode unless they are set within a particular focal range. Most cameras indicate their optimal macro focal length through a display on the camera's LCD.

Check your manual for details and remember to zoom the camera to the appropriate focal length before shooting.

MACRO FOCUSING

Your camera's autofocus mechanism should work normally when you shoot in macro mode. (Figure 9.1) However, be aware that at very close distances, even slight, subtle changes in camera position can wreck your focus.

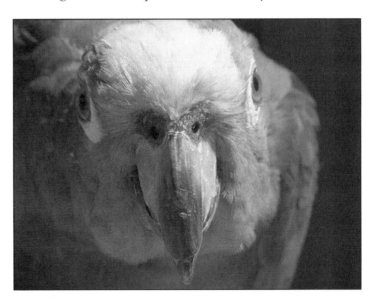

FIGURE *Your digital camera's macro feature lets you take close-up photos that would require*
9.1 *a very expensive lens if you were shooting with a film camera.*

To get the best results when you focus at macro distances, use a tripod. This will ensure that you won't accidentally make slight movements after the camera has already focused.

If you don't have a tripod, then consider activating your camera's continuous autofocus feature, if it has one. This will ensure that the image stays in focus even if you accidentally jiggle the camera.

It's usually easier to hold the camera steady if you *don't* try to press the camera's zoom buttons. Instead of using the camera's zoom controls to frame your shot, simply move the camera in and out. At macro distances, you won't have to move it very far to get a reframing.

The best rule, though, is simply to work quickly. Get the image framed, pre-focus, and then shoot right away. Working quickly will mean there's less time for you to accidentally move the camera. Finally, just to be safe, shoot a few frames. If your first is out of focus, perhaps your second or third will be okay. If your camera has a drive mode (also known as burst mode or continuous mode) that is capable of shooting at the resolution that you want, then consider turning it on. If you're facing a difficult macro shot, shooting a burst of images will improve your chances of getting a good image.

POOR DEPTH OF FIELD

Be warned that, when you are in macro mode, your camera will have a *very* shallow depth of field. Although this can create very nice effects and excellent isolation of your subject, if your subject is large enough, you may have trouble keeping all of it in focus.

Consider the image in Figure 9.2.

FIGURE **9.2** *This calla lily was shot with the macro feature of a Nikon Coolpix 990. Unfortunately, although this is not a really large flower, it is deep enough that the image has a depth of field problem – the flower's stamen is in focus, but the edges of its petals are blurry.*

The depth of field in this image is so shallow that the lily's petals are out of focus. In fact, the depth of field is short enough that this image might have been better served by switching out of macro mode, pulling the camera back, zooming in, and shooting the image normally. Another option would have been to autofocus on the petals and re-frame the shot. However, the stamen in the center of the flower would then be out of focus.

If you're shooting a flat subject, depth of field won't be a problem, of course. If you're shooting something that's even a few inches deep, though, you need to start worrying about which parts will be in focus. Judging depth of field on your camera's LCD can be very difficult as the screen is simply too small to reveal which parts of your subject are in focus. Sometimes you can use your camera's playback zoom feature to examine different parts of your image up close. Even with a 4x magnification, however, you still probably won't be able to determine focus. If you're concerned about depth of field, your best option is to protect yourself by shooting multiple shots with a number of different focal lengths – including some non-macro shots. You should also take some shots with your autofocus locked onto different parts of the subject.

BLACK AND WHITE PHOTOGRAPHY

Some digital cameras offer special black and white modes for shooting grayscale images. Why would you want to shoot in black and white, you may be wondering? After all, you can always convert your color images to grayscale using your image editing program (you'll learn more about this in Chapter 14) so why not shoot color and have the option for black and white?

All of the above is true, yet there are some advantages to using your camera's black and white feature. First of all, because a black and white mode doesn't require your camera to interpolate up to 24-bit color, you can – theoretically – get better detail than when you shoot in color. Since your camera can ignore its color filters and simply treat each pixel as a true pixel, your images might be sharper than when you shoot in color.

In practice, as shown in Figure 9.3, you may find little difference between shooting in a black and white mode, and shooting in color and then converting to black and white.

The main advantage to shooting in black and white is that you can immediately review your image as a black and white image. If you have trouble visualizing a scene in black and white, this immediate grayscale review can be very helpful.

Converted from color image by changing the color mode to Grayscale in Photoshop.

Shot using the Coolpix 990's Black and White function.

FIGURE **9.3** *As you can see, there is often little difference between an image shot in black and white mode, and an image shot in color and converted to grayscale later. If you have trouble visualizing in grayscale, though, the immediate feedback can be invaluable.*

THE ZONE SYSTEM

Serious black and white film photographers often employ a system of special exposure calculation techniques called the *zone system.* Formalized by Ansel Adams, Minor White, and Edward Weston, the zone system can provide a very accurate way of determining the exposure that will capture the greatest tonal range, and preserve the details that the photographer needs to make a good print.

In the zone system, the tonal range is divided into eleven zones, each separated by one complete stop. Middle gray (18% gray, that is) is equivalent to zone V. (Figure 9.4)

FIGURE *Serious black and white photographers often use the zone system to calculate*
9.4   *exposure. In the zone system, the tonal range is divided into eleven different zones,*
each separated by one stop.

Whether you shoot black and white or color, film or digital – and whether you choose to master the zone system or not – there are some good things to learn about these eleven tones. Each zone has different characteristics, as you can see in Figure 9.5.

FIGURE *To get the best dynamic range and the most texture, it's important to realize that only*
9.5   *certain zones hold useful imaging information.*

In other words, any tones in your final image that fall in zones 0, I, IX, or X will not hold any texture. Any tones in your final image that fall in zones 0 or X will be beyond the usable dynamic range of the typical printing process. Zone X tones, for example, will simply be bare photographic paper and the problem with bare photographic paper is that you can't change or control the color of it if you need to.

One of the trickiest things about the zone system is learning to identify which zone corresponds to the real-world object you are trying to photograph. It can be difficult to recognize an object's tonal value, particularly if it's something colored! Figure 9.6 provides some simple examples to show you how objects in the real world fit into the zone system (or, how the zone system represents objects in the real world).

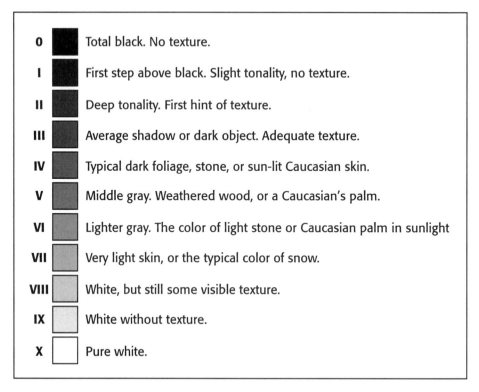

0		Total black. No texture.
I		First step above black. Slight tonality, no texture.
II		Deep tonality. First hint of texture.
III		Average shadow or dark object. Adequate texture.
IV		Typical dark foliage, stone, or sun-lit Caucasian skin.
V		Middle gray. Weathered wood, or a Caucasian's palm.
VI		Lighter gray. The color of light stone or Caucasian palm in sunlight
VII		Very light skin, or the typical color of snow.
VIII		White, but still some visible texture.
IX		White without texture.
X		Pure white.

FIGURE *It can be difficult to recognize which zone best represents an object in the real world.*
9.6 *Here are some examples to help you get started.*

To utilize the zone system, you must have a spot meter with a very tight – 1-3° — focus. As with any light meter, your spot meter will assume that it is pointing at something that is 18% gray (zone V). By carefully spot metering different parts of an image – bright highlights, dark shadows, or areas whose texture you want to preserve – and then determining which zone those tones correspond to, you can calculate exactly how much to over- or underexpose.

For example, let's say you want to meter a very dark stone, a tone that is typically considered to be in zone III. Your meter will, of course, return exposure settings to properly expose that stone *as a zone V tone*. Because the stone really belongs in zone III (and remember that each zone represents a one-stop change in exposure) then you know to underexpose by two stops to preserve the stone's color and tone.

There are a number of good web sites containing detailed zone system information and tutorials. You can find links to them at www.completedigitalphotography.com/zonesystem.

You can further improve your black and white photography through the use of red or orange lens filters that serve to increase contrast. You'll learn more about filters later in this chapter.

INFRARED PHOTOGRAPHY

Infrared light is not visible to the human eye. However, special infrared-sensitive films can be used to capture infrared light, allowing you to see objects in a completely new way. Skies and foliage are particularly well suited to infrared photography as leafy greens will appear white and skies are rendered much more contrasty. Digital infrared photography is possible with any digital camera although some cameras will produce far better results than others.

All digital cameras have an infrared filter in front of their image sensor. Most CCDs and CMOS sensors are too sensitive to the infrared range, and if the incoming light is not filtered for infrared (IR), images can take on strong color casts.

Despite these filters, though, some infrared does get passed through to the camera's sensor, allowing you to use your digital camera for infrared photography. Unfortunately, there's no hard and fast rule for how strong a camera's IR filter is – the only way to find out is to experiment. You can get a rough idea of a camera's infrared sensitivity with the help of the infrared remote control from a TV, VCR, or stereo. Just point the remote at the camera's lens, press and hold a button on the remote, and take a picture. If the camera can see the light of the remote, (Figure 9.7) then you'll know that the sensor is picking up some IR. The brighter the light, the better your camera will be for infrared shooting.

To shoot infrared images, you'll need to put some infrared filters on your camera's lens (the "Filters" section at the end of this chapter has a lot of general information on filters and how to mount them). There are a number of filters

FIGURE
9.7 *You can get a pretty good idea of the infrared capabilities of your camera by taking a picture of a remote control's infrared emitter. Note that, in the second image, the remote's emitter is "lit up" with infrared light.*

available for infrared photography, but the most popular are the Kodak Wratten 89b, 87, and 87C filters. Hoya makes two filters, the R72 and RM72, which are equivalent to the Kodak 89B. B+W also make Wratten equivalents, the 092 and 093.

The right filter is partly a matter of taste, as different filters will yield different levels of contrast. Depending on your camera's infrared sensitivity, you'll either need a brighter or darker filter.

At the time of this writing, the Olympus C2000Z, C2020Z, 2100UZ, Nikon Coolpix 950 and D1 and the Sony F500 are all known to be very good infrared cameras that work with the Hoya filters and the Kodak Wrattan 87 and 87C filters.

The current generation of 3-megapixel cameras, such as the Olympus C3030 and Coolpix 990, have much stronger internal infrared filters. Consequently, you'll need the darker Wratten 89B filter.

Because they are so dark, you can expect an infrared filter to cut four to ten stops from the available light! That means you'll be using very long exposures even in bright daylight. Obviously, a tripod is essential for infrared photography. To pick up some extra stops (and reduce lengthy exposure times) you can set your camera to a higher ISO, but this will make your images noisier. Typically, Wratten 87 exposures in bright daylight at ISO 200 start at around five seconds. Because the filter can confuse your camera's light meter, you may have to do a little experimenting to find the right exposure.

When they shoot film, infrared photographers often have to worry about a focus shift caused by the infrared filter that can result in the camera focusing beyond its focal plane. Fortunately, the deep depths of field of a typical consumer digital camera greatly reduce the chances of focus troubles. Just to be safe, though, you might as well lock your camera on infinity when you shoot landscapes and, if you seem to be having focusing troubles, throw your camera into manual mode and decrease the aperture to increase depth of field.

You don't have to have a black and white mode on your camera to shoot infrared images. When you shoot color through an infrared filter, most images will appear in brick-red and cyan tones, rather like a duotone. You can easily convert these to grayscale later.

Because of the bright light required, you'll typically only shoot infrared outdoors. Any incandescent objects – glowing coals, molten metal – will emit a lot of infrared radiation. The thermal radiation produced by the human body, however, is way beyond the sensitivity of the near-infrared capabilities provided by your camera.

SHOOTING PANORAMAS

At one time or another, you may have tried to capture a wide vista or panoramic scene by shooting a series of overlapping images like the ones in Figure 9.8.

FIGURE *These images were shot separately with the idea that they would later be stitched into*
9.8 *a panorama.*

Although this can be a very nice, stylized way of representing a very wide-angle view, it's obviously not a very *accurate* image. The seams don't join together properly, some elements are repeated from one image to the next, and each frame has its own perspective – notice how all the lines in each image recede to separate vanishing points.

If you want a panorama that looks like a single image, you can use your computer to correct the problems listed above, and produce an image like the one in Figure 9.9.

FIGURE *The finished, stitched and then cropped panorama.*
9.9

Panoramic software can take a series of overlapping images and stitch them together to create a single image. Besides hiding the seams of an image, panoramic software corrects the perspective of each image by essentially mapping the images onto a giant virtual cylinder (Figure 9.10). The curvature of the imaginary cylinder corrects the perspective troubles in your image.

FIGURE **9.10** *Your panoramic software performs complex cylindrical distortions of your images to correct the perspective in each frame.*

In addition to printing out wide panoramic prints of your images, you can also deliver your panoramas as *virtual reality* (VR) movies which present a window onto your panoramic scene, and which allow the user to "navigate" the scene by pivoting and tilting their view (Figure 9.11).

FIGURE **9.11** *If you store your images as virtual reality scenes, users can use special viewing software to pan and tilt around your scene. With more advanced authoring tools, you can build fully navigable VR environments.*

You'll learn all about stitching in Chapter 14, but getting a good-looking panorama begins with your shoot.

PREPARING YOUR CAMERA

To shoot a panorama you need a wide-angle lens. Although you can use a tele-photo lens, you'll have to shoot more images to get the same coverage. And, telephoto lenses tend to compress depth a little too much. The deep sense of space that a wide-angle lens produces is much more appropriate to the proportions of the wide field of view that you'll capture with a panorama.

The good news is that the wide angle on your digital camera's zoom lens is probably wide enough to take good panoramas. For even better results, though, consider purchasing a wide-angle attachment, if the camera supports such an option. With a wider angle, you'll shoot fewer images, which means fewer potential stitching errors.

There are two ways to shoot panoramas: the correct way which involves a lot of special equipment but produces very precise, accurate images for stitching; and the sloppy way which is prone to error but can still produce fine results.

Whether you choose to be precise or sloppy, one of your main concerns when you shoot a panorama is to ensure that you are properly rotating the camera between shots. If you're going for extreme precision, then you'll want to identify the camera's *nodal point*, the optical center of the camera's lens.

Several manufacturers make special tripod heads for shooting panoramic images. These heads include special movable brackets that allow you to precisely position the camera so that its nodal point sits directly above the tripod's axis of rotation (Figure 9.12).

FIGURE *Panoramic tripod head.*
9.12

Note that if you're shooting landscapes, such concern for nodal point rotation is not so crucial. However, a custom panoramic head can still help because most feature special stops that allow you to accurately rotate the camera into the position required for each shot of your panorama. Such heads typically sell for $100 to $300 (depending on the size of the camera they must support) and are worth the money if you do a lot of panoramas.

For most uses, though, you can simply use your normal tripod, or even shoot with the camera handheld. If your camera's tripod mount is positioned so that the camera can be panned around the axis of its lens, then you're in luck: you can simply pan your tripod to frame each shot. If your tripod mount is off-axis, as shown in Figure 9.13, then you might be better off with a monopod, or shooting with the camera handheld.

FIGURE   *If your camera's tripod mount is off-axis from the rotational center of the lens, then*
9.13   *you'll have a hard time shooting panoramas from a tripod.*

When you shoot with the camera handheld, remember to pivot the *camera* and not your head or body. Your eyes are a few inches in front of the center of rotation of your neck, and your camera's lens will be even further removed from your neck or body's rotation, meaning you'll actually be rotating around a point several inches *behind* the camera. So, between shots, rotate the camera around the axis of its lens and then – if necessary – reposition your body behind the camera's new position. Although this sounds complicated, with a little practice it's not too hard. Your main concern when you rotate the camera is to keep its bottom parallel to the ground. If you tilt the camera in addition to rotating it, you'll run into some problems when you are stitching.

When you pivot the camera, remember that your images must *overlap,* not sit adjacent to each other. Most stitching software recommends a 20-50% overlap between images. Many cameras feature panoramic assist modes that offer on-screen cues as to how much to overlap. If your camera has such a feature, it's definitely worth using. A little experience with your stitching program will give you a better idea of how images need to overlap.

PANORAMIC EXPOSURE

Because you will be pointing your camera in a lot of different directions as you shoot a panorama, it's important to plan your exposure ahead of time. Your concern is to have an even exposure across all of the images in your panorama to prevent *banding* – bright strips of incorrect exposure that will appear along the seams of your stitched image. (Figure 9.14).

FIGURE *The original shots in this panorama were not evenly exposed. After stitching, color*
9.14 *differences and banding are visible in the final panorama, particularly in the sky.*

If your camera has some kind of panoramic assist mode, it will, in addition to indicating overlap guidelines, lock the camera's exposure after the first image. Although this exposure may not be appropriate to every image in the panorama – that is, some areas might be under- or overexposed – it will at least provide a consistent exposure across the final image.

If your camera doesn't have an assist mode, but does provide an exposure lock control, then you can simply lock the exposure yourself. If you're using your camera's automatic exposure controls, then try to meter off of an area that will produce an exposure appropriate to the entire panorama – in other words, when you lock exposure, make sure the camera isn't pointed at something brighter or darker than most of the image.

Landscapes pose particular exposure problems because some frame of the panorama might include the sun (unless the sun is completely behind you). Landscapes can also be tricky because the sky can often cause an underexpo-sure of your landscape elements. Be sure to use a metering mode or exposure compensation that will correct for this.

If your camera has manual controls, you can plan your panoramic exposure with more care. Before you shoot, take meter readings from each frame of your panorama, and try to come up with a compromise that will serve the whole image. If your camera has a long enough focal length that depth of field is a concern, then use your manual controls to ensure a deep depth of field.

SHOOT WITH CARE

When you shoot around people, animals, or other moving objects, be careful about where you position the seams of your image. (Figure 9.15) A person who is present in one image and gone in the next may turn partially transparent if they fall on a seam in the final panorama.

FIGURE *Because we were shooting our panorama images from left to right, we inadvertently*
9.15 *shot the Jeep twice. Unfortunately, when stitched, there are now two identical Jeeps in the shot.*

If the objects in your panorama are moving in a particular direction, then shoot in the opposite direction. That is, if a person is walking across your scene from right to left, then shoot your images from left to right. This is assuming that you don't *want* to see multiple copies of them across your panoramic field of view. If you *do*, then by all means, shoot from right to left and ensure that the person is in the middle of each shot when you shoot.

Of course, there are plenty of times when it's fine to violate all of these rules. Figure 9.16 and Color Plate 6 show an example of a technically incorrect panorama.

Finally, learn to think of the panoramic process as a complex – but free – super-wide angle lens. Don't just use panoramas for capturing wide vistas, use them for any occasion where you'd like to have a wide-angle, or fisheye lens. (Figure 9.17)

FIGURE *Technically, this panorama has a lot of mistakes: uneven exposure, bad seams, weird*
9.16 *perspective, not to mention the noise. Nevertheless, despite its technical flaws, it's still*
a good image. The photographic edge was added in Photoshop.

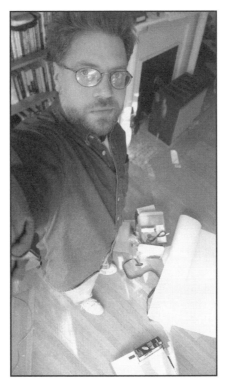

FIGURE *Panoramas aren't just for landscapes. Think about shooting them any time you'd*
9.17 *want a really wide-angle – or even fisheye – lens.*

SHOOTING FOR THE WEB

Shooting with the highest resolution and quality that your camera can manage will allow you to use your images for anything from print to video to the web. However, there may be times when you know your images will be used only for the web. In these instances, there are a few web-specific settings to consider.

IMAGE SIZE AND QUALITY

If you plan to shoot only for the Web, you might as well switch your camera to a lower resolution before shooting, simply to save space and allow for more shooting. Resolution will be discussed in more detail in Chapter 15 but for now it's safe to say that XGA resolution (1024 x 768) will probably be all that you'll ever need for web images (since most users would never be willing to wait for the download of a larger image). Note that if you plan on blowing up part of your image – for example, if you can't get near enough to your subject to get a really good close-up shot – then you might want to shoot at higher resolution, to provide more data for enlarging.

Every time you save an image using JPEG compression you lose some image quality. Hopefully, it's an imperceptible loss of quality, but you never know. Assuming your camera is saving in JPEG format, then your images have already been compressed once before they even leave your camera. Consequently, you want to be careful about compressing them again. You'll most likely make some edits to your image – color or tonal corrections, cropping and resizing – and then save the image out as a JPEG file for web posting, which means it will get compressed again and lose more data. So, it's best to shoot at the compression level that provides the best level of quality. Since you're going to lose some more data later, you might as well start with the highest quality you can manage.

CONSIDER THE LEGIBILITY OF THE IMAGE

Most images on the web are small. To help improve the legibility of the image at small sizes, you'll want to strive for clean compositions with good lighting. Consider shooting with shallow depth of field (if your camera can manage it) to provide good separation of foreground and background.

If you know your images will be highly compressed, then be sure to be wary of content that doesn't compress well. If you are shooting small images (small file size, that is) then go for lower-contrast images as these will compress tighter. Use your exposure controls to capture *less* tonal range.

FINALLY, A USE FOR THAT DIGITAL ZOOM!

If you're shooting at a lower resolution, it might be okay to go ahead and use your camera's digital zoom. Many digital zoom features work by simply taking a smaller area of the image and interpolating it up to full resolution. However, since you'll typically be shooting at lower resolution – XGA or VGA resolution – then the camera won't necessarily have to enlarge its digitally-zoomed crop. The result: no image degradation when you digitally zoom – up to a point.

On the Coolpix 990, for example, you can digitally zoom up to 2x at XGA resolution with no degradation. At VGA resolution, you can go up to 3.2x.

If you'll be shooting a lot of web-resolution images, it's worth experimenting with your digital zoom.

SHOOTING FOR VIDEO

If your still images are destined for video, then you're in luck, because most video is of far lower quality than what even a lower-end digital camera can produce. For most video formats you can get away with shooting at 640 x 480 (VGA) resolution. High Definition footage will require higher, XGA resolution.

When you shoot for video, it's important to remember that the quality of the image will be greatly reduced by the time it hits a video screen. Small details, fine lines, and very bright colors will not render properly as video. In particular, avoid bright reds and magentas as these can have a tendency to smear. If capturing a small detail is important, then go for a close-up.

It's also imperative to be aware that there is are *action-safe* and *title-safe* areas in a video image. Anything outside of these area may be cropped by the viewer's monitor or television. Most video editing programs provide guides that show the boundaries of these areas. Ask your video producer to show you these areas (Figure 9.18).

FIGURE   *If you're shooting images for video, be aware of the action and title-safe areas. Any*
9.18   *important action should be kept within the outer square, while titles (which you*
        definitely want the viewer to see) should be kept within the inner square.

Using Filters

When you edit, you'll often use a lot of filters, small bits of programming code that can add functionality to your image editing program. There's another kind of filter, however, the kind that screws onto the end of your lens and modifies the light passing into your camera. Filters can be used for everything from creating special effects to correcting image problems, but before you can start using a filter, you've got to figure out how to get it onto your camera.

First, check the lens on your camera for lens threads. If it has any, then you're ready to figure out what filters are available in your lens size. The filter size for your lens is probably written on the end of the lens (Figure 9.19). If it's not, just check your manual.

FIGURE *If your lens has threads, you can find out what size filters you need by looking for a*
9.19 *thread-size marking on the end of your lens. The lens shown here needs 49mm filters.*

You should be able to find some filters in the exact filter size of your lens. These will simply screw onto the end of your lens, and most filters will include lens threads of their own, letting you stack up lenses.

Other filters may not be available in the right size for your lens and may require the use of a *step-up ring,* a simple adapter that screws onto the front of your lens and provides a bigger set of threads for accepting bigger filters. (Figure 9.20) Be careful with step-up rings, though - if they're too big, they may block your camera's metering sensors, flash, or optical viewfinder.

Lens filters are completely flat, meaning they don't add any magnification power to your lens. Although optically they are simpler than a lens, you still want to be careful about your choice of filter. There *is* a difference between a

FIGURE *Many cameras, such as this Olympus C2500, require a step-up ring or adapter to use*
9.20 *lens attachments or filters.*

$100 ultraviolet filter and a $35 ultraviolet filter. Just as an element in your lens can introduce aberrations, a poorly made filter can introduce flares and color shifts. Although it can be tempting to go for the less expensive filter, spend a little time researching the more expensive competition. You may find there is a big difference in image quality.

TYPES OF FILTERS

In Chapter 8 you read about neutral density filters, non-colored filters that you can use to cut a few stops-worth of light so as to increase your exposure options. And, earlier in this chapter you read about infrared filters that can be used to photograph objects in infrared light. There are a lot of other kinds of filters – too many to cover here. However, if there is a group of "essential" filters, it would probably include the following:

- **Polarizers.** *Polarizers* don't really do anything to the light that's passing into your lens. Rather, they only allow light that is polarized in a particular direction to enter your lens. The practical upshot is that polarizers can completely remove distracting reflections from water, glass, or other shiny surfaces. To use a polarizer, you simply attach it to the end of your lens and rotate it until the reflections are gone (if you're not using an SLR, then you'll need to watch your camera's LCD viewfinder, as the optical viewfinder won't show the effect of the filter). Polarizers can also be used to increase the contrast in skies and clouds. (Figure 9.21)

- **Ultraviolet filters.** Ultraviolet filters are used to cut down on haze and other atmospheric conditions that can sometimes result in color shifts in your image.
- **Contrast filters.** You can increase contrast and saturation in your images by using simple colored *contrast filters*. Yellow filters will typically darken skies and shadows, and yellow-green and red filters will increase such contrast even further. Conversely, blue filters will lighten skies and darken green foliage and trees.
- **Effects filters.** There are any number of *effects filters* ranging from filters that will render bright lights as starbursts to filters that will soften, or haze an image. Major filter manufacturers such as Tiffen, (www.completedigitalphotography.com/tiffen) B+W, (www.completedigitalphotography.com/b+w) and Hoya (www.completedigitalphotography.com/hoya) publish complete, detailed catalogs of all of their filter options.

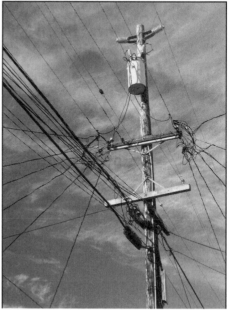

FIGURE **9.21** *These images show the difference in shooting clouds and skies with a polarizer. The image on the left was shot normally, while the right-hand image was shot with a polarizing filter.*

If your camera does not have a TTL light meter, then you're going to have to do some manual compensations when you use a filter. Since the metered light is not passing through the filter, the meter will lead you to overexpose. Most filters will have a documented *filter factor* which will inform you of the exposure compensation (in stops) required when you use that filter.

Similarly, if your camera does not use a TTL white balance system, then your white balance may not be properly adjusted for the filter's effect. The only way to find out for sure is to do a little experimenting.

Obviously, if your camera is not an SLR, then you won't see the effects of the filter when you look through the camera's optical viewfinder. Switch to the camera's LCD.

TIP

Beware of ultraviolet filters. *It's fairly common practice to mount an ultraviolet filter on your lens and leave it there, so as to protect your lens from bumps and scratches. Be aware, however, that an ultraviolet filter can affect the white balance presets on your camera. You may find, for example, that your daylight white balance preset becomes far too warm, as the camera will be expecting more ultraviolet light to be coming through the lens. If this seems to be true of your camera, either remove the filter when you use this setting, or use automatic white balance or a manual white balance when you shoot with the filter in bright sunlight.*

Cheap filters

Gels are thin pieces of plastic that are usually placed in front of lights to create colored lighting effects. Available at any theatrical lighting supply store, and at many photography stores, gels can also be used as inexpensive filters. Simply hold the gel in front of your lens and fire away.

On the downside, gels are not as optically pure as a fine piece of glass and holding them in front of your lens can introduce even more aberrations, as any buckles, folds, or reflections in the gel will introduce distortion into your image. You'll also need to be careful to not get any fingerprints on the gel material. To avoid such troubles, you can always try sandwiching gel material between a couple of ultraviolet filters and mounting the whole contraption onto your lens.

LENS EXTENSIONS

Some cameras support screw-on lens extensions that attach to your camera's filter threads to create a more telephoto or wide-angle lens. As with filters, these extensions may require a step-up ring. Also note that some cameras require you to tell them – usually through a menu option – that a lens extension is being used. If you don't let the camera know, then its focus and metering operations can become confused.

Spend some time experimenting with your camera's extensions to determine their idiosyncrasies. For example, some lenses may have bad barrel or pincushion distortion or vignetting problems.

Finally, if the extension or step-up ring is very large, it may obscure the camera's optical viewfinder or, more importantly, the onboard flash. If the extension protrudes too far in front of the flash, it will cast a shadow when you take the shot. Usually, the only solution is to use an external flash.

SHOOTING IN EXTREME CONDITIONS

One great advantage of film cameras over digital cameras is that they can be incredibly simple machines and, thus, very durable. Since all of the imaging and storage technology in a film camera is tied up in the film, the camera itself can be little more than a box. This is not true with a digital camera, which requires batteries, silicon chips, LCD screens, and many more potentially fragile components.

When you shoot in extreme heat or cold, or in very wet or dusty situations, you need to take a number of precautions to ensure that you don't damage your camera. Obviously, like any mechanical apparatus, dirt, dust, sand, water, and extreme temperatures are definite hazards.

DIRT, DUST, OR SAND AND DIGITAL CAMERAS

Be particularly cautious about dirt, dust, or sand because, even if it doesn't get inside the camera, a single grain of sand can be abrasive enough to scratch your lens. With their deep depths of field, minor lens scratches are usually nothing to worry about, but why take chances.

WATER AND DIGITAL CAMERAS

Digital cameras and water definitely do not mix. Although a few sprinkles are nothing to worry about, you absolutely do *not* want to submerge your camera. The rule of thumb for manual film cameras has always been: if it falls in the water, grab the camera and put it in a bucket of that same water. Keeping a film camera submerged will prevent rust until you can get the bucket and camera to a repair person who can take it apart, clean it, and dry it.

Unfortunately, this doesn't apply to today's electronics-laden digital cameras (or even to modern film cameras). If your camera goes in the drink, fish it out immediately and do everything you can to get it dry. Immediately remove the battery and media card; open all port covers, lids, and flaps; and wipe off any water you can see, no matter how small. Set the camera in a warm place and do *not* turn it on until you're sure the camera has had time to dry off, both inside and out.

If you know you're going to be using your camera in potentially wet situations (kayaking, canoeing, taking your convertible to the car wash) then consider buying a *drybag* - a sealable, waterproof bag that will keep your camera dry even if it gets submerged.

If you absolutely have to shoot in the rain, try sticking your camera in a Ziploc bag. You'll still be able to access the controls, and you can always cut a hole for the lens. (Figure 9.22)

FIGURE   *If you're shooting in light rain, consider a Ziploc bag to protect your camera. Be*
9.22   *warned, though, that your camera is very sensitive to cold and damp.*

THE CAMERA THAT CAME IN FROM THE COLD

Shooting in cold weather presents a number of problems for the digital photographer. First, there are the LCDs on your camera. Remember that the "L" in LCD stands for liquid. As temperatures drop, your LCD will become far less "L" and the last thing you want is for it to turn into a solid crystal display. Although the LCD won't necessarily be damaged by cold weather, it may prove to be unusable.

Other, smaller, electronic components might actually be damaged if you try to use them in cold weather. Extreme cold may cause small electronic components to expand or contract enough that using them will cause them to break. Your camera's manual should list a range of operating temperatures and, although you *might* be able to push these an extra 20° on the cold end, it's safe to say that such use won't be covered by your warranty.

Even if you're shooting within your camera's prescribed operating temperatures, be very careful when you move the camera from cold temperatures to warm. Walking into a heated house from a day of shooting in the snow can cause potentially damaging condensation to form inside the camera. If you know you're going to be shooting in cold weather, take a Ziploc bag with you. Before you go into a warm building, put the camera in the bag and zip it up. Once inside, give it 20 or 30 minutes to warm up to room temperature before you let it out of the bag. If you don't have a bag, then be sure not to turn it on until any condensation has had time to evaporate.

If the temperature is cold enough to freeze your camera, then it's probably cold enough that you'll be wearing gloves. Given your reduced dexterity when you wear gloves, be absolutely certain your camera has a neck or wrist strap and that it's securely attached to some part of your body.

As discussed in Chapter 7, batteries can be greatly affected by cold weather. Take a look at the cold-weather battery tips in Chaper 7 under the topic Power and Storage Management.

HOT WEATHER AND DIGITAL CAMERAS

Hot weather can also affect your camera and, again, the first thing to go will be your LCD screens. If you turn on your camera and your LCD appears black, then it's safe to say that your LCD has overheated – they're really not reliable above 32°C (90°F). Turn your camera off and try to get it somewhere where it can cool down. If you must shoot in high temperatures, then consider keeping your camera in some kind of dry cooler (an ice chest with some blue ice) until you're ready to shoot.

If you haven't exceeded the camera's recommended operating temperature, but your LCD has overheated and isn't working, it's probably safe to keep shooting using the camera's optical viewfinder (if it has one). Turn off the picture review function since your LCD won't be visible anyway.

HALFWAY THERE

Like a film camera, to get the best prints from your digital camera you'll need to manipulate your image to turn its tonal information into the image you originally envisioned. That process begins by making some preparations on your computer. In Chapter 10 you will learn how to transfer your images to your computer and how to configure your image editing software.

ASTROPHOTOGRAPHY

Although you may not have the massive space program necessary to shoot like the Apollo astronauts, there's no reason you can't photograph the same subject matter. Because of its extreme sensitivity to light, your digital camera is an ideal camera for photographing astronomical objects through a telescope. In fact, many astronomers are finding that even cheap $100 web cameras produce pretty good astro photos.

In addition to providing you with a way of recording your astronomical observations, your digital camera can help you capture images of things that you normally couldn't see. Your eye has to gather a lot of light to discern the color of an object and it simply cannot gather light fast enough to see the color of objects millions of miles (or light years) away. Because your digital camera can sit and gather color for a long time, it can help you see the color of objects that would appear black and white if you simply looked at them through a telescope.

Some quick astrophotography tips include the following:

- Obviously, you'll need a lens mount that will allow you to attach your camera to your telescope. There are many such mounts and adapters; check with your telescope dealer or camera manufacturer for details.
- Your camera will need to have a manual mode that allows for shutter and aperture control and that provides for long exposures (greater than 30 seconds). Open your aperture all the way. Your light meter will be useless for this type of photography, so you'll be doing everything manually.
- To prevent vibration, you'll want to use a remote control or self-timer to fire your camera's shutter release.
- If you're using a digital SLR with removable lenses, consider using a very fast prime lens rather than a zoom lens. Because zooms are usually slower than primes and not quite as sharp, a prime lens will yield better resolution when you shoot point light sources such as stars. Also, if your camera has a *mirror lock-up* feature, use it, as this will further reduce camera vibration when you shoot.

There are a number of good astro-photography web sites. You can find links to them at www.completedigitalphotography.com/astro.

CHAPTER

10

Preparing Your Images for Editing

IN THIS CHAPTER

- Moving Pictures: How to Transfer and Organize your Images
- Preparing your Image Editor
- Preparing your Image

In the rest of this book, you will learn about what happens after you've finished shooting. From color correcting to editing to printing, the following chapters will cover the things that have traditionally happened in the darkroom, but that now happen inside your computer.

Although your image editing application is capable of amazing photographic feats, it's also capable of producing really lousy images. To get the best results in a manner that is predictable and reproducible, you need to make some preparations to both your images and to your computer. In this chapter, you will learn how to configure your system to get the best results from the processes you'll learn in the rest of the book.

Before you can begin editing, though, you need to move your images into your computer.

MOVING PICTURES: HOW TO TRANSFER AND ORGANIZE YOUR IMAGES

No matter how serious you are about your photography, there has probably been some time in your life when you've gone on vacation, shot a bunch of pictures, brought your film back home, and never developed it. For some reason – jet lag, going back to work, or some other reason – you just never got around to taking the film down to the lab, and so the film sits in a drawer where it will remain for years until your children eventually inherit it, develop it, and have no idea what they're looking at.

Okay, perhaps this is something of an extreme example, but it does have a parallel in the digital world. Because you only have a limited supply of the rather expensive media that your digital camera uses, you may find yourself frequently dumping a card full of images to your computer to free up the card for more shooting. In no time at all, you can have hundreds of images on your hard drive, each with a weird name like DSC00453.JPG that gives you no idea of what the image is.

With just a little effort, and some special software, you can save yourself (or your descendents) from one day facing a 30-gigabyte drive full of unlabeled images.

MAKE THE TRANSFER

As discussed earlier in this book, there are a number of ways that you can transfer images from your camera to your computer. Your camera probably includes a serial port of some kind, either RS-432 or USB, or possibly even a Firewire port. Using the special cable and software included with your camera, you can dump your pictures onto your computer.

This is usually the least convenient, and most time-consuming method of transferring your digital images. Depending on the size of your images and the speed of your connection, transferring a single image can take anywhere from a few seconds to several minutes. Emptying a whole card can take up to half an hour (or longer, depending on the size of the card). In addition, using your camera's cable connection will drain your camera's batteries, which may not be a big deal if you're at home and can simply recharge the batteries when you're done. If you're in the field, though, you may not want to spend battery power on simple image transfers.

A speedier option is to use a media drive or CompactFlash adapter like those shown in Chapter 5. With these devices, your media card will appear on your desktop just like any other volume. You can then quickly drag and drop files to your hard drive.

If you must transfer your images through a cable, your main concern will be to not recompress your images before saving them. For example, some transfer programs give you the option to download an image to your hard drive, or to open it up on-screen. Be warned that if you open the image on-screen, the only save options available might be to resave the image as a JPEG file, introducing more JPEG compression and, therefore, more loss. Some programs will allow you to save in a non-*lossy* format such as TIFF, but these files will be much larger than JPEG files. Note that this process is usually slower than a direct transfer to disk.

Not all programs work this way, but if yours does, you might want to consider downloading all of the images to your hard drive first, and then looking at them later.

No matter how you move your images, it's essential to stay organized and keep your images labeled. If your camera's image transfer software includes a *light table* or *image cataloging* function, then you can quickly generate a page of thumbnails showing the contents of an entire media card.

ON THE CD
If your camera's included software doesn't include such a function, or if you'd like more power, consider using a third-party media cataloging application such as iView Multimedia, Thumber, or Extensis Portfolio. Demos and evaluation copies of several media catalogers are included on the Complete Digital Photography CD-ROM.

ORGANIZE YOUR DIGITAL MEDIA

Although everyone will have different ideas about organization and workflow, here are a few tips and suggestions for managing your digital media.

- Get a cataloging program that allows you to rename or move files. Being able to rename a file from within your cataloger is easier than having to switch back to your operating system's File Manager.

- Start by grouping images into folders, by subject. If you're in a hurry, don't worry about naming every file, just quickly sort by subject. You can always label individual files later.
- If you have a series of bracketed images, label each file with the appropriate exposure. Because Photoshop does not provide EXIF support (see Chapter 8), labeling your bracketed images is the easiest way to keep track of how each image was exposed (Figure 10.1). You can look up the settings using your camera's information display, or by using an EXIF-compatible application.

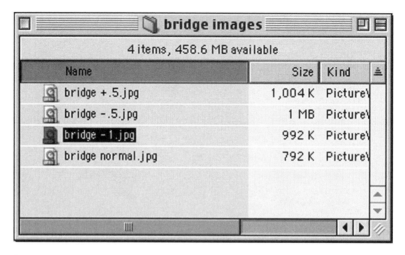

FIGURE **10.1** *If you've got a group of bracketed images, change their file names to reflect the degree of exposure adjustment in each image. This will make it easier to keep track of which image is which.*

- Similarly, sort panoramic images into folders. Whether you stitch them right away or not, it's a good idea to keep related images together.
- Lock valuable images before editing. Because most images are stored as JPEG files, you want to be sure that you don't accidentally save them again as a JPEG file and introduce more compression. Using your File Manager to locking your original file turns gives you the equivalent of a digital negative. You can then save new copies as you make edits. If you're storing images on a removable medium such as a Zip disk, go ahead and lock the entire disk after you've moved your files.
- Most likely, your image cataloging software won't be able to display images stored in a Raw data format. Cameras that offer Raw data support usually save tiny JPEG thumbnails for viewing. When you transfer images, be sure to copy the thumbnail files as well as the Raw files as you'll need these for cataloging and sorting.

Once you settle on a system of organization, use it! Although it may seem strange to devote several pages to this one topic, it's very easy to get overwhelmed by the number of images that your camera will produce in a heavy day of shooting. With a well-designed system of organization, you can quickly keep image glut under control.

PREPARING YOUR IMAGE EDITOR

Before you can get started editing, you'll need to do a little work to make sure that your image editing software is configured to accurately display colors. Color management and calibration is a complex subject, and how far you should delve into it depends largely on your printing and output needs. Most likely, no matter what software or printer you're using, you're going to need to spend a little time trying to manage the display and output of color.

In this section, you'll learn how to configure the color management tools in Adobe Photoshop 6 to more accurately represent colors on your monitor and printer. Although the methods discussed herein are specific to Photoshop, much of the theory applies to any application, and should be helpful no matter what application you ultimately decide to use. Even if Photoshop is not your image editorof choice , it's worth installing the Photoshop 6 demo from the Complete Digital Photography CD-ROM, just to follow the instructions in this text more easily.

ON THE CD

A LITTLE MORE COLOR THEORY

As you saw in Chapter 3, light mixes together in an additive process so that as colors are added together they appear more and more white. Ink, on the other hand, mixes in a subtractive manner. That is, as colors are mixed they appear darker. While the primary colors of light – the fundamental colors from which all other colors can be made – are red, green, and blue, the primary colors of ink are cyan, magenta, and yellow.

This simple difference is what makes accurate printing of your images so difficult. Each time you print, your computer has to figure out how to take your image – which it understands as a combination of red, green, and blue light – and convert it into a mix of cyan, magenta, and yellow ink.

Special K. As you may already know, color printing actually uses four colors: cyan, magenta, yellow, and black. Black is not a primary color, of course, but black ink is added to the mix because it is impossible to create perfectly pure ink pigments. So, although the theory says that if you mix cyan, magenta, and yellow together you will eventually get black, the truth is you'll just get very dark brown because of impurities in your color pigments. Adding a little black ink is the only way to get true black. This is why four-color printing is called CMYK.

As if converting colors between these two different color spaces wasn't difficult enough, accurate color reproduction is further complicated by the fact that not every monitor or TV is the same. If you've ever looked at a wall of TVs in an appliance store, you've seen that an image can vary greatly even between identical models. There are a number of reasons why, ranging from differences in color adjustments on each set, to differences in age, to differences in manufacturing. Computer monitors vary in the same way, which is why a digital image or web page on your monitor might look completely different on someone else's monitor.

Printers have the same trouble. Each manufacturer may take a different approach to reproducing colors, plus different brands of ink have unique color qualities. Similarly, different types of paper respond differently to ink. Further complicating matters is the fact that printers often use completely different approaches to reproducing color. Some printers use four colors, some add an extra two colors to reproduce lighter tones, some use ink, some use solid wax, and so on.

So how in the world will you manage and account for all of these variables? Fortunately, if you properly configure your software, you won't have to.

COLOR MANAGEMENT SYSTEMS

There are a number of ways that you can try to calibrate your monitor with your printer (or another monitor if you will be moving your images to different computers). Some people simply print a sample from their printer and then mess around with their monitor controls until the color on-screen matches the print. This is just about the worst way to approach color management because, in addition to being wildly inaccurate, your monitor adjustments won't necessarily be appropriate for all colors.

Another approach is to print an image using your preferred printer and paper, and then look at what's wrong with the print and adjust the color in your image accordingly. This works okay (and even in the best of circumstances, you'll always have to do test prints and make adjustments) and over time you'll probably begin to better understand the idiosyncrasies of your monitor and printer. However, you'll have to do a lot of printing to get good results, and if you ever change monitors or printers everything you will have learned about what looks right on-screen will be wrong.

The best approach to color management, therefore, is to use a *color management system* or *CMS*. A CMS is a set of software components that work together to compensate for the differences in your monitor, printer, and scanner, so that your images appear as accurately as possible on your display.

Using a CMS is pretty simple, but it does require a little time to gather the appropriate data and configure your software properly. With this small investment of time, though, you'll have a much better chance of reproducing the image you tried to capture when you were shooting.

COLOR MANAGEMENT WORKFLOW

A color management system works by adjusting the display of the colors in your image file (also referred to as your document in this text) so that they appear correct on the particular monitor you are using. To make these adjustments, your color management system needs to know some details about the color characteristics of your monitor, your printer, and the device that produced your image. Once it has this information, it can adjust the colors in your original image so that they display more accurately on your monitor and print more accurately on your printer. What's more, with Photoshop 6 and a properly configured color management system, you can make your monitor do a fairly accurate job of simulating a particular printer, allowing you to perform on-screen proofing.

To perform these color manipulations, your CMS needs to have accurate *device profiles*. Also referred to as *ICC profiles* or simply as profiles, these small files describe certain color characteristics of each device in your color management workflow. Obviously, for your CMS to work properly, you'll need accurate device profiles.

In Chapter 3 you learned about color models - the different approaches to representing color in an image. Different color models have different *gamuts*, or ranges of colors that they are capable of representing. For example, a CMYK offset printing process has a very particular gamut of colors that it can reproduce. If any of the colors in your image are outside the color gamut of the press, they won't print properly. Part of the job of your color management system is to properly adjust colors between different gamuts.

Photoshop 6 performs most of its color calculations and manipulations in an RGB color space. Although you can choose to convert to another color space – *CMYK* or *L*A*B*, for example – for most digital photography and desktop printing applications, you'll stick with RGB. However, there are many different RGB color spaces, and each one has a different gamut. For example, Microsoft and

Hewlett Packard defined the *sRGB* color space, a rather small RGB color space that attempts to reflect the color gamut of the average color monitor. Adobe, meanwhile, created the Adobe 1998 color space, a slightly larger color space that is more appropriate for typical desktop and offset printing jobs.

To ease its color management chores, Photoshop asks you to select a default RGB color space that it will use for its color management calculations. Adobe provides several options and you can even add more if you want. In general, though, you simply want to choose a space that is large enough to support the colors produced by your camera. Photoshop also adds an extra wrinkle to the normal color management process: it attaches a profile to your image. This profile contains information about the RGB space used by the image.

Once you've selected a color space and installed your device profiles, Photoshop – with help from your *color matching engine* – can start managing your color. By examining the profile from your camera (if you have a camera profile) as well as the profile attached to your document, the CMS has a much better idea of what the colors in your image are supposed to be. By examining the profile for your monitor, it can figure out how to represent your colors on-screen, while your printer profile will provide the information necessary for your CMS to more accurately print those original colors.

What's more, if you take your image to another monitor and printer, it should look exactly the same on those devices as it did on yours – assuming those new devices have accurate profiles.

It's important to realize, however, that although a CMS can do a very good job of accurately displaying colors, it still can't exactly represent printed output on your screen – or vice versa. After all, color created by a self-illuminated computer monitor is going to be inherently brighter than color ink on paper.

In the next section, you'll learn how to configure your color management system.

CONFIGURING YOUR COLOR MANAGEMENT SYSTEM

There are a number of different color management systems, but the most popular are ColorSync, which comes built into the Macintosh operating system and Windows' Integrated Color Management, which comes built into Windows. One of the nice things about color management in Photoshop 6 is that, from the Color Settings dialog box, you can choose to use any CMS, and Photoshop even includes a built-in CMS of its own. Although extreme color maniacs will argue the merits of one CMS over another, it's safe to say that for almost any application, the CMS that's built into your operating system – or Photoshop's built-in color manager – will be all that you ever need.

Your most important CMS-related concern is that you configure your CMS settings properly by specifying which profiles you want to use for your monitor and printer (and, ideally, your camera, although you probably won't be able to

---

WHAT A COLOR LOOKS LIKE VS. WHAT IT IS MADE OF

Unfortunately, although CMYK or RGB color spaces can represent a lot of colors, they don't describe what a color actually looks like; rather, they simply describe what a color is made of. In other words, a set of RGB values is nothing more than a recipe for displaying a certain color. In theory, this may seem like a great idea. In practice, though, it doesn't really work very well because there's no guarantee that your chosen monitor or printer has the right ingredients to properly make your color recipe.

For example, if your computer says that a particular pixel is supposed to be 50% red, 30% green, and 70% blue, but the red gun in your monitor is no longer the nice pure red that it once was, then what gets displayed may be closer to 40% red, 50% green, and 75% blue.

Fortunately, in 1976 CIE, the Commission Internationale de l'Éclairage (the International Commission on Illumination) came up with the Lab color model (actually Lab is a modification of a color model created by CIE in 1931). Rather than describing how a color is made, Lab describes what a color looks like. Because Lab has nothing to do with any actual color reproduction method (such as the red, green, and blue electron guns used by your monitor, or the four different inks used by a printer) it is referred to as a device-independent color space.

A CMS works by using the profile of your camera or scanner to convert your image into a device-independent color space such as Lab. In other words, your camera's profile helps the CMS understand what the colors in your image are supposed to be and Lab mode provides a reference space for modeling those colors.

---

find a camera profile) and tweaking a few settings. Most of your CMS configuration will happen inside Photoshop, but before you head there, you need to select a profile for your monitor.

If you're a Macintosh user using an Apple-brand monitor, then your operating system probably shipped with an appropriate profile. If you're a Mac or Windows user using a 3rd-party monitor, though, check your vendor's web site to see if they offer a profile for your CMS. If they don't, you can build one yourself as described below.

Specifying a Monitor Profile on a Macintosh
If you're using Macintosh operating system 8.6 or later, then ColorSync, Apple's color management system, is probably already installed on your computer. If you don't see a ColorSync control panel in your Control Panel folder, then you need to install ColorSync from your original operating system disk. Color-Sync ships with pre-defined profiles for most of the monitors that Apple makes,

including iMacs and PowerBooks. If you're using a 3rd-party monitor, then you should check with your vendor to see if they offer ColorSync profiles.

If you don't have a profile for your monitor, you can always create one of your own. Special hardware calibrators - such as the $400 OptiCal system from ColorVision - can be used to measure the characteristics of your display and create a monitor profile. Or, you can build a profile by eye using Apple's Monitor Calibration Assistant software as shown in Figure 10.2.

FIGURE *Apple's Monitor Calibration Assistant provides a way of building a monitor profile by*
10.2 *eye. Although less accurate than a hardware-calibrated profile, it's better than nothing.*

Although it is not as precise as a hardware calibrator, Apple's calibrate-by-eye approach is still much better than not using a profile at all. Even if you have a pre-defined profile for your monitor, you might want to build a new profile from scratch. If your monitor is old, it may have changed enough from its original design specifications that the pre-defined profile no longer matches. To use the Monitor Calibration Assistant, simply follow the on-screen instructions.

Once you've found or created a monitor profile, you simply install it in the ColorSync Profiles folder inside your System folder. Then, open up the Monitors control panel, click on the Color button, and pick the appropriate profile from the list of available options (the Monitor Calibration Assistant will do these two steps for you).

That's it. Your monitor profile is now configured and you're ready to move on to the settings in Photoshop's Color Settings dialog box.

Specifying a Monitor Profile in Windows

Before you can specify a monitor profile in Windows, you'll need a profile. Windows ships with only one default profile -which is unlikely to be the perfect match for your monitor - so it's better to try to build your own. You'll get the most accurate profile by using a hardware calibrator of some kind. You can also build a reasonable profile using the Adobe Gamma Control Panel (Figure 10.3). Simply follow the instructions on-screen to build a profile by eye.

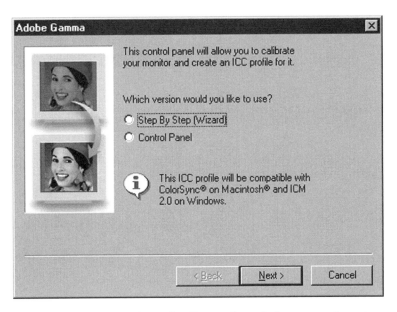

FIGURE *The Adobe Gamma control panel walks you through the process of creating a*
10.3 *monitor profile by eye.*

Monitor profiles in Windows 98 and 98 Second Edition need to be stored in the Windows/System/Color folder while monitor profiles for Windows 2000 and Millennium Edition (ME) need to be stored in the Windows/System32/Spool/Drivers/Color folder.

Once you've placed your profile in the right folder, you need to attach it to your monitor. Open the Display control panel and click on the Settings tab. Click on the Advanced button at the bottom of the window and then click on the Color Management tab. (Figure 10.4) From this screen you can simply hit the Add button to choose a profile.

As on the Macintosh, the rest of your color management settings will be defined from within Photoshop.

FIGURE *Once you've installed your monitor profile in the proper folder, you can use the*
10.4 *Display control panel to define it as your current profile.*

MONITOR CALIBRATION TIPS

Before you calibrate your monitor, whether by eye or with a hardware calibrator, let the monitor warm up for half an hour, or so. This will give it time to get up to its usual operating temperature. For best results, turn the lights in the room down and block off any reflections or glare that might be striking the monitor.

Set your desktop background or pattern to a neutral gray (when you do any precise color manipulation or editing, you should set your desktop to gray to keep your eyes from getting confused). If you want to get really picky, then it's a good idea to move any large, bright-colored objects out of your field of view. In general, you want your working space to be neutrally colored.

Photoshop 6's Color Settings Dialog Box

Figure 10.5 shows the Photoshop 6 Color Settings dialog box. Although it may look a bit complex, you really only need to make one or two adjustments if you're printing to a desktop printer. If you have more complex, offset printing jobs, then you'll need to delve into your Photoshop manual to learn more about CMYK settings.

FIGURE   *In Photoshop 6, almost all of your color management settings can be entered in the*
10.5   *Color Settings dialog box.*

Your first choice is to configure your working spaces. A color space is really just a mathematical model of a particular range of colors. As such, you can simply tell your computer to use one model or another. When you work in a particular color space, you won't be allowed to pick colors outside of that space, and when you perform corrections and other color-altering operations, your colors will be kept "legal." That is, they won't ever extend beyond the colors of that space.

The Working Spaces section of Photoshop's Color Settings dialog box lets you specify the color spaces you want to use for different types of editing. So, you can select a particular color gamut for all of your RGB editing, another for all of your CMYK editing, and others for your grayscale editing or spot color work.

(Figure 10.6) Because digital cameras and desktop color printers are RGB devices, you only need to worry about choosing an RGB color space.

FIGURE *You define the color spaces you want to use for different types of editing using the*
10.6 *Working Spaces section of the Color Settings dialog box.*

TIP

"I thought my printer used CMYK inks?" *Although your desktop printer uses CMYK inks (or, in the case of a six-color inkjet photo printer, CMYK with extra C and extra M) the driver software for the printer expects to receive RGB data. It then does the appropriate conversion to a CMYK color space. So, from your computer's point of view, your color printer is an RGB device.*

Photoshop provides four different RGB spaces that differ slightly in the size of their gamuts. For most uses, the Adobe RGB (1998) space is probably the most appropriate. It's bigger than the sRGB space and has a wide enough gamut to handle all of the colors a digital camera can produce.

If your work is ultimately destined for output to a CMYK offset printing process, then you'll need to choose a CMYK space. For most uses, the best CMYK choice is to choose one of the Prepress Default presets from the Settings pop-up menu in the Color Settings dialog box. (Figure 10.7) Before getting too far into your work, though, you should consult with your printing service bureau to learn more about the color gamut of their particular press.

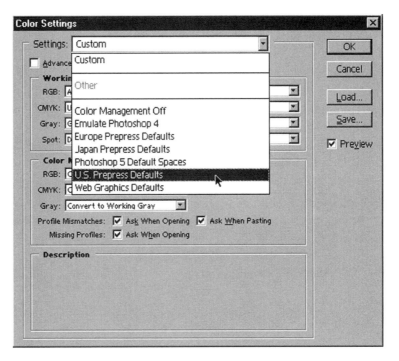

FIGURE   *Photoshop 6 includes several color management presets which will automatically*
10.7   *configure your color settings for specific printing situations.*

Photoshop 6 tags your documents with the working space that you define in the Color Settings dialog box. These tags are part of the document's profile and any new documents that you create will automatically be tagged with this working space profile. Later in this chapter, you'll see how these tags are used to proof your documents on-screen. First, though, you need to learn a little bit about profile management.

Making Policy

Because not everyone will choose to use the same color space, Photoshop allows you to set policies as to how to handle documents that are tagged with a different color space than your chosen working space. For example, let's say you've chosen to use Adobe RGB (1998) as your default working space, and a friend who does a lot of web design gives you a Photoshop document. Most likely, they will have selected sRGB as their default working space and their document will be tagged as such. Photoshop will handle the document in different ways depending on how you've set your color management policies.

With version 6's default policy options, any time you open a document that has been tagged with a color space that is different from your default working space, Photoshop will present the message box shown in Figure 10.8.

FIGURE *If a document's profile doesn't match your default color working space, Photoshop*
10.8 *lets you change to a new profile upon opening.*

Simply put, Photoshop doesn't know what to do with the discrepancy between the document's color space and your stated color space preference. So, it lets you choose to either use the attached (embedded) document profile, change the profile to your working space, or discard the profile completely. In Figure 10.8, the discrepancy has occurred because the document's attached sRGB profile doesn't match the AdobeRGB working space defined in your Color Settings dialog box.

You could choose to use the document's profile, but your printed results may not be as good as they would be if you converted the document to your chosen RGB space. It's better to go ahead and re-tag the document with your working space. Be aware, however, that you may want to warn the owner of this document that you've changed the working space, if you have to return the document to them.

The Color Settings dialog box lets you specify how mismatches in profiles should be handled. The bottom of the Color Settings dialog box provides detailed descriptions of each setting, and it's worth spending some time learning about the different policies. In general, though, Photoshop's default settings are the best for general use.

Finally, if you open a document that doesn't have a profile attached, Photoshop will present the message box shown in Figure 10.9 (unless you've specified different behavior in the Color Settings dialog).

FIGURE *If a document has no profile, Photoshop will let you assign one upon opening.*
10.9

At this point, you can choose to not attach a profile, meaning Photoshop will perform no color management functions, or you can attach your default working space, or another profile of your choice. In most cases, you'll probably want to attach your default color space. Photoshop presents similar documents if there is a profile mismatch when you paste something from one document into another.

When you change the profile of a document, Photoshop converts the document's colors into the new color space. Thanks to your color management system, this is a nearly lossless process, but there is – technically – a little loss of data when this occurs. Although you probably won't ever notice this loss, it's best not to go wantonly converting your images from space to space.

Trouble moving images into other applications. *If you're using Photoshop's color management features, then you may find that an image looks different in Photoshop than in another application. This is because Photoshop is "correcting" the color before it hits your monitor. This can create problems if you're trying to pick or edit colors to match color elements in another application – for example, a page-layout or web design package. To prevent this, you can choose to not tag an image with a profile when you first open the image, or you can select Color Management Off from the Settings pop-up menu of the Color Settings dialog box.*

"Aaaarrrgh! This is Too Confusing!"

You can choose to ignore color management altogether. Although there's no way to completely disable Photoshop's color management, choosing Color Management Off from the Settings pop-up menu at the top of the Color Settings dialog box will select some good, all-purpose color spaces, and will disable Photoshop's color management policies. However, if you open a document with a profile that's different from your chosen working space, Photoshop will still present you with the Embedded Profile Mismatch message box shown in Figure 10.8. When this happens, choose the Use the embedded profile option. This will prevent color conversions and will leave the document's profile intact so that, if you return the document to its original owner, it will still behave as they expect.

Changes from Photoshop 5. *It's important to realize that Photoshop 6's Color Settings dialog box is very different from the color settings in Photoshop 5, which were spread across four different dialog boxes. Photoshop 6 also differs from version 5 in its ability to have multiple documents open, each with a separate RGB space, and in its ability to easily perform soft proofing.*
So, if you're using version 5, you'll probably need to review your Photoshop manual to learn more about that version's color settings. If you're using a previous version, now is a good time to upgrade. Earlier versions of Photoshop used a very different, greatly inferior method of color management.

SOFT PROOFING IN PHOTOSHOP 6

Here's the payoff for all of this tedious color management theory. With your color settings configured and your profiles assigned, Photoshop can now do a pretty good job of generating a screen image, or a *soft proof* of what your image will look like when it is printed on a particular printer. Although Photoshop's soft proofs won't exactly match your printed page, they'll be in the ballpark, and most likely will save you a few test prints.

To generate a soft proof, you'll need the appropriate printer profiles. These are most likely available from your printer vendor's web site or were included in the software that shipped with your printer. Epson, HP, Canon, and many other vendors are diligent about generating profiles for their color printers, and you should install these profiles in the same folder as your monitor profiles.

With the proper profiles installed, open the document you want to soft proof and choose View>Proof Setup from the Photoshop menu bar. In the Proof Setup dialog box select Custom from the Setup pop-up menu. (Figure 10.10) Choose the appropriate printer profile from the Profile pop-up menu. Select Perceptual from the Intent pop-up menu. (Figure 10.10) Click the Save button and give this proof setup the same name as your printer, then click OK.

FIGURE *With the Proof Setup dialog box, you can create special soft proof settings for all of*
10.10 *your printers.*

Now choose View>Proof Colors. You should see the colors in your image shift and the resulting image should be closer to what your printed output will look like. Note that you can select a default proof setup by choosing View>Proof Setup when there are no documents open. A discussion of the other Proof Setup settings is beyond the scope of this book, but you can learn more from your Photoshop manual, Photoshop's on-line help, or by simply checking the settings and doing some test prints to determine which configuration generates the most accurate proof.

Your CMS also comes into play when you print. You'll learn more about this in Chapter 15.

TIP

The right profile for the job. *Note that many vendors include printer profiles designed for specific types of paper. Be sure to choose the profile that matches the type of paper that you'll be using, as different types of paper can produce very different colors.*

PREPARING YOUR IMAGE

In the next chapter, you will begin to correct and adjust the tone and color of your images. However, there are a few things that you might need to do to your image before you start editing. No matter how many pixels your camera captures, it probably doesn't create files that have a resolution that is right for your printer, and your image as you shot it may not be cropped quite the right way.

In this section, you're going to learn how to get your image sized and cropped the way you like.

NEW IMAGE RESOLUTIONS

Although your camera may capture millions of pixels, it doesn't necessarily create files that have a resolution which is appropriate for your intended output. In imaging terms, resolution is simply the measure of how many pixels fit into a given space. So, if your image has a resolution of 72 *dots per inch* or *dpi* (sometimes referred to as *pixels per inch* or *ppi*) then the pixels in the image are sized and spaced so that 72 of them lined up alongside each other cover a distance of one inch.

The average computer screen has a resolution somewhere between 72 and 96dpi.so, almost all digital cameras output files at 72dpi. At 72 dots per inch, a 2048 x 1536 pixel image covers 28.4 x 21.3 inches – far larger than either the average computer screen or printer. Although you can zoom in and out of an image on your screen, for printing you'll need to make some adjustments.

RESIZING AN IMAGE

Most image editing applications let you resize an image in two ways. You can either *resample* the image, or you can choose to not resample the image.

Imagine your image as if it were projected onto a normal piece of graph paper. As it comes out of the camera, it has a resolution of 72 dots per inch and so it requires a piece of paper that is roughly 20 x 30 inches. Let's say, though, that you want to fit the image onto a piece of paper the size and resolution of your monitor, which is perhaps 14 x 10 inches at 72dpi. To do this, you'll have to squeeze your image onto a smaller piece of 72dpi graph paper. So, to fit your 20 x 30 inch image onto your new 14 x 10 inch piece of paper, you'll have to throw out every third pixel or so to reduce the number of pixels in the image so that the whole picture can fit into a smaller area. (Figure 10.11)

This is called *resampling* (or, more specifically, *downsampling*) because you are taking a new sample of pixels from your original image to create a new, smaller image. Resampling can also be used to scale images up but, just as downsampling requires your computer to throw away data, *upsampling* requires your computer to make up data.

For example, if you have an image that is 4 x 6" at 200dpi and you want to enlarge it to 8 x 10" at 200dpi, then you'll need to resample it upwards, which will force the computer to interpolate new pixels to create the bigger images. Most applications offer a variety of interpolation techniques. Photoshop, for example, offers three interpolation methods: *nearest neighbor*, *bilinear*, and *bicubic*. For 99% of your resampling needs, bicubic interpolation is the best choice. As you can see in Figure 10.12, other interpolation methods produce far inferior results.

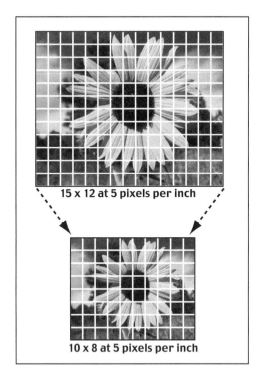

15 x 12 at 5 pixels per inch

10 x 8 at 5 pixels per inch

FIGURE **10.11** *To resize an image down to a smaller size with the same resolution, you have to throw out some pixels (or resample) to fit your image into the smaller size.*

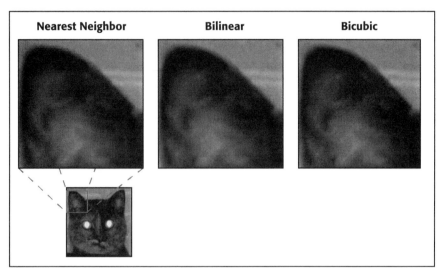

Nearest Neighbor   **Bilinear**   **Bicubic**

FIGURE **10.12** *Many image editing programs provide different methods of resampling, or scaling an image up and down. Of Photoshop's three choices, bicubic interpolation is the best option for most images.*

Now imagine the same 20 x 30" image projected onto a sheet of rubber graph paper. If you wanted to shrink this image to 14 x 10" you could simply squeeze the sheet of paper down. You would not throw out any pixels, but now your pixels would be much smaller, and more of them would fit into the same space. That is, the resolution of your image – the number of pixels per inch – would have increased. This is what happens when you resize image *without* resampling. (Figure 10.13)

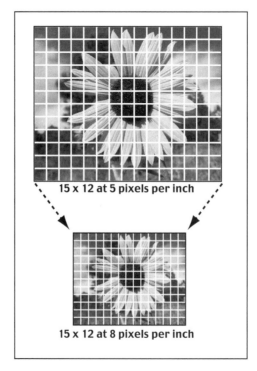

15 x 12 at 5 pixels per inch

15 x 12 at 8 pixels per inch

FIGURE *If you don't resample an image when you resize, then all of its pixels are kept, but*
10.13 *they're squeezed closer together, resulting in a smaller, higher-resolution image.*

Similarly, if you have a 4 x 6" image with a resolution of 200dpi and you scale it up to 8 x 10" without resampling, then you're effectively stretching the image. Its pixels get larger and fewer of them fit into the same space – that is, the resolution goes down – as the image gets larger. This is what happens when you resize up without resampling.

Most of the time, when you scale up, you'll want to resize without resampling to prevent the computer from making up new data. However, if your camera did not produce a big enough image to start with, you may not be able to achieve the size you want with the resolution you need unless you resample.

CROPPING AND RESIZING AN IMAGE

TUTORIAL

Because you usually can't get both you and your camera into exactly the right position to frame an image, your pictures usually need to be cropped. And, because most cameras spit out images at 72dpi, your images usually need to be resized before they are printed. In this tutorial, we'll cover both topics by cropping and resizing an image for printing.

Although Adobe Photoshop is used in this tutorial, you can use any image editor that provides a Crop tool and a resizing/resampling function.

STEP 1: OPEN THE IMAGE

ON THE CD

The image for this tutorial is included on the Complete Digital Photography CD-ROM and is located in the Tutorials>Chapter 10>cropping folder. Open the image *kittycrop.tif* (Figure 10.14). You should be able to open the document in any editor that supports TIFF files.

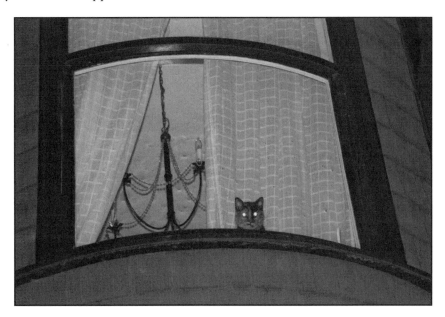

FIGURE *Although this is not the most compelling image, with a little cropping we can make it*
10.14 *more interesting, while a little resizing will make it more appropriate for printing.*

STEP 2: EVALUATE THE IMAGE

Let's take a quick look at the image so that we can formulate a plan of action. The original intent when we were shooting this image was to frame the picture so that only the window was visible. Unfortunately, our camera – a Canon EOS D30 – didn't have a long enough lens to zoom into this second-story window.

Even after zooming in all the way, the image area was too large. It will need to be cropped.

Next, open up the Image Size dialog box (Figure 10.15) by choosing Image > Image Size from the menu bar in Photoshop. This image was taken straight out of the camera and, as you can see, it has a resolution of 72dpi and an area of 30 x 20 inches. Because we plan on printing the image on a desktop color inkjet, we will want it to have a resolution of about 200dpi (Chapter 15 will cover the details of choosing a printer resolution). Obviously, some resizing will be in order.

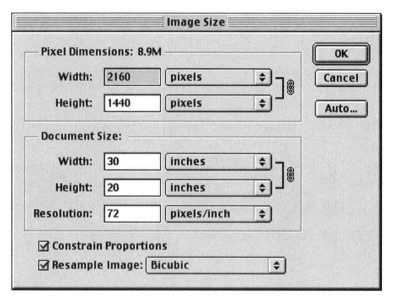

FIGURE *When the image came out of our 3 megapixel camera its three million pixels were set*
10.15 *to a resolution of 72dpi, giving the image an area of 30 x 20 inches.*

STEP 3: PERFORM THE FIRST RESIZING

Before we do anything else, let's get the image set to the proper printer resolution so we can get an idea of how big it would print, as is. If the Image Size dialog box is not still open, open it now.

Make sure that the Resample Image checkbox is *not* checked. We don't want Photoshop to add or remove any pixels, we just want it to squeeze the pixels it has closer together.

Notice that the Image Size dialog box has two areas, Pixel Dimensions and Document Size. When Resample Image is unchecked, we can no longer change the Pixel Dimensions of the image, as changing the number of pixels requires the ability to resample. We simply want to change the document's print size.

Make sure the Units box next to the Resolution field is set to pixels/inch and then change the Resolution box to 200. Photoshop will immediately calculate a new image size and display the new values in the Width and Height fields. (Figure 10.16)

FIGURE *Adjusted Image Size dialog box.*
10.16

As you can see, at 200dpi, our image is now 10.8 x 7.2 inches. Click OK to accept the changes.

STEP 4: CROP THE IMAGE

Photoshop provides a couple of ways to crop an image, but the easiest is with the Crop tool. Click on the Crop tool in Photoshop's tool palette. Use your mouse to drag a rectangle that crops out everything outside the window pane (Figure 10.17).

When you get the crop the way you like it, press the Enter key on your keyboard, or double-click inside the crop area to perform the crop.

STEP 5: RESIZE AGAIN

As you can see, cropping can make a world of difference. Already, our image is more interesting. (In case you're wondering, those strange black spots in the image are shadows from the camera's flash that are being cast by irregularities in the poured glass window pane.)

FIGURE *Photoshop's Crop tool shows you a preview of your crop while you're cropping.*
10.17

Open the Image Size dialog box again to see how big the image is now. After you have cropped, your image should be somewhere around 5.5 x 4 inches. This is a little small, so let's resize the image up a bit.

With Resample Image unchecked, enter 6 inches into the Width field. Because the Constrain Proportions box is checked, Photoshop calculates the appropriate height, which turns out to be approximately 4.3 inches.

However, notice that the resolution of our image has gone down. Because we told Photoshop not to resample the image, as we stretched the image out to make it bigger, our resolution went down. Let's boost it back up to our requisite 200dpi.

Click the Resample Image checkbox to turn it on and make certain that the box next to Resample Image is set to Bicubic. Notice that the Pixel Dimensions fields are no longer dimmed and can, therefore, be edited. This is because re-sampling enables us to change the number of pixels in the image. (Figure 10.18)

Enter 200 in the Resolution field. The Pixel Dimensions and Document Size readouts should now be larger. Click OK to accept the changes. Now the image should be ready to print. Figure 10.19 shows the final image as it will print.

Image Size

Pixel Dimensions: 2.98M (was 2.48M)

Width: 1200   pixels

Height: 865   pixels

Document Size:

Width: 6   inches

Height: 4.323   inches

Resolution: 200   pixels/inch

☑ Constrain Proportions
☑ Resample Image: Bicubic

OK
Cancel
Auto...

FIGURE 10.18   *With your final Image Size command, you'll resample the image up to a slightly larger print size.*

FIGURE 10.19   *The final image, resized for printing.*

Obviously, most images will need more adjustments than simple resizings and croppings. In the next chapter we'll begin to improve the quality of an image by performing tonal adjustments.

11

Correcting Tone and Color

IN THIS CHAPTER

- Histograms Revisited
- Color Correction with Levels
- Color Correction with Curves
- Levels and Curves and Color

With your image editing software, you can perform some amazing manipulations (some would say "deceptions") of your images. The most powerful features of your image editor, however, are not its abilities to alter the content of an image, but to alter the tone and color so that the image – no matter what its content – looks better on the printed page.

In chapter 8, you read a lot about histograms and dynamic range. In this chapter, you're finally going to get to take advantage of all that work you did when you were shooting. Using the tools in your image editor, you will be able to take advantage of all that range that you meticulously exposed for, and use it to produce images with the best possible contrast and color.

The main tools you'll use to achieve these adjustments are Levels and Curves controls. Fortunately, most quality image editing programs include these types of controls so, even if you're not using Photoshop, you should have no trouble following along with the concepts and tutorials in this chapter.

To get started, let's quickly revisit the histograms that you saw in chapter 8 and take a look at how the information in the histogram is manipulated by the Levels control.

HISTOGRAMS REVISITED

In chapter 10, you learned about histograms - graphic representations of the tonal values within an image. If you'll recall, a histogram is essentially nothing more than a bar chart of the distribution of different colors or tones in a picture. Some cameras can produce histograms of images you've shot, making it easier to determine if you have over- or underexposed an image.

Your image editor can also produce a histogram of an image, but it can also go a few steps farther. Consider the image in Figure 11.1.

Figure 11.1 is a simple gradient from black to white, created using Photoshop's Gradient tool. The histogram confirms that the image goes from completely black to completely white, with most of the tones distributed at either end of the spectrum. You can also see from the histogram that there is a lot of contrast in this image – that is, the range of black to white covers the entire spectrum of the histogram.

Now take a look at Figure 11.2.

Also created in Photoshop, this gradient was specified as being 80% black to 20% black instead of pure black to pure white. And, if you look at the histogram, you can see that the tones in the image fall more toward the middle of the graph. There are no dark or completely black tones, nor are there any really light or completely white tones. In other words, there's not a lot of contrast in this gradient.

FIGURE *This gradient from black to white generates a simple histogram.*
11.1

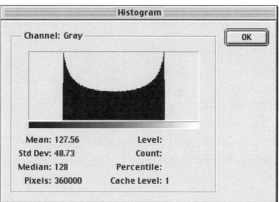

FIGURE *This grayscale ramp from 80% black to 20% black generates a similar histogram to*
11.2 *the one shown in Figure 11.1, but the tones are centered in the middle of the tonal*
spectrum.

What if we wanted to adjust this image, though, so that it *did* go from black to completely white? That is, what if we wanted to greatly improve the contrast and tone of this image?

CORRECTING AN IMAGE WITH BRIGHTNESS AND CONTRAST (OR TRYING TO, ANYWAY)

TUTORIAL

Many applications include a brightness and contrast control that is similar to the brightness and contrast controls on a television set. Photoshop is no exception; you can open the control by choosing Image>Adjust>Brightness and Contrast. In this tutorial, you will use Brightness and Contrast to try to correct the grayscale ramp in Figure 11.2 so that it looks like the grayscale ramp in Figure 11.1. As you may have already guessed from the title of this tutorial, you're not going to have much success in this endeavor.Like many less enjoyable activities, however, you'll probably learn a lot from this effort.

ON THE CD

STEP 1: OPEN THE IMAGE

Open the file grayramp.tif, located in the tutorials/Chapter 11 folder of the Complete Digital Photography CD-ROM. Use your image editor's Histogram feature to view a histogram of the image. In Photoshop, you can open the control by choosing Image>Histogram. The histogram should look something like the one in Figure 11.2.

STEP 2: ADJUST THE IMAGE'S BRIGHTNESS

Now open the Brightness and Contrast control in your image editor. In Photoshop, choose Image>Adjust>Brightness and Contrast. The control looks like the one in Figure 11.3.

Brightness and Contrast provides two sliders, one for brightness and the other for contrast. By sliding each slider in either direction, you can increase or decrease either property.

In this image, the black is not black enough, so begin your adjustments by lowering the brightness, to drop the darkest tone down to black. To get full black using Photoshop's control, slide the Brightness control until it reads approximately –75.

Unfortunately, in doing this, you also lowered the brightness of all the other tones in the image, including the whites. (Figure 11.4) Take a look at the histogram, and you'll see that the image has no more contrast than it did before. Rather, the whole tonal range has just been shifted down toward the bottom of the scale.

FIGURE   *Photoshop's Brightness and Contrast control.*
11.3

FIGURE   *After a −75 brightness adjustment the blacks in the gray ramp are darker, but*
11.4   *unfortunately so are all of the gray and white tones. All of the tones have been*
uniformly shifted down the gray spectrum.

This is one of the main problems with a brightness and contrast control: every pixel is adjusted in exactly the same way. So, if you only want to correct the shadows or highlights of an image, you're out of luck. What's more, if you enter a brightness change that is too extreme, some tonal values may get pushed completely off the scale, resulting in clipped highlights or shadows.

STEP 3: ADJUST THE CONTRAST OF THE IMAGE

So far, you've darkened the entire image to restore the blacks to true black. Now you need to try to restore the whites by increasing the contrast of the image. Move the contrast slider to around +66. You have now restored the white to full white, but the image is a far cry from the gray ramp shown in Figure 11.1. A quick check of the histogram (Figure 11.5) shows why.

FIGURE *After both brightness and contrast adjustments, the image has lost a lot of tonal*
11.5 *information and the distribution of the remaining tones has been changed.*

First, notice how there are far fewer lines in the histogram than there were before. In the process of stretching the tones out to create more contrast, Photoshop has actually had to throw out some tonal information. In other words, it has had to redistribute the tonal values in the image to make them stretch all the way down to black, and all the way up to white.

Data loss is an unfortunate side effect of any tonal adjustment and you'll read more about it later. However, a brightness and contrast control is particularly bad with data loss because it doesn't throw out data in a very intelligent manner. Rather, it simply uniformly removes data across the entire tonal range.

What's worse, though, is the distribution of the curve of the histogram. Notice that it no longer has the same shape that it had before. Colors are not predominantly distributed at the top and bottom of the curve, but have been flattened out over the entire range of the curve. The original image had much more black and much more white, while this image has a pretty even distribution of everything. This is why the ramp itself appears less contrasty.

STEP 4: GIVE UP

That's really about the best you can do with Brightness and Contrast. Yes, you could try to not stretch the blacks or whites so far, so that fewer tones would drop out, but there's simply nothing you can do to preserve the original distribution of tones. The fact is, Brightness and Contrast is simply a bad tool. Don't worry, though, there is something better.

LEVELS

In Chapter 8, you saw that different exposure settings let you capture more or less tonal information. Through the use of a histogram on your camera, you saw that it is possible to measure this tonal information, both to determine how much contrast is in an image, and where that contrast lies along the tonal spectrum.

If you followed along with the last tutorial, though, you saw that, when you are correcting and adjusting an image, preserving the distribution of those tones is fundamentally important, as is ensuring that too much data doesn't get thrown out while you are making adjustments. Typically, the problem with a brightness and contrast control is that its actions affect the entire tonal spectrum resulting in edits that are too broad in scope and thus severely alter the tonal relationships within the image.

Fortunately, if your image editor has a levels control, you have a solution to these problems. Photoshop's Levels control can be opened by choosing Image>Adjust>Levels. It produces the dialog box shown in Figure 11.6.

Input levels
(black point, gamma, white point)

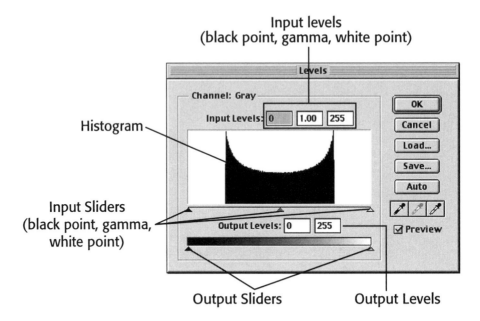

Histogram

Input Sliders
(black point, gamma,
white point)

Output Sliders   Output Levels

FIGURE *Photoshop's Levels control offers a number of features. Right now, you'll only be using*
11.6 *the histogram, input sliders, and Input Levels fields.*

First off, you can see that a Levels control is built around a histogram of your image. In this figure, the histogram is from the grayscale ramp shown in Figure 11.2. Directly beneath the histogram are three input sliders. The left-most slider shows the position of black in the histogram – that is, it points at the location on the graph that represents 100% black. The right-most slider shows the position of white, while the middle slider shows the *gamma*, the midpoint of the image. The Input Levels fields above the histogram are simply numeric readouts of the positions of the three input sliders.

The easiest way to understand what these sliders do is to use them. So let's go back to the image shown in Figure 11.2 and try again to correct it so that it looks like the one shown in Figure 11.1.

USING LEVELS INPUT SLIDERS

TUTORIAL

Once again, we're going to try to correct the grayscale ramp shown in Figure 11.2 so that it has better black and white values and improved overall contrast. This time, instead of using a brightness and contrast control, we're going to use a levels control. Although we'll be using Photoshop for this example, you can easily follow along in any image editor that provides a levels control.

STEP 1: OPEN THE IMAGE

ON THE CD

Once again, open the same gray ramp image that you used in the Brightness and Contrast tutorial (grayramp.tif, located in the tutorials folder of the Complete Digital Photography CD-ROM). Once the image is up, open your Levels control. In Photoshop, it's opened by choosing Image>Adjust>Levels.

STEP 2: ADJUST THE BLACK POINT

As you can see from the histogram in the Levels dialog box shown in Figure 11.6, the darkest tone in this image is not full black, but is closer to 80% black. Make sure the Preview checkbox in the Levels dialog box is checked. Drag the black triangle at the far left of the histogram to the right until it is directly beneath the left-most value of the histogram (Figure 11.7). The black point read-out should be around 52.

FIGURE *Setting the black point.*

11.7

Now take a look at your image. The left-most side – that is, the black side – of the grayscale ramp should be black. With our Levels adjustment, solid black is no longer at 0 on the histogram, it's now at 52 (remember, the histogram is a graph of values from 0 to 255). So, everything to the left of our new black point is considered black. Notice that our gamma point – the middle slider – has automatically moved to the right to preserve the relationship between black, midpoint, and white.

Take a look at the right side of the image. Our lightest value has not changed! Unlike a brightness and contrast adjustment, which adjusted every value in the image uniformly, our Levels adjustment has affected only the areas between the black point and the gamma point.

To understand this better, click OK to accept the changes. Now open the Levels control again to see a new histogram of the image (Figure 11.8).

FIGURE *After our black point adjustment, our histogram looks different. The darker tones*
11.8 *have been stretched all the way to black, but the overall shape of the histogram has remained the same.*

You may be a little surprised to see that the histogram looks different than it did when you closed the Levels box before. Remember, though, that even after you performed your black point adjustment, the image still had a full range of tones from 0 to 255. This histogram is a graph of those new, adjusted tones.

As you can see, some bars are missing, indicating that we've lost some data. This makes sense when you think about what your black point adjustment did. You moved the black point in to indicate the value that you wanted to be black. The Levels control placed that value at 0 and stretched all of the values between 0 and your midpoint (the gamma slider) to fill the space. Unfortunately, there wasn't enough data to fill the space (if there had been, you probably wouldn't have needed to make this adjustment in the first place) so some tonal values were left empty or dropped.

The good news is that, so far, the distribution of tones within the image is better preserved than it had been with the Brightness and Contrast control.

STEP 3: ADJUST THE WHITE POINT

Now we need to do the same thing to the white point that we did to the black point. Open your Levels control and take another look at your histogram. The white values are not really white, they're light gray.

Drag the white slider to the left so that it points to the right-most data in the image. The white point display should read approximately 190. (Figure 11.9)

FIGURE *After adjusting the white point, your Levels dialog box should look something like this.*
11.9

Now take a look the right side of your image. It should be a brighter white. The good news, though, is that your shadows are still nice and dark! As with the black point adjustment, adjusting your white point only affected the values between the white point and the midpoint.

Clicking the Auto button in the Levels dialog box does the same thing that you have just done in these two steps. It moves the black point to the left-most tonal value in the histogram, and it moves the white point to the right-most value. Why not just use Auto every time? Because some images may not need such meticulous adjustments made to their white and black points. As you'll see later, sometimes you may want to leave a little "headroom" above and below your tonal range.

The Load and Save buttons allow you to save your Levels adjustments for re-use later. For example, if you find that your camera is consistently off with its white and black points, then you can save a Levels standard adjustment that can be loaded and applied to all your images.

STEP 4: PLAY WITH THE GAMMA SLIDER

This particular image doesn't really need a gamma adjustment, but there are some interesting things to learn by moving it around and watching what happens to your image. Slide the gamma slider to the left and watch what happens to your image. As you move it, the midtones in your image become much lighter. Slide it back to the right, past its original location, and you'll see your midtones get darker. As you move the gamma slider, though, your black and white values stay locked down at black and white. Gamma lets you adjust the midtones of your image to shift contrast more toward shadows or toward highlights. With it, you can often bring more detail out of a shadowy area, but you'll never have to worry about your blacks or whites turning gray.

Type 1.0 into the gamma readout (the middle text box above the histogram) to return the gamma slider to its original location.

With the Levels dialog box still open, zoom in on your image (in Photoshop you can do this by pressing Command-+ on a Mac, or by pressing Ctrl-+ if you're using a Windows version). Now drag the gamma slider to the left. Again, you'll see your midtones lighten, but now watch what's happening in the shadow areas. If you look closely, you'll probably see some slight banding.

This banding is the result of the data that's being thrown out as the Levels control stretches the tonal values in your image. Drag the slider in the other direction and you'll begin to see banding in the highlights of your image as you darken the midtones, causing the highlights to stretch to fill in the now empty space.

Play around with these controls to get a feel for their effect, and to see how the image changes and degrades. These changes and problems are particularly easy to see in this document, since it is a simple linear gradient.

SHOULD YOU WORRY ABOUT DATA LOSS?

In the last two tutorials you've engaged in image editing operations that removed data from your image. That really sounds like something you should be worried about, doesn't it? In some cases it is.

Fortunately, the kind of data loss that you saw in the last tutorial was not readily apparent on-screen – you had to make a fairly extreme adjustment and zoom in very close to the image – and the data loss was certainly far too slight to appear in a printout. Most of the printers you'll be using can't generate a complete range of 256 shades of gray anyway, so if you've thrown out 5% of them it won't really matter.

However, if you were to make the change you just made, and then go back and make two or three more edits, things might start to get a little hairy. This is why it's so important to capture as much data as you can *when you're shooting*. If your image has more tonal range to begin with, then you won't have to make adjustments that are too extreme when you're editing, and your image editor won't have to throw out so much data as it stretches the image's tonal range. Controlling data loss is just one more reason that it's important to choose a good exposure at the time the picture is taken.

Once you've got your image in your image editor, though, you'll want to think carefully about your edits to minimize your data loss. When you are editing, try to achieve as much as possible with the fewest tonal corrections. In other words, don't do a Levels command to fix your black point, and then go back later to adjust your white point. Make your tonal corrections count by accomplishing as much as you can with each correction.

Also, keep an eye out for *posterization* in your image. Posterization occurs as the number of tones in your image is reduced. If you start to see these types of artifacts, there's a good chance that your tonal corrections have eliminated too much image data.

REAL-WORLD LEVELS ADJUSTMENTS

TUTORIAL

Hopefully, working in the controlled space of a linear gradient helped you better understand what, exactly, a Levels control does. In this tutorial, we're going to apply that knowledge to an image we looked at earlier.

STEP 1: OPEN THE IMAGE

ON THE CD

Open the street.tif image located in the Tutorials>Chapter 11>levels folder of the Complete Digital Photography CD-ROM. (Figure 11.10) As you'll recall from Chapter 8, there was a very particular vision in mind for this image, that of the dark line of the street cutting across the gray and white field of houses. To achieve that goal, this image was intentionally underexposed so as to plunge the street into deep shadow. Unfortunately, the whole image is a little dark.

FA quick look at the histogram (Figure 11.11) shows that the image has a good amount of tonal information (dynamic range) even though it doesn't go to completely black or white.

A second, slightly overexposed image was also shot, and its histogram showed that it had a wider dynamic range. However, its shadow detail was not as strong, making it more difficult to achieve our original intent. Wide dynamic range isn't everything; you've got to be sure that your exposure places the tones in your image in the correct tonal zone. For this reason, it's better to choose the underexposed image.

STEP 2: SET THE BLACK POINT

In Photoshop, choose Window>Show Info (Figure 11.12). When it is used in conjunction with Photoshop's Eyedropper tool, the Info palette can provide very handy information about the colors and tones in your image. We'll use this information to refine some of our settings. As discussed in Chapter 6, an Eyedropper tool and Info readout are essential image editing tools. If your application doesn't have these, you might consider finding another image editor.

FIGURE **11.10** *Our goal when we were exposing this image was to emphasize the shadowy line of the street. Unfortunately, the same underexposure that rendered the street in shadows resulted in the rest of the image being too dark.*

FIGURE **11.11** *The histogram shows a good amount of tonal information, but poor highlights.*

FIGURE *As you move Photoshop's Eyedropper tool over an image, it displays the values of each*
11.12 *pixel in the Info palette. Pixel values are presented using a number of different*
measures.

Open the Levels controlin your image editor. In the Levels dialog box histogram, you can see that the black levels in the image don't descend all the way to 0. That is, they don't go to completely black, but end at about 10 (or about 4% if you want to think in percentages of black).

We're going to leave the black level where it is because we intend to print this image. Unfortunately, most images tend to get darker when they go to print so it's a good idea to leave a little room for the shadows to darken up a bit. As you'll see later, the same is true for highlight areas.

STEP 3: SET THE WHITE POINT

There are a couple of simple considerations to make when you are setting the white point for this image. First, we know that we want to generally brighten the image, since it was underexposed. The question is, how far do we want to go?

Drag the white point to the left until it is at the edge of the right-most histogram data. The white point readout should read about 198.

This definitely removes the underexposed pall that covered the image before. Our shadows have brightened up a bit, so let's make a quick gamma adjustment. However, we're still not through with our white point adjustments.

STEP 4: ADJUST THE GAMMA

Although our blacks are still good and black, our white point adjustment did affect enough of the midtones that the image has lost some of the nice dark areas that it had before. Drag the gamma slider to the right until it reads about .83.

This should darken the image up rather nicely without affecting our blacks or whites.

STEP 5: READJUST THE WHITE POINT

With the gamma adjusted properly, we have a better idea of what our whites really look like. Your white point should still be set around 198. Although the image looks good with this white point, there are a few considerations to weigh.

The whitest thing in the image at this point is the white house in the lower-right center of the image. The question to ask at this point is: Just how white do we want it to be?"

Click on the Eyedropper tool from Photoshop's Toolbox and hold it over the white in the house. The K field in the Info palette shows you the actual black value of the pixels in that area. (Figure 11.13).

FIGURE **11.13** *With the Eyedropper tool and the Info palette, you can find out the exact black values of any pixels in your image. With this information, you can make more intelligent decisions about your tonal adjustments.*

The house is reading about 5% black. If you hold the eyedropper over the door, you'll see that the house is reading 0%, meaning that area will simply be paper white, with no ink.

As bright as it is, the house is a little distracting with this white point. What's more, there is little detail between the house and the door. Pull the white point to around 210. This takes the harsh whiteness out of the house as well as some of the other white details throughout the image. What's more, it restores some contrast between the house and its door. If you measure the house now, you'll see that it reads about 12% while the door is still at 0. The door will now provide a nice specular highlight in the image.

STEP 6: SAVE THE IMAGE

Click OK to accept your Levels changes and you're done for now. Go ahead and save this image to your drive. Although the tones are now properly adjusted, the image could use a little sharpening before printing. You'll learn more about sharpening in Chapter 13.

CURVES

Although the Levels control is very powerful, your image editor probably provides a tool that offers more control over your editing process: Curves. You can open this control by choosing Image>Adjust>Curves. Although you can achieve the same thing in Curves that you can in Levels, it is not a replacement. Both tools are appropriate for different tasks.

A typical Curves interface (Figure 11.14) is really just a different approach to the exact same adjustments that you were making with the Levels control.

The Curves dialog box also presents a graph of the data in your image.Instead of graphing distribution of tones, however, it shows a graph of the unaltered vs. altered pixels in your image. The horizontal gray ramp along the bottom of the Curves dialog box represents the pixels in your image before they are altered by the Curves command. The vertical gray ramp along the left side of the Curves dialog box represents the pixels in your image *after* they are altered.

When you first open the Curves control, the Curves graph shows a 45° line from black to white, indicating that the input pixels (the ones along the bottom) are identical to the output pixels (the ones along the top). If you change the shape of the line, you change the correspondence of the input pixels to the output pixels (Figure 11.15).

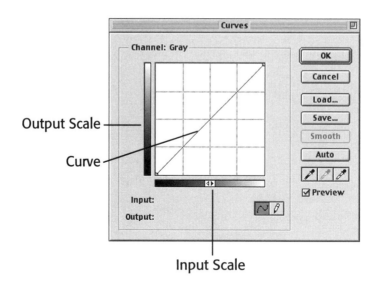

Output Scale

Curve

Input Scale

FIGURE *Photoshop's Curves dialog box is typical of most Curves tools, offering a simple graph*
11.14 *of input (before) values to output (after) values.*

When you adjusted the black point using your Levels control, you told your image editor that there was a new value that it should consider black. The image editor then stretched and squeezed the values in your image to make your desired adjustment. The curve in the Curves dialog box, which starts out as a straight line, lets you see very clearly how the tones in your image are being stretched and squeezed.

To redefine your black point using Curves, for example, you simply move the black part of the curve to a new location (Figure 11.16).

The main advantage of Curves is that, while Levels lets you edit the white, black, and midpoints of an image, Curves lets you edit as many points as you want.

A QUICK WORD ABOUT TONE

When you are correcting and adjusting color, it's important to remember that when you add more red, green, or blue to an image, you're adding more light – your color will get lighter. In other words, some colors are inherently brighter than others. A light blue, for example, in addition to being a different hue, and having a different saturation, is also lighter than a dark red or dark blue. So, if you perform adjustments that change the color in your image, you might also be changing the overall lightness or darkness of your image.

FIGURE **11.15** *In the upper diagram, before editing, each point on the input ramp corresponds to the same spot on the output ramp. After adding a point, the corresponding spot on the input graph in the lower diagram is equal to a lighter spot on the output graph. What's more, all of the surrounding points have been altered along a smooth curve.*

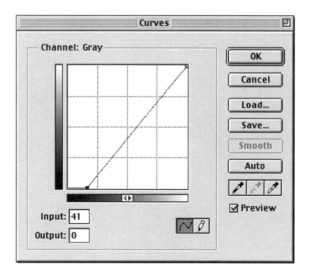

FIGURE *Black point adjustment in Curves*
11.16

CORRECTING AN IMAGE WITH CURVES

TUTORIAL

The easiest way to learn how the Curves control works is to try it out. In this tutorial, we're going to make the same sorts of adjustments we made using the Levels control, but we'll have a little more flexibility.

STEP 1: OPEN THE IMAGE

We're again going to return to an image we shot in Chapter 8. This time, it's the greenhouse image which presented an interesting exposure challenge in that we wanted to overexpose enough to render the whites as white, but not so much that shadow detail would be lost. Open the image greenhouse.tif located in the Tutorials>Chapter 11>Correcting an Image with Curves folder on the Complete Digital Photograph CD-ROM. (Figure 11.17)

ON THE CD

As you can see from the histogram, the image has a good amount of dynamic range. As you can see from both the image and the histogram, however, the picture lacks contrast and is generally too dark. We need to reset the white and black points.

STEP 2: SET THE BLACK POINT

Open up the Curves control. In Photoshop, you can open it by choosing Image>Adjust>Curves. The black point on the curve is the point at the bottom of the 45° line. This point is indicating that black on the input scale corresponds to black on the output scale. We want to change it so that dark gray – the darkest

FIGURE *The histogram confirms what your eyes will tell you: this image is too dark and needs*
11.17 *better contrast.*

tone in the image – on the input scale corresponds to black on the output scale. Because the input scale goes horizontally from black to white, we need to move the black point to the right.

Click on the black point and drag it to the right until the Input box reads about 27. Output should stay at 0. With this move, you're saying that values at 27 or lower are equivalent to 0, black. The dark areas in your image should now look black.

What do those numbers mean? *The 27 value that you just selected in the Curves dialog box is equivalent to about 10% black. Remember that, to your computer, tonal values span from 0 to 255. So, 27 is equal to 27 ÷ 255, or about 10%.*

STEP 3: SET THE WHITE POINT

The white point is the point at the other end of the curve, in the upper right-hand corner. Just as you moved the black point directly to the right, you want to move the white point directly to the left to indicate that light gray should become white.

Click on the white point and drag it to the left until the Input box reads about 218 (85%). The Output value should now read 255. In other words, the value 218 has been stretched out to 255. (Figure 11.18)

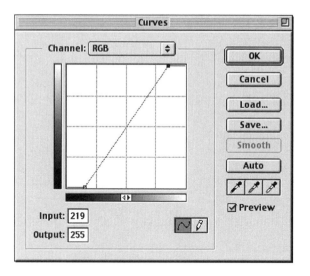

FIGURE *Black and white points are set in Curves by sliding the end points toward the center*
11.18 *of the graph.*

STEP 4: ADJUST THE GAMMA

The image is looking better, but it could use a slight gamma adjustment to help the midtones. Right now, the shadow tones in the roof and the misty tones in the sky are a little dark.

The gamma point is the point on the curve in the middle of the graph. Normally it lies at the intersection of the two middle grid lines, but because of our white and black point adjustments, the midpoint has shifted up and to the left a bit. Move your pointer over the curve until the Input display reads about 124. This is roughly the midpoint. Now click anddrag up and to the right a tiny bit to lighten the midtones. Drag the point until the readouts show roughly Input 119, Output 135.

As you move the point, notice that the curve changes shape. Remember when you tried to use the Brightness and Contrast controls and were hampered by the fact that your adjustments were applied evenly to the whole image? With Curves, as you can see, your adjustments create a smooth curve of change throughout the tonal range. What this means is that in addition to adjusting that single gamma point, you have also adjusted the nearby points to varying degrees. Levels works the same way, but with Curves you can really see how other tones are affected.

STEP 5: MAKE ANOTHER ADJUSTMENT

The image is looking much better now. However, our gamma adjustment, in addition to lightening the rooftop, lightened up the greenhouse, rendering it a little less contrasty. If we were working in Levels we'd be out of luck as Levels only lets you adjust the black point, white point, and gamma. With Curves, though, we can reshape the curve as much as we want.

With the Curves dialog box still open, move the mouse over the front part of the greenhouse in the image. The mouse pointer should turn into an eyedropper. Click the mouse and drag the eyedropper around. A circle will appear over the parts of the curve that correspond to those tones in your image. You now know which part of the curve you need to adjust.

Click the mouse in this part of the curve (around 98) to create a point, then drag down slightly, to around 101. This should darken up the greenhouse enough to restore some contrast. Unfortunately, it also has also lightened the sky enough that some of the cool striations in the mist have been washed out.

STEP 6: ADJUST THE SKY

With one or two final adjustments, we can darken the sky up. Click on the image to determine where the sky falls along the curve. You'll probably find it registers between 185 and 200. Click somewhere in this area to set a point and drag down slightly to darken the sky a bit. Hopefully, this will restore some contrast to the sky. If not, you can try to set separate points for the dark and white parts of the mist, as shown in Figure 11.19. Click the Save button to save your final Curves adjustments.

FIGURE *With our final Curves adjustment, we've selectively altered several tonal areas of the*
11.19 *image. This is far more than we could have done with Levels.*

That's it. You're done. Typically, at this point you'd want to do a test print and make refinements to your adjustments. You'll learn more about printing in Chapter 15. In the meantime, you can see color versions of these edits in Color Plate 8.

LEVELS AND CURVES AND COLOR

So far, you've seen how Levels and Curves controls can be used to adjust tone and contrast, whether in color or grayscale images.These tools, however, can also be used to adjust, correct, and change color. In previous chapters you've read about a lot of ways that color can go wrong when you are shooting with a digital camera. Levels and Curves are two tools that allow you to fix color problems that arise from bad white balance, improper exposure, or a bad camera.

To understand how Levels and Curves affect color, you have to understand how color is stored in an image. In Chapter 3, you learned that digital cameras make color by combining red, green, and blue information. These separate red, green, and blue components are referred to as *color channels* or just *channels* and most image editors allow you to perform corrections and adjustments on individual color channels.

In Photoshop, you can access the different color channels through the Channels palette (choose Window>Show Channels). The Channels palette includes separate rows for each Red, Green and Blue channel as well as for your image – the RGB channel. (Figure 11.20) By clicking on each channel you can view its contents.

So, if you click on the Red channel in the Channels palette, you'll see a grayscale image that represents all of the red in your image. Why is it grayscale? Because, if you'll recall, one *24-bit image* is made up of three separate *8-bit images*, and with 8-bit images you can have up to 256 shades of gray. So, a dark black spot in a Red channel equates to full red in your final image. Combine a dark black spot in a Red channel, with identical spots in the Green and Blue channels, and you'll have a white spot in your final image.

When you view a channel in Photoshop, you can use all of the editing, painting and manipulation features that you can use when you edit your document the normal way. This is a very handy feature for digital camera users as digital cameras often have troubles with a specific channel. For example, many cameras produce inordinate amounts of noise in the Red channel of an image. With your image editor, you can try to attack the noise in the Red channel directly by applying special noise reducing filters or blurs, or even by hand painting noisy areas.

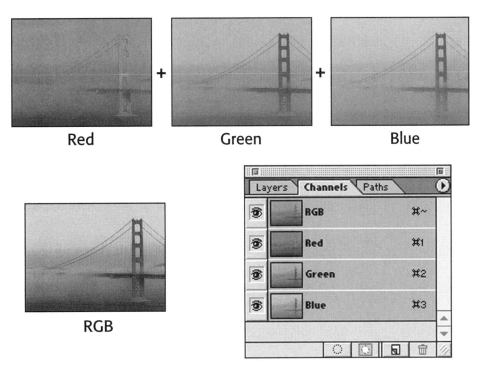

Red   Green   Blue

RGB

FIGURE **11.20** *The Channels palette lets you view and edit the individual Red, Green, and Blue channels that comprise your RGB documents.*

Similarly, many digital cameras have trouble accurately capturing blue. If you find the blues in your image are a little bit off, you can try to correct them by editing the Blue channel directly.

In the next tutorial, you'll see how you can target Levels and Curves corrections in specific color channels.

TUTORIAL

USING BOTH LEVELS AND CURVES TO CORRECT COLOR

Although Curves offers the same functionality as Levels, you'll probably find that it's often easier to use a combination of the two tools. Some adjustments are simply easier to perform in Levels than they are in Curves.

When you are using multiple adjustments, it is important to consider the data loss that we discussed earlier in this chapter. However, if your adjustments are small, and you're only performing a few of them, this type of loss shouldn't be a concern.

In this tutorial, you'll use both a Levels and a Curves adjustment to correct a bad white balance.

STEP 1: OPEN THE IMAGE

Open the image meerkat.tif located in the Tutorials>Chapter11>levels folder of the Complete Digital Photography CD-ROM. Right away, you should be able to tell what's wrong with this image: it's way too red! This picture was shot with the camera's daylight white balance setting. Unfortunately, the camera had an ultraviolet filter on the front of the lens which confused the white balance.

White balance problems can be hard to deal with, as the color troubles typically run through the entire range of colors and tones within the image. Figuring out how to correct this image is further complicated by the fact that both the dirt and the meerkat naturally have a lot of red in them.

The image also needs some simple white and black balance adjustments, both to improve the contrast and to brighten up the image. However, because the white balance problem has messed up the tone in the image, let's save the white and black point compensation until after we've corrected the red cast.

STEP 2: GET A CLOSER LOOK

We can tell just from looking at the image that there's too much red. However, it's also interesting to take a look at some histograms just to see what's going on. Choose Window>Show Channels to open the Channels palette and click on the Red channel to see just the red information in the image. Now choose Image>Histogram. Because you are only looking at the Red channel, the histogram is only a graph of the red information. Now look at the histograms for the Green and Blue channels. (Figure 11.21)

Sure enough, there's more red data than blue or green data, particularly toward the lighter end of the tonal spectrum. We need to darken the Red channel so that its tonal range slides down to be more like that of the Blue and Green channels.

In the Channels palette, click on the RGB row to return to the full RGB display of the image.

STEP 3: MAKE A CURVES ADJUSTMENT

Open your image editor's Curves control. Notice that there is a Channel box at the top of the dialog box, above the curve graph. Opening this pop-up menu lets you select the channel you want to modify with your Curves adjustment. Open the Channel pop-up menu and select the Red channel.

We want to darken the Red channel, so drag the black point in the lower-right corner of the image to the right until the Input box reads about 33. (Figure 11.22) This should immediately cut a lot of the red from the image.

FIGURE *By looking at the histograms for each color channel, we can get a better idea of what*
11.21 *corrections are needed.*

Now, however, the image is too green. Select the Green channel from the
Channel pop-up menu at the top of the Curves dialog box. Drag the white point
(the point in the upper right-hand corner) to the left until the Input box reads
about 247.

This helps the green, but now our image is too blue. Switch to the Blue
channel and drag the white point to the left until the Input box reads about 205.

Your image should be looking pretty good now. Yes, there's still a lot of red
in it, but most of this is red that was actually in the image. However, we could

FIGURE *Most of the red cast can be removed with a simple Red channel Curves adjustment.*
11.22

cut a tiny bit more red from the midtones, both to remove some more red, and to improve the contrast of the image.

Switch back to the Red channel and click on the middle of the red curve to create a control point. Click at around Input 168 and drag down to Output 147. This should remove a little more red. If you find that the image is a bit too green, then switch to the Green channel and make a similar midpoint adjustment. (Figure 11.23)

Click OK to accept your Curves adjustments. Notice that we were able to make all of these Curves changes with a single command. This is another advantage to operating on individual channels.

STEP 4: MAKE A LEVELS ADJUSTMENT

With our color correction completed, we have a better idea of just how bright or dark our image is. Now we can adjust our white and black points. This type of adjustment is always easier with Levels, so open the Levels control and drag the white and black points to their appropriate locations. If you think the image needs it, make a slight gamma tweak to improve the midtones. (Figure 11.24)

There you have it, much less red, brighter and better contrast.

FIGURE   *The final Curves adjustments for each color channel.*
11.23

FIGURE *With a simple Levels tweak to adjust our white and black points, our image is*
11.24 *finished.*

DON'T TOUCH THAT DIAL

In Chapter 13 you're going to see many more editing and correction techniques
while Chapter 14 will cover a number of techniques for creating "special" effects. Before heading into those areas, however, there are a few more tools you
need to learn. Many of these tools will not only enable you to perform more sophisticated edits, but will allow you to easily change and undo your edits as you
work.

Building Your Editing Arsenal

12

IN THIS CHAPTER

- Brushes and Stamps
- Masks
- Layers
- Other Editing Tools

As you've seen, Levels and Curves are powerful tools. They're so powerful, in fact, that you'll be reading much more about them later. There's much more to your image editor, of course, and before moving on to more sophisticated editing, there are a few more tools you need to learn about.

In this chapter, we're going to cover the basic tools and functions that you'll use in all of your everyday – and not so everyday – editing tasks. These are the features you'll turn to again and again - in many different combinations - to perform your corrections, adjustments and modifications. And, as in previous chapters, although the examples and tutorials in this chapter are built around Photoshop, any decent image editor should provide equivalent functions. Even if you're using a different set of tools, you should have no trouble translating the workflows and approaches presented in the following chapters to any image editor.

BRUSHES AND STAMPS

Many of the retouching and editing tasks that are performed in a real darkroom are dependent on brushes, masks, and paint. Your image editor is no different, except that your brushes and tools are digital. To get good results from them, you still need a good hand, a trained eye, and well-designed tools – just as in a real darkroom.

The documentation that came with your image editor should offer all the details you need on how to use the tools included with your application. In this section, therefore, you're going to learn about what each set of tools is good for and when you might turn to each type of tool. Knowing which tool is the right tool for the job will often save you a lot of time.

BRUSHES

Hopefully, your image editor includes a good assortment of paintbrushes and airbrushes. A good brush tool is one that offers an easy way of selecting different brush sizes and shapes, has anti-*aliased* (smooth) edges, pressure sensitivity when you are using a drawing tablet, and variable opacity. (Figure 12.1)

You'll use these tools for everything from painting out unwanted elements in a scene, performing certain types of color correction, creating masks, and "brushing in" different special effects.

To use a brush tool well you need – obviously – good hand-eye coordination and a feel for the brush. This will develop over time and is greatly aided by the use of a drawing tablet. In addition to providing a more intuitive interface, a drawing tablet is *much* easier on your hand than is a mouse. If you plan on doing a lot of image editing, consider investing in an inexpensive pressure-sensitive drawing tablet.

FIGURE   *Photoshop's Brush controls – scattered between the Brush palette and the toolbar – let*
12.1   *you select brush size, transfer mode, and opacity.*

You'll also want to spend some time learning the different keyboard shortcuts that augment your brush tool. Learn your brush's features including parameters such as *spacing* and *repeat rate*.

AIRBRUSHES

Airbrushes are very similar to normal paintbrushes, the main difference being that they don't lay down a full load of paint with one pass. Instead, they work like an airbrush – they spray on a fine layer of paint which can be thickened by repeated strokes. Airbrushes are ideal for very fine shading and detail work. Touching up shadows and highlights, trying to match the color and tone of an existing element in your image, or trying to soften an effect or composite are all potential uses for your application's airbrush tool. In general, the airbrush is ideal for any application where you don't want to "commit" to a particular color or tonal value, but want to build up color or tone with multiple strokes.

The airbrush requires a finer touch than the normal paintbrushes and the tool's sensitivity can usually be adjusted with simple parameter sliders. As with the paintbrush, learn to control your airbrush's and sensitivity and spend some time practicing with your airbrush to get a feel for how it applies color.

RUBBER STAMP OR CLONE

One of the most powerful – and seemingly magical – tools in your image editing toolbox is a rubber stamp tool (also known as a clone tool) which provides a brush that performs a localized copy from one part of your image to another as you brush. (Figure 12.2)

FIGURE *When you paint with a rubber stamp (clone) tool, your image editor copies paint*
12.2 *from your source area (the crosshairs) to your target area (the circle).*

You'll use your rubber stamp tool for everything from removing dust and noise to painting things out of your image to painting things in to your image. The advantage of a rubber stamp tool over normal copying and pasting is that the tool's brush-like behavior lets you achieve very realistic composites and edits.

Study your rubber stamp tool's documentation to learn the difference between absolute and relative cloning and to learn how to set the source and destination points. When you are rubber stamping an area, you want to be able to quickly select a source area and then start painting.

Your image editing application provides many more tools and functions, but brushes and stamps are the ones that you'll be using the most. These are also tools that will not be heavily discussed or documented in the rest of this book. For the rest of these tutorials, it is assumed that you know how to follow an instruction like "Rubber stamp out the telephone wires." If you don't know how to use these tools, consult your manual.

MASKS

People are often confused by the mask tools provided by their image editor. Really, though, there's nothing to be afraid of. A mask is just like a stencil that you would use in a real darkroom or painting studio. The only difference is that digital masks are much, much better.

As in the real world, you'll use digital masks for controlling the extent and range of your edits and adjustments. If you only want to color correct the background of an image, for example, you might build a mask over the foreground elements. You could also use that foreground mask to paste a new background behind your foreground elements.

Many photographers feel that masking is not such an essential tool because they're not interested in creating weird special effects or wacky composites. Masking, however, can be an essential color correction tool, allowing you to create adjustments and corrections that would otherwise be impossible.

Like many editing tasks, knowing how and when to use a mask is a skill. However, learning the basics of your mask tools is pretty simple once you understand a few simple concepts.

MASK TOOLS

Most image editing applications offer many different tools for creating a mask and you'll often find yourself using these tools in combination. Some tools, for example, are more appropriate for masking complex subjects like hair or fine detail. Other tools are more appropriate for masking geometric shapes or large areas of color.

Selection Tools

The simplest mask tools are the selection tools – the lasso, rectangular and circular marquees – that let you create simple selections by outlining areas of your image. You may not think of these as mask tools, but the selections they produce work just like a mask. Create a rectangular selection around an object, for example, and your editing tools will only work inside that selection. Everything outside of the selection is masked out.

What makes these effective mask tools is that most applications let you add and subtract from a selection. Photoshop, for example, lets you add to a selection simply by holding down the Shift key while you select more image. This allows you to use different tools for different parts of your image. For example, you can use Photoshop's Circle tool to select a curvy section of an object, then hold down the Shift key and use the Lasso tool to outline the rest of the object. (Figure 12.3)

Similarly, Photoshop lets you use the Command key (Control if you're using Windows) to subtract from a selection. The ability to keep adding to a selection with different tools is essential for building complex masks.

In the same family as the selection tools are magic wand tools that automatically hunt down similar colors to create selections automatically. As with other

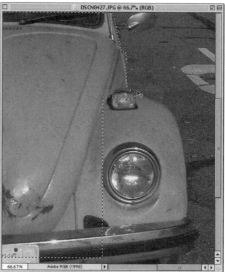

FIGURE *By holding down the Shift key, you can add to a selection, so you can use different*
12.3 *selection tools for selecting different types of shapes.*

selection tools, in Photoshop you can combine Magic Wand selections with other selection tools by simply holding down the Shift or Command (Control) keys.

Mask Painting

Photoshop's QuickMask mode lets you create a mask by painting. To use Quick-Mask, you simply click on the QuickMask icon at the bottom of the main tool palette. In QuickMask mode, any areas that you paint black will be selected when you exit QuickMask mode, and any areas that you paint white will be un-selected. (Figure 12.4)

You can switch in and out of QuickMask mode as much as you like, meaning you can combine its mask selection tools with your image editor's other mask tools.

Color-Based Selection Tools

Many applications provide special tools for automatically selecting certain colors. Photoshop, for example, includes a Color Range command that can automatically select all occurrences of a particular color in an image. (Figure 12.5)

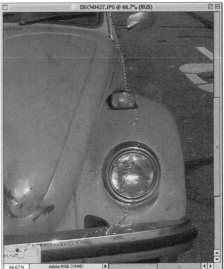

FIGURE *In QuickMask mode, you can select areas simply by painting.*
12.4

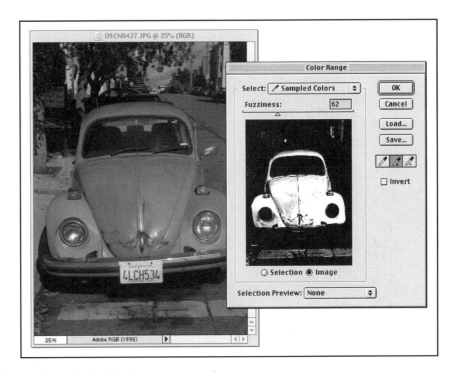

FIGURE *Photoshop's Color Range command.*
12.5

Color Range will almost always select more pixels than you want, but the extra pixels can usually be easily removed with another selection tool.

Special Mask Tools

Some applications include special dedicated tools, such as Photoshop's Extract tool, which can perform complex extractions of difficult subjects like hair, or transparent surfaces (Figure 12.6). Extract doesn't create a mask, but it does let you isolate an image for compositing with another image.

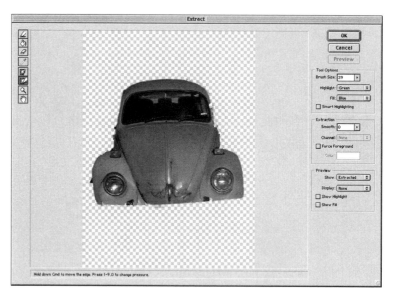

FIGURE **12.6** *Photoshop's Extract tool provides sophisticated edge detection routines for extracting part of an image. The results can then be composited with other images.*

There are also several third-party masking plug-ins that can be added to any image editor that supports Photoshop plug-ins. Programs like Corel's KnockOut or Extensis' Mask Pro provide a simple way of creating complex masks. If you find yourself consistently trying to mask difficult subjects, it may be worth your while to look into one of these options.

SAVING MASKS

Once you've used the various selection tools at your disposal to create a selection, you can save that selection as a mask for later use. In Photoshop, selections can be saved by choosing Select>Save Selection. At any time, you can use the Select>Load Selection command to restore your selection.

In Chapter 11 you saw how separate red, green, and blue channels are used to create a full-color image. You also saw that you can access and manipulate individual color channels. Selections, or masks, are stored in a similar fashion. When you save a selection, your image editor creates a new channel in your document – called an *alpha channel* – and stores an image of your selection. (Figure 12.7)

 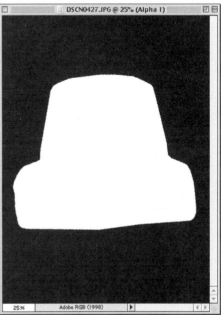

FIGURE **12.7** *When you save a selection, Photoshop stores a grayscale, 8-bit alpha channel. Black areas are masked, white areas are selected.*

As you can see, any selection can be represented by a grayscale image – areas within the selection are stored as white pixels, areas outside are stored as black. In Photoshop, you can create as many different selections as you want, and each will be stored in its own alpha channel. From the Channels palette which you access by choosing Window>Show Channels, you can access each of these masks by simply clicking on its name. (Figure 12.8)

SORT OF MASKED

So far, we've discussed masks as if they were simple stencils. Digital masks, however, are much more powerful than real-world masks because, in addition to masking an area, they can *partially* mask an area. Just as black pixels in a mask are completely opaque, gray pixels are only *partially* opaque, meaning you can use masks to apply effects and adjustments that vary across an image.

The easiest way to understand masks is to use them. In the following tutorial, you'll use a series of complex masks to alter an image.

FIGURE *You can see and access the alpha channel from Photoshop's Channels palette.*
12.8

CREATING COMPLEX MASKS

TUTORIAL

Masks are used for everything from constraining painting and filter effects, to controlling how different images composite together. In this tutorial, you'll see that you can also use masks to create complex color corrections and adjustments.

STEP 1: OPEN THE IMAGE

ON THE CD

Open the image tree.tif, which is located in the Tutorials>Chapter 12>Creating Complex Masks folder on the Complete Digital Photography CD-ROM. (Figure 12.9) Your goal in this tutorial is to try to emphasize the foreground elements – the tree and the bent wrought-iron cage – by softening the background. To edit the background without disturbing the foreground, therefore, you need to mask out the tree.

STEP 2: CREATE A MASK

ON THE CD

Using your choice of masking techniques, create a mask for the tree as well as the entire wrought-iron cage that surrounds the tree. Save the mask using Select>Save Selection. To save time, the file *tree with mask.psd* has been included in the Tutorials>Chapter 12>Creating Complex Masks folder. This image includes a pre-built mask that you can use for the rest of this tutorial.

FIGURE   *Because we want to edit the background of this image without disturbing the tree, we*
12.9   *need to create a tree mask.*

(Figure 12.10) (In case you're wondering, this mask was created by simply painting over the tree and fence using Photoshop's QuickMask tool.)

STEP 3: LOAD THE MASK

Before you can use a mask, you have to load it. Open Photoshop's Channels palette. You should see separate channels for red, green, blue, and your mask (called Alpha 1). At the bottom of the Channels palette are a series of buttons. The far left button is the Load Channel as Selection button. Drag the Alpha 1 channel on top of this button and Photoshop will load your selection.

Sometimes, after loading a mask, it can be difficult to tell what is selected and what isn't selected. For example, with the tree mask loaded, it's difficult to tell whether the foreground or background is masked. To find out, click on the paintbrush tool and brush it around on the image. You should see that the paint is only going into the background. The tree is completely masked. Click Undo to remove your brush strokes. (If Undo doesn't undo all the strokes, use the History palette to remove the brush strokes.)

FIGURE *This mask was built using the QuickMask tool and is included in the*
12.10 *Tutorials>Chapter 12>Creating Complex Masks folder.*

ON THE CD

STEP 4 FADE THE BACKGROUND

With your mask loaded, you can now start manipulating the background. If the
goal is to emphasize the foreground, then you should try lightening the background using a simple Levels command.

Choose Image>Adjust>Levels to open the Levels control. In previous tutorials,
you've exclusively used the Input controls and have learned how they allow you
to change the distribution of tones within your image. So far, though, your Levels adjustments have redistributed the tones in your image so that they fit
between full black and full white.

What if your printer can't print full black, though? Many offset printers can't
hold more than 85% black – any more ink and they jam up. So, Levels includes
a pair of output sliders which allow you to adjust the limits of the tonal range in
your image. The distribution of tones specified by the input levels remains the
same.

Let's eliminate many of the darker tones without changing the tonal relationships in our image. Slide the left-most output slider to roughly the midpoint
(around 126) and hit OK. This should create a faded background. (Figure 12.11)

FIGURE *We've faded everything but the tree. Unfortunately, we've faded more than just what*
12.11 *was behind the tree in the scene. The sidewalk in front of the tree has faded as well.*

STEP 5: ASSESS THE CHANGE

Now it's time to assess if this was the right edit. With all those selection lines marching around, it can be difficult to see the image clearly. Choose Select>Hide Selection to hide the selection lines. The selection is still active, you just can't see it. You can always choose Select>Show Selection if you need to double-check that the selection is still active.

Sure enough, as we planned, the adjustment caused the background to recede. Unfortunately, because we faded everything but the tree, our edit has also caused elements in front of the tree to fade. This is not really the desired effect. Click Undo to remove the Levels adjustment.

What we want is a Levels adjustment that won't affect the entire image uniformly, but that will appear to be stronger in "deeper" parts of the image. It's time to create another mask.

STEP 6: CREATE A GRADATED MASK

Although you can use any number of selection tools to create masks, you can also paint them by hand, directly into an alpha channel. In the Channels palette, click on the Create New Channels button (the second one from the right). A new channel will be created, selected, and filled with black.

Remember that black areas in a mask are completely opaque, while white areas are completely transparent, and gray areas are somewhere in between. We want a mask that fades from fully opaque to fully transparent.

First, choose Select>Deselect to deselect the previous selection.

Set Photoshop's foreground and background colors to black and white by clicking on the black/white swatch next to Photoshop's color swatches in the main tool palette.

Now select the Gradient tool and drag from the bottom of the image to the top. This will create a complete black to white gradient. Choose Select>Save Selection to save this as a new alpha channel (Alpha 2).

STEP 7: TRY THE NEW MASK

Click on the RGB channel in the Channels palette to switch back to full-color view. Now load the new channel by dragging the Alpha 2 channel to the Load Channel as Selection button. A selection will appear that covers about half the image. Don't worry, Photoshop has loaded the complete mask, it's only choosing to outline areas that are more than 50% masked. Choose Select>Hide Selection to hide the selection and then apply the same Levels adjustment we made in Step 4. (Figure 12.12)

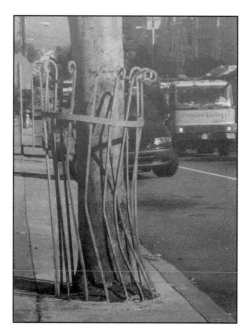

FIGURE *We get a better fade with a graduated mask, but now our tree is fading along with*
12.12 *the background.*

This is the effect that we wanted – a lightening of the image that gets stronger from bottom to top. Unfortunately, the effect is no longer confined to just the background. Click Undo to remove the Levels adjustment and let's make a new mask.

STEP 8: CREATE YET ANOTHER MASK

Go back to the Channels palette and delete the Alpha 2 channel by dragging it to the tiny trash can at the bottom of the palette. Now let's make a new channel.

We want to create a gradient that fills all of the document *except* where the tree is. Unfortunately, the Gradient tool will fill the whole channel unless we *use the tree mask* we've already created. Load the first mask (the tree) by dragging the Alpha 1 channel to the Load Channel as Selection button. You should see the outline of the tree mask.

Now click on the Gradient tool and make a bottom to top, black to white gradient. (Figure 12.13)

FIGURE   *This mask provides the gradient we need to create our fade, but also masks out our*
12.13   *tree.*

STEP 9: FADE THE BACKGROUND

Now load your new mask and apply your Levels adjustment. You should see a Levels change that affects only the background, but varies from the bottom to the top of the image!

With this mask, you can now independently edit the foreground and background of your image. Try experimenting with different color corrections and filters. The image in Figure 12.14 has had a more severe Levels adjustment applied to it, as well as some subtle desaturations of the foreground and background.

FIGURE   *Our final tree image includes some extra desaturations of the foreground and*
12.14 *background.*

LAYERS

Layers are pretty easy to understand. If your image editor provides a layer facility, then you'll be able to stack images – and parts of images – on top of each other to create effects. Layers allow for much more than simple collages and composites. A robust layer facility provides you with the ability to more easily make the types of corrections you saw in the last tutorial, and – if you structure your layers properly – allows you to go back and adjust and tweak your edits later.

SOME LAYER BASICS

If your image editor provides layer controls, then you'll need to spend some time learning how they work. Below are some of the basics of using the Layers control in Photoshop. (Note that Layers weren't added to Photoshop until version 3. If you're using an earlier version, then it's time to upgrade!)

Creating, deleting, and moving layers

Fortunately, layer management is very simple in Photoshop; you simply use the Layers palette. On the bottom of the palette are all of the controls you need to create and delete layers. (Figure 12.15) Right now, you only need to worry about the Create layer and Delete layer buttons located on the right side of the palette.

Create layer   Delete layer

FIGURE   *Photoshop's Layers palette includes simple button controls for creating and deleting*
12.15 *layers.*

When you create a new layer, it will appear stacked in the palette. Because new layers are empty, your image won't look any different. All edits – whether painting, filters, or image adjustments – happen in the currently selected layer. Note that you can turn off the visibility of a layer by simply clicking its Eyeball icon.

Layers that are higher in the Layers palette obscure any lower layers and you can re-arrange layers by dragging them up or down the stacking order. Note that you cannot change the order of the lowest layer - the Background - unless you double-click on it to turn it into a normal, floating layer.

New layers are completely transparent while the Background layer is completely opaque. (Obviously, as you paint into a layer, Photoshop changes the opacity of that part of the layer so that your paint is visible.)

Opacity and Transfer Modes

You can change the opacity of the currently selected layer by simply sliding the Opacity control back and forth.

You can also change how the currently selected layer interacts with layers that are lower in the stacking order by selecting a *blending* (or *transfer*) mode from the pop-up menu in the Layers palette. Normally, the pixels in a layer simply overwrite any pixels that are lower down the stack. By changing the blending mode you can force layers to blend with lower layers. Each pixel in a layer is mathematically combined with the pixels that are lower in the stack to create new pixels. (Figure 12.16)

As you work more with blending modes, you'll get a better idea of what they do. At first, don't worry about being able to predict their results. Just start playing around with them until you find the effect you like. To lessen the effect of a mode, lower that layer's opacity.

Watch that RAM! As you add layers to your image, its RAM requirements will quickly skyrocket. Nothing affects Photoshop performance as much as RAM, so if you find your computer getting sluggish, it may be that Photoshop is running out of memory. The easiest way to shrink the RAM requirements of your document is to eliminate extra layers. If you think you've finished editing an individual layer, consider merging it with other layers using Photoshop's Merge Linked or Merge Visible commands, located in the Layers menu.

ADJUSTMENT LAYERS

One of Photoshop's most powerful editing features are its adjustment layers which let you apply Levels, Curves, and many other image correction functions *as a layer*. For example, when you add a Curves adjustment layer to your document, Photoshop presents you with a normal Curves dialog box. You can adjust your image as desired but, when you click OK, instead of applying the Curves adjustment to the image, it stores the adjustment in a new adjustment layer which appears in your Layers palette.

FIGURE   *A few of Photoshop's blending modes.*
12.16

An adjustment layer affects all of the layers laying beneath it. The best thing, though, is that you can go back at any time *and change the settings* of the adjustment layer. So, if you decide later that you need a different Curves adjustment, you can simply double-click on your Curves adjustment layer and change its Curves parameters. In addition to providing flexible editing, Adjustment

Curves Adjustment Layer

FIGURE *The upper layer in this image is a Curves adjustment layer, which applies a Curves*
12.17 *function to the lower layer.*

Layers keep you from re-applying effects that result in data loss to your image. You'll be using adjustment layers extensively throughout the rest of this book.

LAYER MASKS

In the last tutorial, you saw how alpha channels can be used to create masks. As powerful as alpha channels are, there is an easier way to perform many types of masking operations.

Photoshop allows you to attach a layer mask to any layer to create complex mask effects. From the Layers palette pop-up menu (Figure 12.18) you can choose to attach a layer mask to a layer.

In the Layers palette, for each layer you can click on the document thumbnail or on the layer mask thumbnail to switch between editing the layer or editing its thumbnail. As you paint or edit a layer mask, you create masking information that works exactly like the alpha channel masks you saw earlier. Paint black into a layer mask and the pixels in that part of the layer will be masked and, thus, invisible.

The complex masking effects that you created in the last tutorial could have also been created using layer masks and adjustment layers. If you were to go back and create the same image using Layers tools, your Layers palette would look like Figure 12.19.

You'll get a lot of first-hand layer masking experience in the next chapter.

Layer Content   **Layer Mask**

FIGURE **12.18** *You can paint masking information directly into a layer's layer mask by clicking on the layer mask thumbnail in the Layers palette.*

FIGURE **12.19** *If you had used adjustment layers in the previous Tree tutorial, your Layers palette might have looked something like this.*

OTHER EDITING TOOLS

Levels and Curves are the most powerful tone and color correction tools that you'll find. In addition to their editing controls, these tools provide such clear visual feedback that they help you ensure that your edits are not wrecking your image by blowing out your highlights, darkening your shadows, or tossing out too much image data.

Although powerful, these tools are not always the easiest choice for certain types of corrections. For example, perhaps one part of your image needs to be more purple, or another part has a yellow-green cast. Although Levels and Curves provide controls for editing individual color channels, targeting a specific range of yellow can be difficult when you have to think in terms of red, green, and blue.

Fortunately, most image editors provide other tone and color correction tools. Here is a brief rundown of other tonal correction tools provided by Photoshop. In addition to their regular use, each of these functions can be applied through an adjustment layer.

HUE/SATURATION

Raising or lowering saturation in an image is very difficult to do with Levels or Curves, but with the Hue/Saturation control, it's a snap. Just slide the Saturation slider left or right to raise or lower the saturation of your image. Like Levels and Curves, Hue/Saturation can operate on individual color channels, or you can target particular color areas.

If your camera tends to shoot some colors too "hot" – that is, too saturated - or, if it tends to produce images that are undersaturated, you can easily change the saturation with the Hue/Saturation slider. See Color Plate 9 for examples.

SELECTIVE COLOR

Photoshop's Selective Color control lets you adjust the cyan, magenta, yellow, and black levels of a specific tonal range. The Selective Color dialog box provides a choice of nine different tonal ranges (red, yellows, greens, cyans, blues, magentas, whites, neutrals, and blacks) which can be adjusted using simple sliders. (Figure 12.20)

Because the colors ranges it targets are so broad, Selective Color is not a very subtle tool – you'll almost always need to run this operation through a mask to limit its effects.

FIGURE   *Photoshop's Selective Color lets you adjust the individual channels of selected color*
12.20   *ranges within your document.*

THE RIGHT TOOL FOR THE JOB

These are just a smattering of the tools that you'll find in a high-end image editor like Photoshop. However, with this basic arsenal, you can correct and adjust most of the problems that you'll find in your digital images. In the next chapter, you'll begin to use these tools in combination to tackle the most common digital imaging problems.

13 Essential Imaging Tactics

Now that you have a handle on how to use some of the tools and functions of your image editor, it's time to put those tools to work. The creative possibilities inherent in a program as powerful as Photoshop – or any other state-of-the-art image editor – are endless. However, as a digital photographer, there are certain issues and problems that you will run into fairly consistently. In this chapter, you'll learn how to handle these problems and how to perform the type of corrections that you'll most certainly need to make during your digital photographic career.

Every editing task is different, of course, and there's no way to predict all of the issues and troubles you might run into. Consequently, the tutorials in this chapter are intended to provide you with a set of fundamental skills that you can repurpose and recombine to solve other problems you may run into. Hopefully, in working through this chapter, you'll get an idea for how to approach a problem.

WORKFLOW

For maximum flexibility, and to preserve image quality, you should perform your edits in a particular order. For example, you almost always want to perform any sharpening operations *after* you've performed all of your other corrections and edits. Because sharpening can be a very destructive operation, you only want to do it once, after you're sure nothing else in your image will change.

Typically, your image editing workflow will progress something like this:

- **Initial clean-up.** You'll attempt to remove any excess noise as well as remove any spots or dirt from the image. By removing these elements first, you won't exaggerate them with later operations. This is also the stage where you'll correct any *barrel* or *pincushion* distortion caused by your camera's lens. You might also crop your image at this stage, and possibly perform an initial resizing to get a better idea of what your final image will look like.
- **Color and tone adjustment.** Once your image contains only the pixels you're interested in, you can begin to perform your first color and tone adjustments. These operations are typically where you'll determine the tonal range of the image. After a few adjustments, you may find that your shadows have brightened enough to reveal some noise that was not removed earlier. Consequently, color and tone adjustment will sometimes be followed by a little more clean-up.

- **Saturation adjustment.** Because it's hard to adjust saturation with a Levels or Curves adjustment (the tools you'll usually use in your color and tone adjustments), you'll often need to tweak the saturation of your image. As you boost saturation, you may find that your colors need further refinement.

- **Editing**. With all of your colors adjusted, you can begin to perform any additional editing such as compositing, collage work, special effects, or other manipulations. Often, to make these edits blend seamlessly together, you'll need to perform additional color and saturation adjustments.

- **Scaling.** If you didn't crop and scale your image during the initial clean-up, then you can perform those operations after you've finished all of your adjustments and edits. For the web, you'll probably need to scale your image down, while printing may require sizing up.

- **Sharpening.** Finally after everything's finished and your image is the correct size, it's time to apply any requisite sharpening. If you scaled your image down in the previous step, then that process probably served to sharpen the image. If you scaled your image up, it could very well need additional sharpening.

*A **note on saving.*** *Unless you're shooting in a special Raw or TIFF mode, the images that come out of your camera are compressed using JPEG, a compression scheme that degrades your image. So, once you start editing, you don't want to resave your image as a JPEG file as you'll introduce more degradation. Lock your original JPEG file (think of it as a negative) and, once you start editing, resave your image in Photoshop's native format or in another lossless format such as TIFF. The only time you need to resave your image as a JPEG file is if you're going to post it on the web or send it via e-mail.*

Obviously, this process is not carved in stone and, as described above, you'll often move back and forth between different steps. If you follow the procedures on the following pages, you'll learn how to apply your edits and adjustments so that they remain editable and can be undone at any time, allowing you to easily move back and forth from step to step, as well as making it simple to go back and make changes to your document later.

INITIAL CLEAN-UP

No matter how careful you were when you were shooting, your document will probably have some troublesome artifacts that will need to be removed before you begin more complex edits. These artifacts can include anything from noise to lens flares and dirt.

REMOVING NOISE

Noise is the most troublesome artifact to get rid of and, unfortunately, the most prevalent. Although modern digital cameras are getting much better in their ability to generate images with low noise, most cameras will still generate some noise, particularly in shadow areas and bright skies, and especially when you shoot at higher ISOs.

The problem with trying to remove noise from an image is that it's often very difficult to separate noise from fine detail. So, in removing noise, you'll often end up softening very finely detailed areas. And, depending on the noise reduction method you use, removing noise can also lower the contrast or saturation of your image.

Nevertheless, a slightly softer or less-saturated image is usually preferable to an image covered with distracting, ugly noise. In this section you'll learn several methods of removing noise. Why so many? Because some methods are more effective against particular types of noise than others. In addition, some methods will be more appropriate to your particular image.

After some experimentation, you'll probably discover that some methods work better than others to eliminate the particular type of noise your camera creates, so don't worry about mastering all of these techniques. Give them all a try and then focus on the ones that work best for you.

Identifying Noise

Before you can remove noise you have to find it. In some images – particularly those shot at high ISOs – the noise will be strong enough that you won't have any trouble identifying it. In other images, noise might be less pronounced. Determining which parts of the image have noise problems will make it easier to develop a plan of attack.

Daylight skies are particularly susceptible to noise, as are any flat, colored objects. Shadow areas, even the lighter shadows under a person's chin, are also havens for noise. When you are identifying noise, pay attention to what the noise looks like. Is it a simple grainy noise, or is it loaded with specks of color?

Some of the individual color channels in your image can have more noise than other channels. (Figure 13.1) The Blue and Red channels are very susceptible to noise – daylight sky noise will usually live exclusively in the Red channel, for example – while the Green channel is usually very clear. Examine your image's color channels individually by clicking on their names in Photoshop's Channels palette. You can also look at individual color channels by pressing Command-1 for Red, Command-2 for Green, and Command-3 for Blue (substitute Control for Command if you're using Windows). To return to RGB view, press Command-~. Try to get in the habit of looking at the individual color channels and making a note of which channel is noisiest.

Red Channel   Green Channel   Blue Channel

FIGURE *Different color channels will often have different amounts of noise. Consequently,*
13.1 *when you remove noise from an image, it's often most effective to attack an individual color channel.*

As mentioned earlier, because your image has not yet had any tonal or color correction, there may be parts of it that are so dark that you can't see if they're noisy. You can always apply a Levels adjustment layer to brighten up your image while you remove noise, and then discard the adjustment later. However, don't brighten the image too much. You don't want to worry about removing noise that will be too dark to see in the final image.

Another approach is to remove the noise you can see now, and then go back for another noise removal pass *after* you've made your tonal corrections.

Also, don't obsess too much about fine-grained noise. Depending on your printer, you may not be able to see the noise anyway. For example, if your inkjet printer produces fairly large, visible ink dots, then these dots will obscure any noise in your image.

Once you know where the noise is, you can begin to use any combination of the following procedures to remove it.

Noise reduction with Dust and Scratches, Median, or Despeckle

Photoshop includes a Dust and Scratches filter that averages adjacent pixels that have a sudden contrast change. You can set the pixel size of the noise you are targeting and the threshold of contrast that you want the filter to search for.

The Median filter offers a function similar to Dust and Scratches, but without control over the threshold. Despeckle is another similar filter, but lacks any control over pixel size and threshold.

The problem with all three filters is that they tend to soften your images. Although you can sharpen your images to restore some of the detail, this introduces other problems, as we'll see later. These filters are best used with a mask to constrain their effects.

TUTORIAL

REDUCING NOISE WITH MEDIAN

Fortunately, noise in a picture is obscured by image detail. This is the case in the image rooftop.tif, located in the Tutorials>Chapter 13>noise folder of the Complete Digital Photography CD-ROM. Unfortunately, there is also a big expanse of sky in the image that shows clearly visible noise. In this tutorial, you'll see how to quickly eliminate the noise from the sky.

ON THE CD

STEP 1: EXAMINE THE IMAGE

With the image open, take a look at the sky. The noise isn't bad, but it is visible. If you look at the building itself, you'll see that any noise there is obscured by detail and texture on the building. What little remains most likely won't be visible when it is printed, so you really only need to worry about cleaning up that sky.

STEP 2: BUILD A MASK

We're going to use a Median filter to eliminate the noise, but we want to constrain the filter to only the sky, so we need to build a mask. Fortunately, this one's pretty simple, just click on the Magic Wand tool in the main tools palette, and set the Tolerance setting in the Toolbar to around 32Then click on the sky. (Figure 13.2) Choose Select>Feather and *feather* the selection by 2 or 3 pixels.

TIP

Make selections in channels. *Sometimes the Magic Wand tool won't work as well as it does here. For those instances, try using the Magic Wand on an individual color channel. Look through the channels and try to find one that isolates the area you want to select. Click on it with the Magic Wand and then return to your RGB view.*

FIGURE *Fortunately, creating a mask for this image involves nothing more than a quick click*
13.2 *of the Magic Wand tool.*

STEP 3: REMOVE THE NOISE

Now apply a Median filter (Filter>Noise>Median) with a radius of 3 pixels. This should eliminate all of the noise in the sky. Click OK, deselect, and you're done.

At the end of this section, you'll see a simple way to selectively apply an editable noise reduction that can be altered later.

Noise Reduction Through Selective Blurring

Similar to the previous technique, you can simply select noisy areas of your image and apply a gentle Gaussian Blur or Smart Blur filter. These processes soften the contrast between pixels to create a smooth blur. Because the Gaussian blur filter provides a very fine control over the blur's pixel size, you can usually minimize noise without compromising texture. (Figure 13.3) You will, however, soften or destroy any fine detail in your image, so you'll want to make your selections carefully.

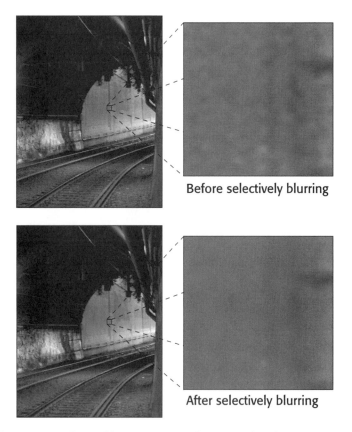

Before selectively blurring

After selectively blurring

FIGURE *With some very selective blurring, we can eliminate a lot of noise without softening*
13.3 *fine detail.*

If you have bright-colored, noisy specks in your image – bright red dots of
noise, for example – a soft blur on the image's Green channel will often eliminate these.

Smart blur provides a finer degree of control than does Gaussian blur and is
often more intelligent about preserving edge detail. An aggressive Smart blur –
with a Radius of 1.7-2.2 and a Threshold of 7.5-8, High Quality and Normal
Mode – applied directly to the Blue channel is often a good solution to Blue
channel noise.

Preserving Editability When you Remove Noise

Unfortunately, Photoshop does not offer blurs, despeckle, Dust and Scratches or
other filters as adjustment layers. Instead, these filters are *destructive effects*. That
is, they actually modify the pixels in your image, so there's no easy way to go
back and change their settings or undo their effects if you change your mind
about them later.

However, by creating duplicate layers of your source image, you can often isolate these destructive effects so that you can remove or replace them later. For example, let's say you want to use one of the noise reduction techniques described above to remove some noise from your image. Rather than simply blurring your image, try this:

- Create a new, duplicate layer of your image by dragging your background layer to the New Layer button in the Layers palette (this is assuming that your image is currently a single-layer image).
- Apply a noise-reducing blur or filter to the upper layer by selecting the appropriate filter from the Filter menu. Your entire image will now look blurry, and will probably exhibit some fine detail loss.
- Now add a layer mask to your upper, blurred layer. Set the mask to be empty by choosing Layer>Add Layer>Hide All to create the mask. This will create a layer mask that hides your entire blurred layer.
- With your upper layer active, click on a white paintbrush and begin painting into the layer mask of the upper layer. This will selectively reveal the blurred image and it will appear as if you are painting in the blurred effect.

With this technique, you can go in and repaint the mask any time you want to change the blurred area. If you want to change your blur settings, just delete the layer, duplicate your base layer again, re-blur it, and paint a new mask.

You can use this approach for any type of edit or effect. When it is combined with adjustment layers, this approach allows you to keep nearly every editing action discrete and editable. It will, however, result in huge files and require a good amount of memory. However, as you feel that certain effects are finished, you can merge their layers together to reduce the size of your file.

Noise Reduction in Lab Mode

As discussed in Chapter 3, Lab mode stores your image as three channels, a Luminance channel and two color channels. Just as you can attack the separate Red, Green, and Blue channels of an RGB image, Lab mode lets you selectively de-noise the color information in your image independent of the luminance. Converting to Lab mode, and back again, does result in a tiny bit of quality loss, but this loss will not be perceptible until you change modes a dozen times or so.

To reduce noise in Lab mode:

- First, convert your image to Lab by choosing Image>Mode>Lab color.
- In the Channels palette, switch to the A & B channel.
- Use a Smart or Gaussian blur (or any of the averaging filters discussed above) to attack the noise. (Figure 13.4)

FIGURE *If you convert your image to Lab mode, you can attack the color information in your*
13.4 *image independently of the lightness or detail of your image.*

- Now switch back to RGB.

Using Photoshop's History palette, you can easily jump back to the Blur operation to try different settings. This method of noise reduction often tends to reduce saturation in your image. Once you get back into RGB mode, you can try to use Hue/Saturation to restore lost saturation.

Noise Reduction with a Luminance Copy

In the previous method, noise was eliminated by blurring the color channels independently of the Luminance information. There's another way of doing the same thing without having to convert your image to Lab mode.

- Using Photoshop's Layers palette, duplicate your image by dragging it to the New Layer button at the bottom of the palette. You'll now have two identical copies stacked on top of each other. (Figure 13.5)

Be sure to set the blending
mode to Luminosity

FIGURE *If you don't want to convert your image to Lab mode, you can target just the color in*
13.5 *your image by using the Luminosity blending mode between two identical layers.*

- Use the Blending pop-up menu at the top of the Layers palette to set the blending mode to Luminosity. With this mode, the hue and saturation of the lower layer is preserved, while all luminance information comes from the top copy. Luminance equates to brightness, which is a measure of contrast. So, the detail in your image will come from the top layer, while the color will come from the bottom.
- Now apply a blur filter to the lower layer to eliminate the noise. Because your contrast information is coming from your upper, unblurred layer, your noise-reducing blur shouldn't soften the details in your image.

A quick click on Undo after you apply your Blur filter makes it easy to go back and try different blur settings.

Using Third-Party Utilities to Eliminate Noise
There are several programs that are specifically designed to eliminate noise. If your camera produces conspicuously noisy images, or if your application demands that your images be very low in noise, then it might be worth an investment in one of these applications.

- **QImage Pro.** If you're a Windows user, you're in luck! QImage Pro is one of the best image editing utilities available for any platform. In addition to excellent noise reduction tools, QImage provides extraordinary white balance correction, sharpening, cataloging, color correction, and batch processing tools. For the digital camera owner, it's a must-have. You can find out more at www.completedigitalphotography.com/qimage.
- **Quantum Mechanic.** Macintosh users have an excellent tool in Quantum Mechanic, a Photoshop plug-in that provides excellent noise, artifact, and moiré removal tools. More information is available at www.completedigitalphotography.com/quantummech.

Dark Frame Subtraction

In Chapter 8 you learned about shooting for dark frame subtraction, a method of removing the excess noise that can happen with long exposures. As you'll recall, on very long exposures, (greater than one second) the pixels in your camera's sensor can get stuck "on," filling your image with bright white specks.

When you were facing such a situation, you learned to shoot a separate frame immediately following the first image, using the exact same exposure settings, but with the lens cap on. The idea was to take a second image of only the noise that appeared in the first image.

For that second frame to be useful, you now need to subtract it from the first frame. This won't eliminate the noise from your image, but it will replace the distracting bright white specks with less distracting darker specks.

Open both your image and your corresponding dark frame. Copy the dark frame and paste it into a new layer in your image file. Give the dark frame a slight Gaussian blur and set its blending mode to Difference. This should remove much of the noise from your image.

REMOVING DUST AND BLOTCHES

If you have a digital camera with removable lenses, then it is possible for dust to get to your camera's sensor and cause dark blotches or spots on your final image. Check your manual for instructions on cleaning your sensor (don't just assume that you can blast it with compressed air!).

Unfortunately, sometimes a pixel or two on the CCD in a digital camera can go bad. If one of the pixels in your camera's sensor dies, your images will consistently have a white or blue spot at the location of the bad pixel (Figure 13.6)

Unfortunately, there's nothing you can do to fix the camera, and most vendors won't replace or repair a camera with only one or two bad pixels. However, just like dirt or smears, you can quickly remove these erroneous pixels with your image editor's clone tool, by simply cloning from the immediately surrounding area. (Figure 13.7)

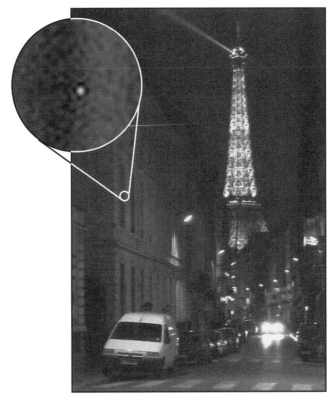

FIGURE *This image was shot with a Canon S100 Digital Elph that, unfortunately, has a bad*
13.6 *pixel.*

When you clone, remember to clone with the "grain" of the light. If the image gets darker diagonally from upper left to bottom right, then be sure to clone along that angle; otherwise, your clone color won't correspond to the image into which you're cloning.

CORRECTING BARREL AND PINCUSHION DISTORTION

Barrel and pincushion distortions are simple distortions that occur in images shot with extreme wide-angle or telephoto lenses. If you had to zoom way out when you were shooting your image, then there's a good chance that the lines in your image will be bowed outward. Conversely, if your lens was zoomed in all the way, there's a chance that your image will be bowed inwards. If you're using a wide-angle or fisheye attachment on your lens, your images will almost certainly be distorted (unless you're using a very expensive *rectilinear* wide-angle lens on an even more expensive digital SLR).

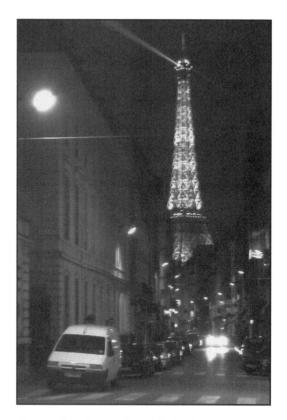

FIGURE *A quick retouching with a clone tool and the bad pixel is gone.*
13.7

These distortions don't occur in all lenses – in fact, the lack of them is the mark of a very good lens. In the following tutorial, you'll see how to correct a simple barrel distortion.

CORRECTING BARREL DISTORTION

TUTORIAL

Your lens may not have a big problem with barrel or pincushion distortion and, even if it does, the distortion may not be visible on all images. Sometimes, if the distortion is slight, it can be hidden by other curves and geometry within the image. Usually, you'll spot the distortion in architectural photos or other images that have very obvious horizontal and vertical lines. In this tutorial, you'll correct an image that was shot with an Olympus C2100UZ. With the lens zoomed out to full wide, the image barreled just a little bit.

STEP 1: OPEN THE IMAGE

Open the image graphwall.tif, located on the Complete Digital Photography CD-ROM in the tutorials>chapter 13>barrel folder. Barrel distortion is easy to spot in this image because of the horizontal and vertical lines painted on the wall of the building. Nevertheless, the distortion is slight, so it's a good idea to create some guides to help in our adjustments.

STEP 2: CREATE GUIDE LINES

To make it easier to gauge the effects of your correction, it's a good idea to create some simple vertical and horizontal guide lines. Choose View>Show Rulers to display Photoshop's rulers at the top and left side of your document.

Click in the top ruler and drag to pull down a guide line. Drop it along the top horizontal line on the wall.

Next, click on the left ruler and drag to the right to place a vertical guide on the left side of the building. With these guide lines in place, all you have to do is correct your image until the painted lines on the wall match up with your guide lines. (Figure 13.8)

FIGURE   *Graph wall with guide lines in place.*
13.8

STEP 3: EXPAND YOUR CANVAS

To correct this distortion, we're going to use a filter that will cause the image to distort to a size that's larger than the current image's canvas size. So, before you can start correcting the image, you need to add a little working room.

Choose Image>Canvas Size, and set the Width to 10 inches and the Height to 8 inches. This is more canvas than you need, but you can always crop it later.

STEP 4: CORRECT THE IMAGE

Photoshop's Spherize filter can apply a bulging, spherical distortion to your image. Fortunately, it can also create a depressed, bowl-like effect that is ideal for correcting barrel distortion. If you look closely at the graph wall image, you'll see that the distortion radiates from the center of the image in a spherical fashion. You'll also notice that the distortion gets worse toward the edges of the image.

Open the Spherize filter: choose Filter>Distort>Spherize. (Figure 13.9).

FIGURE *Photoshop's Spherize filter is a great tool for correcting barrel distortion.*
13.9

The Spherize filter is very simple. Simply enter a value for the amount of spherification that you want to apply. Positive percentages will cause the image to bulge outward, while negative values will bow the image inward. In other words, positive values will add barrel distortion while negative values will create pincushion distortion. You're simply going to use the Spherize filter's pincushioning ability to reduce the barrel distortion in the image.

How much spherizing to apply is simply a matter of trial and error. Enter a value of –50 and click OK. Figure 13.10 illustrates the results.

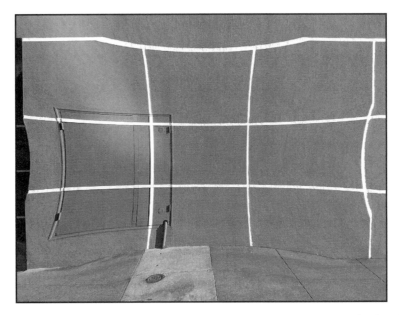

FIGURE   *Well, the image doesn't have any barrel distortion anymore. Apparently, though, our*
13.10   *Spherize value was too high.*

STEP 5: TRY AGAIN

Obviously, -50 is way too much, but you can at least see what the filter does. Click Undo and open the Spherize filter again. Let's try something less extreme. This time enter –10.

Check out the results and you'll probably find that this effect is still a little strong. Keep experimenting, but be certain that you examine the entire image when you evaluate your results. Don't just look at the guide lines. You want to find a setting that provides the best results overall, not just a correction along the two guide lines.

A Spherize setting of –6 is probably about right.

STEP 6: CROP

Obviously, the spherizing effect has rather changed the shape of the image. Click on the Crop tool in the main tools palette and crop off the curved edges of the image. (Figure 13.11)

FIGURE　*With a tiny bit of spherizing, and a little cropping, our distortion is gone.*
13.11

You can correct pincushion distortion in exactly the same way; just use positive values in your Spherize command to add barrel distortion. Once you've found a value that works for a particular focal length of your camera, it should work for any image shot at that focal length since your lens will always distort the same amount at a given focal length. To expedite your corrections, consider creating a Photoshop action that expands your canvas, performs the Spherize command and then shrinks your canvas to your desired crop size.

COLOR AND TONE ADJUSTMENT

After scrubbing the noise off your image and correcting any optical distortions, you're ready to move on to the color and contrast.

As you saw in the last two chapters, a good image editor provides color correction tools that pack incredible power. However, none of these tools are a "magic bullet" that can fix your image in one shot. Although you might, ideally, like to correct an image with a single, well-crafted Curves adjustment, the reality is that you'll often have to apply several different kinds of adjustments and corrections to get your image adjusted to your liking.

In the following tutorial, you'll take all of the color correction and masking skills that you learned in the last chapter, and apply them to the color correction of an image.

COLOR CORRECTION

TUTORIAL

Color Plate 9 shows two digital color photos of a bald eagle. Although an okay image, the top image has some troubles. First, the "bald" white color of the eagle's head has gone blue. In fact, most of the white tones in the image have gone blue. The file's EXIF information (see Chapter 8) reveals that the image was shot with a Daylight white balance setting. Given that the scene was plainly shot in shadow, it's obvious that we're facing a bad white balance. Unfortunately, the daylight setting has emphasized the blue of the shadows.

In addition to the color troubles, the bright colors in the background slightly overpower the black and white of the eagle, so we'll want to tone down the background colors. And finally, the image is a bit underexposed and so it will need some black and white point adjustments.

STEP 1: OPEN THE IMAGE

ON THE CD

Open the image eagle.tif, located on the Complete Digital Photography CD-ROM, in the tutorials>chapter 13>color correction folder.

STEP 2: REMOVE THE BLUE CAST

Let's begin by removing the blue cast caused by the bad white balance. We want to begin here so as to have the color as accurate as possible before we begin adjusting white and black points, or before trying to assess the foreground/background troubles. If we make contrast adjustments first, they may not be appropriate after we then make color changes.

It's pretty easy to see that this image is too blue. There are a number of ways to handle this problem. We could use a Curves or Levels adjustment targeted at the Blue channel, but we're going to use Photoshop's Hue/Saturation tool, simply because it's very easy to use for a situation like this, where the offending color is so easily identified.

From Photoshop 6's Layers palette, create a new Hue/Saturation adjustment layer: on the bottom of the palette, click on the third button from the right and select Hue/Saturation from the pop-up menu.

To remove a color using Hue/Saturation, we first need to target the color. From the Edit pop-up menu at the top of the Hue/Saturation dialog box, select Blues. The color ramp at the bottom of the dialog box will show you the range of colors that Hue/Saturation will target. As you can see, the default target is a little darker than the blues that we're facing. We need a lighter blue.

Move your mouse over the eagle – your pointer should change to an eyedropper – and click somewhere on the white of the eagle's head, in an area that is too blue. (Figure 13.12)

FIGURE *Selecting a color range in the Hue/Saturation dialog box.*
13.12

The color selector should slide further down the left of the color ramp. The left-most read-out should read approximately 178°/208°. You have now targeted the proper range of blues in the image.

To remove those blues, simply drag the Saturation slider to the left. A desaturation of about –81 should be all you need. You want to be careful about going too far, as you might posterize some of the blueish tones a little too much.

As you desaturated the blues, the eagle's head probably darkened in tone slightly. Remember, your operation has simply changed the color of those pixels from a heavily blue-hued color to a lightly blue-hued color. In this case the new light blue color is a little darker than the dark blue color that was there before. To lighten the eagle's head back up a bit, drag the Lightness slider to the right to about +16. Click OK.

That pretty much takes care of the blue. Our bald eagle now looks, well, bald.

STEP 3: DESATURATE THE BACKGROUND

The background is still a little too colorful for the black and white eagle in the foreground. Let's use another Hue/Saturation layer to desaturate the background.

With your last Hue/Saturation layer selected, create another Hue/Saturation adjustment layer. New layers are created above the currently selected layer and we want the layers in this image to stack up on top of each other. In other words, we don't want to insert a layer between the background and our first adjustment layer. This time, leave the Edit pop-up menu set to Master because we want to desaturate everything, not just a particular color range. Drag the Saturation slider down to about −61 to suck the color out of the background.

Unfortunately, this will also suck the color out of the eagle, rendering the whole image a little flat. To protect the eagle from the effects of this adjustment layer, you need to mask him. Choose Layer>Add Layer Mask>Reveal All and the mask will be selected for painting.

Click on a big paintbrush, select Black as your foreground color, and begin painting over the eagle. Each brush stroke will appear to brush in more saturated color. This is because each brush stroke is actually *masking out* the adjustment layer's desaturation effect. As you paint, you should also see a thumbnail of your mask appear in the layer mask thumbnail of the Layers palette (Figure 13.13).

FIGURE *Photoshop's Layers palette after painting a mask.*
13.13

After masking, your eagle should be back to his normal level of saturation. This looks better, but now the background just looks washed out and the entire image is a little flat. Let's darken the background to lend more weight to the foreground and to boost its colors back up a bit.

STEP 4: ADJUST THE LEVELS OF THE BACKGROUND

Create a Levels adjustment layer (make sure it's the top-most layer) and drag the middle input slider to set the gamma to about 5. (Figure 13.14)

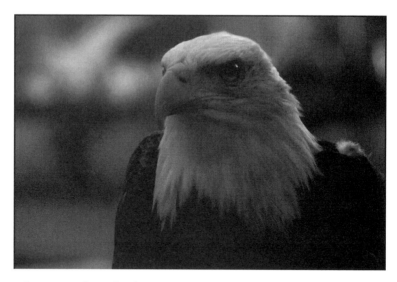

FIGURE *Eagle image with Levels adjustment before any Levels masking information is applied.*
13.14

Unfortunately, because the Levels adjustment is affecting the whole layer, it's difficult to see what is a proper adjustment. Add a layer mask to your Levels adjustment layer and paint out the eagle, just as you did in Step 3.

With the eagle masked, double-click on the Levels adjustment layer in the Layers palette to re-open the Levels dialog box. Now you can readjust the levels without affecting the eagle. Try a gamma adjustment of around .7. Click OK when you're finished.

STEP 5: ADJUST THE WHITE POINT AND BLACK POINT

Now that you've got the color and contrast right, you can look towards brightening the whole image. Add another Levels adjustment layer – this time with no mask – and adjust the levels to your taste. We used a black point (the left-most input slider) of 9, gamma (the middler slider) of 1.14, and white point (the right-most slider) of 229. Click OK when you're finished. (Figure 13.15)

You can see the final image in the bottom image of Color Plate 9.

As you can see, performing even simple color corrections on an image can often take several color correction functions filtered through a variety of masks. It's also important to think about the stacking order of your adjustment layers. For example, if you move the first Levels layer you created *below* either of the Hue/Saturation layers, your image will get darker as it will be operating on colors before they've been desaturated.

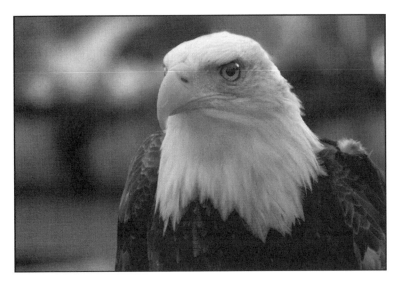

FIGURE   *The final eagle image after color correction.*
13.15

REMOVING RED-EYE

Because of their small size, many digital cameras are particularly prone to *red-eye*, that demonic look that can appear in your subject's eyes when the flash from your camera has bounced off their retinas and back into the camera's lens. Although there are ways to avoid red-eye when you shoot (see Chapter 7), there will still be times when you'll face this problem in an image and need to remove it.

The easiest way to deal with red-eye in Photoshop is to simply brush it out with a paintbrush. It's very rare for a flash to turn your subject's entire eye to red, so you can usually find a good color sample by zooming in and using the eyedropper to sample the original eye color.

Do your painting into a new layer so that you can throw it out if you mess up. You'll also probably want to lower the opacity of the new layer, or of your paintbrush to create a more subtle shading. The airbrush is also a good tool.

When you repaint the eyes, be sure to paint in a *catchlight*, the white highlight that appears in people's eyes. Without this extra detail, your subject's eyes will look lifeless. Examine some non-red-eye flash photos to see what this highlight should look like.

You can also try a masked desaturation on your base layer to try to eliminate some of the red from the original image.

Some programs offer special red-eye reduction tools. If you find yourself – your subjects, rather – plagued by red-eye, then consider investing in one of these special tools.

REMOVING CHROMATIC ABERRATIONS (PURPLE FRINGE)

In Chapter 8 you read about weird purple fringing artifacts that can occur in 2- and 3-megapixel cameras when you are shooting high-contrast areas with a wide-angle lens. Although opinions differ as to what causes this problem, everyone agrees that the results are ugly! Fortunately, there are several methods you can use to eliminate these weird color fringes.

Desaturating Fringe

Most fringing artifacts can be eliminated with a simple Hue/Saturation adjustment layer. The idea is to simply target the color of the fringe and drain the saturation out of it to make it blend better with the background. The trick is to not mess up any of the other color in your image.

TUTORIAL

ON THE CD

DESATURATING A CHROMATIC ABERRATION

Open the image Palace.tiff, located in the tutorials>chapter 13>chromabb folder on the Complete Digital Photography CD-ROM. The chromatic aberrations are not terrible, but they are there. Take a look between the two right-most columns and you'll see a nasty red fringe on the left side of the right column, and a bad green fringe on the right side of the left column.

Although the fringes aren't huge, the predominant colors in the image are red and green, so you'll have to be careful when you remove the extra colors.

STEP 1: SELECT THE FIRST FRINGE

Using the Marquee or Lasso tool, select the right-most, red fringe. You don't have to be really precise in this selection; (Figure 13.16) your main goal is to protect the other red tones in the image.

STEP 2: CREATE A HUE/SATURATION ADJUSTMENT LAYER

With your selection active, use the Layers palette to create a new Hue/Saturation adjustment layer. Notice that the Layers palette shows your adjustment layer with a layer mask that matches your selection.

STEP 3: TARGET THE OFFENDING COLORS

Now you need to select the colors of the fringe. To do this, you'll need to zoom in to your document to see some individual pixels. Press Command-+ (Control-+ in Windows) a few times to zoom in to 200%. Because the fringe is kind of a pinkish-red you want to limit the effects of the adjustment to reds. Select Reds from the Edit pop-up menu at the top of the Hue-Saturation dialog box.

FIGURE   *Select the area of bad red fringe in the image.*
13.16

Now you need to sample the color of the fringe in the image. Using the eye-dropper, select one of the very light-colored pink dots within the fringe. The color selection scale will shift to the left to encompass the color that you sampled. Because the palace columns contain a lot of red, you want to narrow your red selection so as to not desaturate the columns. The color selection scale has four sliding controls, two on the left and two on the right. The inner sliders control the range of colors to select, while the outer controls create a color selection drop-off to ensure smooth color shifts.

Slide all four sliders inward to create a very tight color selection (Figure 13.17).

STEP 4: DESATURATE THE FRINGE

Now drag the Saturation slider to the left to suck some of the saturation out of the selected red tones. As they lose saturation, they may turn more gray. If so, try backing off on the desaturation by moving the Saturation slider back to the right and instead add a little lightening by moving the Lightness slider to the right.

FIGURE *Targeting the fringe color.*
13.17

STEP 5: TARGET MORE COLORS

Although the image is probably looking better, there's still most likely a lot of red or pink. You want to now expand the target color range. Click on the middle eyedropper, the one with the + next to it, and click on some of the remaining fringe colors. This will add these colors to the range of colors that is being deselected. You may have to go deep into the shadows of the columns to get all of the colors. You may also have to adjust your Saturation and Lightness settings after you select more color.

STEP 6: CHECK THE RESULTS

When you're all finished, click OK, and zoom out to check the results. In addition to looking at the quality of the fringe reduction, look closely at the surrounding area of your selection to ensure that you haven't inadvertently desaturated any other parts of the column. If there's still visible fringing, double-click on the adjustment layer to tweak your settings.

When you're all done, do the same thing with the other fringe, but this time target the greens.

This approach will work for most chromatic aberrations, although you have to be careful. Sometimes the color of your aberration will very closely match the background of your image. For example, you'll frequently run into blue aberrations against a blue sky. Be certain to select and feature your aberration first, to protect the rest of the sky. You'll also probably want to do less desaturation and more lightening to match the hue of the fringe to the sky.

Removing Chromatic Aberration by Hand

Sometimes your aberrations might be bad enough that you simply need to go in and paint them out using a paintbrush or clone tone. With the Clone tool you can clone in color from the surrounding area, but you'll need a steady hand. Use a very soft-edged brush and set the opacity low. Using a paintbrush is a similar process, but you'll need to sample the paint color by hand using the Eyedropper tool.

You can also use the Blur tool to blur a fringe out of existence. Set the Blur tool's opacity very low – around 15-20% - and change its mode to Color. Brush along the fringe and you should see it slowly fade away.

Removing Fringes by Shrinking Channels

Fringes are often very pure red, green, or blue colors. Consequently, they're often confined to an individual color channel. If you examine your individual channels and find this to be true, you can always go in and edit the channels directly.

Fringes sometimes look just like a mis-registration from a printing press. That is, if your image has red fringing, it can often appear as if the Red channel has slipped out of registration with the Blue and Green channels. It hasn't, but we can try to correct it using the same procedures we'd use to fix a mis-registration.

- Select the offending color channel.
- Shrink it to "scoot" the fringe under the other color channels. You can do this by choosing Edit>Transform>Numeric and entering a tiny value—99.7 or 99.8, for example. This will reduce the size of the channel and hopefully hide the aberration.

After shrinking a channel, be sure to examine your image closely for any new artifacts that may have been introduced by the transformation. In particular, make sure no new fringing has developed in other parts of the image.

There are one or two applications that will do this for you, most notably Picture Window and Panorama Tools. You can learn more about them at www.completedigitalphotography.com/panotools.

ADJUSTING TONAL RANGE WITH LAYERS

You can also improve the tonal range of an image by stacking a duplicate of the image and using a special blending mode. For example, if you have an under-exposed image that lacks punch, duplicate its layer. Then set the blending mode of the upper copy to Screen. The blending should help boost the tone of the image.

Similarly, if you have an image that's overexposed, stack a second copy and set the blending mode to Multiply. If you want to know more about what, exactly, these transfer modes are doing, Photoshop's Help file has full descriptions.

CORRECTING WHITE BALANCE

In Chapter 11 you learned how to use Levels and Curves controls to correct color in an image, and even used the controls to correct an image with an incorrect white balance. There's no set method or rule for correcting a bad white balance as each situation will be unique. Levels, Curves, and Hue/Saturation adjustments will usually be your best tools for white balance correction and each image will usually have its own unique correction needs.

In general, though, there are some guidelines to follow when correcting white balance.

- Don't expect to be able to use a single correction to fix a bad white balance. Though white balance usually affects all areas of an image, it often affects one color range (highlights or midtones, for example) more than another. You might need to use separate adjustments for each color range in your image.
- Use masks to isolate areas for corrections. If an area of your image is particularly out-of-whack, color-wise, then you may have to mask it off and apply a strong color correction to fix it.
- Don't expect to restore accurate color. Though you can greatly improve the white balance of an image, you probably won't be able to restore absolute color accuracy. In addition to changes in hue, you'll probably find that it's difficult to achieve full brightness in your colors.

As you may have guessed, the best way to achieve good white balance is when you're shooting. For those, hopefully rare, times when your images are poorly white balanced the above tips should help you on your way to restoring proper color.

CORRECTING VIGNETTING

Hopefully, you kept an eye out for *vignetting* when you went shopping for a camera. If not, you'll probably need to develop a method for removing this darkening of the corners of your image (Figure 13.18).

The easiest way to handle vignetting is to build a mask that mimics the darkening in your image. You can then apply a Levels filter to this mask to compensate for the darkening. It may take some time to refine your mask, but once you have one that works, you can probably re-use it for any image with vignetting troubles.

You can paint a vignette mask by hand using a large airbrush or a very soft-edged paintbrush, or a gradient tool. Or, you can use a selection tool such as Photoshop's Pen tool or Lasso tool to outline the edges of your vignette corners. Then, apply a strong feather to your selection to fade its edge.

Once you're satisfied with your selection, save it as an alpha channel. (Figure 13.19) With your mask still selected, create a Levels adjustment layer and try to

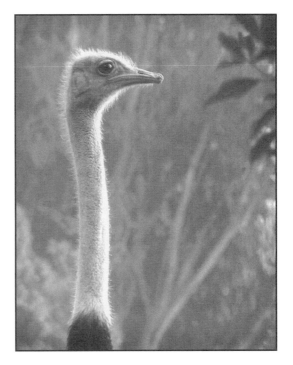

FIGURE
13.18
This image suffers from vignetting, a darkening of the corners.

FIGURE
13.19
If you have trouble with vignetting, consider building a mask that matches your camera's vignette, like the one shown here, on the left. By applying a Levels filter to the mask, you can usually correct the darkened corners of your image.

lighten the vignettes. If your mask needs adjustment, throw out the adjustment layer, edit your mask and start over.

Once you have a mask that works, you can copy it into any image that has a vignetting problem.

SATURATION ADJUSTMENT

Once you've made all of your color adjustments – which you'll typically do with Levels or Curves controls – then you'll want to consider a separate pass to adjust saturation. Why not adjust saturation at the same time that you're correcting tone and color? Because it's hard to change saturation using Levels and Curves and because you don't what your saturation concerns will be until you've corrected your image and arrived at your final colors.

The easiest way to adjust saturation – whether increasing or decreasing – is through the Hue/Saturation control which can be applied as a straight, destructive filter, or as an adjustment layer.

When you correct saturation, keep an eye out for posterization and be aware that your monitor can produce images that are much more saturated than what your printer can print. As with color correction, you'll want to make test prints and, ideally, use your color management software, to keep an eye on your final results. Increasing saturation is usually the easiest way to push colors out of the printable range of your printer.

INCREASING CONTRAST AND SATURATION WITH LAYER STACKING

There's another way to increase contrast and saturation without using an adjustment layer or correction function. By stacking and blending copies of an image, you can build up saturation in color images, and contrast in grayscale images. (Figure 13.20)

To create the effect in Figure 13.20, we duplicated our base layer and set its Blending mode to Soft Light. We then dialed down the opacity to control the degree of saturation increase. Now, just as in an adjustment layer, we can go in and erase or mask parts of the image to control the application of an effect.

Why use this approach over a Saturation command? Because in color images you often get a nice alteration of hues in addition to an increase in saturation.

DECREASING CONTRAST AND SATURATION WITH LAYER STACKING

If you want to decrease the saturation of an image, either because your camera goes a little too "hot" on some colors, or because you simply prefer muted tones, you can perform a trick similar to the one above.

FIGURE   *By duplicating an image layer and setting the Blending mode of the copy to Soft*
13.20   *Light, you can create a much higher-contrast image.*

Create a new layer and fill it with a color. Change its Blending mode to Soft
Light or Hard Light, and adjust its opacity to control the intensity of the effect.
Depending on the color you choose for your desaturation layer, you can tone or
cast the colors in your base image at the same time that you're desaturating
them. For even stranger, more pronounced effects, experiment with the other
blending modes.

EDITING

Your image is cleaned, your colors are adjusted, so you now have an image that
is perfect raw material for your artistic license. Now is the time where you'll
begin to create any composites or collages, or any radical touch-ups (removing
Russian astronauts, that sort of thing). If you had performed any of these edits
earlier, then any cloning or painting that you did might have duplicated any
noise or chromatic aberrations that were already in your image. You would then
have a much more difficult time removing them.

There's also a good chance that the edits you perform are going to lead you
to create many new layers in your document. Color correcting can be much
more complex when different elements are on different layers, which is just one
more reason why it's good to get those operations out of the way.

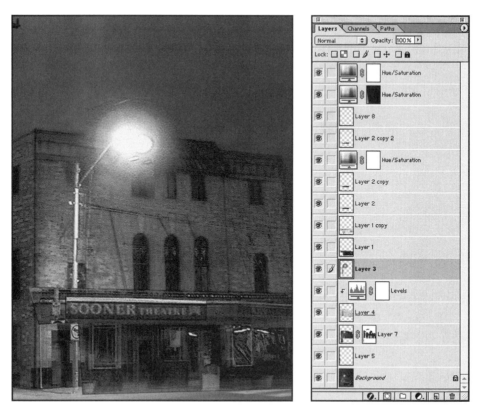

FIGURE
13.21
This complex, heavily manipulated Coolpix 990 image is comprised of over 16 layers, each of which isolates an individual color correction or painted object. This layered approach makes for easier edits and revisions.

However, after your edits, you may find that you need to tweak your color correction settings or perform another color correction pass to blend and smooth out your edits.

In the next chapter, you'll explore many of the things that might transpire in this editing stage, from compositing to adding texture and tone to your image. For now, let's concentrate on the remaining steps of your image editing workflow.

SCALING

In Chapter 10 we discussed the differences in sampling and resampling when you scale your images. In most cases, it's good to save the scaling step until now because you don't want to blow up your image if it's full of noise and color artifacts, as you'll blow up those artifacts along with the image.

If you're stuck working on a low-resolution image, let's say 640 x 480, then you might want to enlarge your image some before you start editing because you may need some extra pixels to perform your painting and editing tasks.

Why else might you need to resize an image? At the very least, you'll probably need to change the resolution setting of your image to something more appropriate for your printer (see Chapter 15). If your final destination is the web, then you'll definitely need to scale your image down, assuming you were shooting at one of your camera's higher resolutions.

You'll need to scale up if your image came out of your camera smaller than you'd like to print it. You might also need to scale the image up if you're printing to a printer that demands higher resolution. Although your image editor can do a good job of scaling an image up, you can only go so far. Follow the tips below for best results.

SCALING DOWN

If your images need to be output to the web, video, or for display on a computer, then they most certainly will need to be scaled down, or *downsampled.*

Downsampling is a fairly worry-free process because your computer is throwing data *away* rather than having to make it up. About the only thing you need to know when you downsample an image for use is what size, in pixels, does the final product need to be.

Talk to your designer, webmaster, producer, or whoever is responsible for your final graphics (if you're responsible, then you're on your own) and find out the desired pixel dimensions of your final image.

From Photoshop's Image Size dialog box, check the Resample Image checkbox, enter a Resolution of 72 pixels per inch and enter your desired pixel dimensions in the Pixel Dimensions fields. Click OK and then choose File>Save As to save a *copy* of your smaller file with a new filename (be sure to type in a new name or you might save over your original!). You never know if you'll need a bigger image someday, so it's a shame to throw away all that extra resolution by writing over your original file.

SCALING UP

As explained in Chapter 10, when you scale an image up, Photoshop has to interpolate new pixels to get the image up to your desired size. Fortunately, Photoshop's bicubic interpolation algorithm is very good at upsampling images up to about one-and-a-half times their original size. After that, the results can be a little soft. Fortunately, with today's high-resolution cameras, you usually don't have to scale up too much to boost your image up to a fairly big print size.

To scale up, you need to know the target resolution of your printer (more on this in Chapter 15) as well as your desired print size. Open the Image Size dialog box, be sure that Resample Image is checked, enter the appropriate resolution in the Resolution field, and your desired print size in the Document Size fields. Click OK, and Photoshop will calculate your new image.

As with sampling down, it's a good idea to save your new, larger image as a copy. Your original size image is going to be a little cleaner and you might want to re-use it for something else later.

After scaling up, you may find that your image has softened somewhat. You'll get a chance to sharpen it up in the next stage of the workflow. Poke around your image and look for any other artifacts that may have been exaggerated in the upsampling. In particular, look for *aliasing* (stair-stepping) along diagonal lines, as well as exaggerations of any noise or aberrations that may have been left in the original image. These can be retouched using the techniques discussed earlier. Aliasing can usually be handled by brushing over the offending areas with a very small Blur tool.

WHEN 1.5X ISN'T ENOUGH

Of course, there might be times when you need to blow up an image to colossal proportions. Although you can try pushing Photoshop's bicubic interpolation to larger sizes, you may be disappointed by the results. Fortunately, there are some other solutions.

AltaMira's GenuineFractals PrintPro uses a technology called *wavelet compression* to convert your image from a series of raster dots into a collection of tiny fractal curves. Because fractals reveal more detail as you expand them, and because they can be mathematically enlarged (rather like vector artwork) you blow up a wavelet-compressed image by fairly extreme factors.

AltaMira doesn't claim great results on images smaller than 2 megabytes, and yet the program still does a very good job of enlarging digital camera images up to three or four times without great degradation. Wavelet compression can't perform miracles, though. After a point, if you need larger files, you'll have to upgrade to a higher-resolution camera.

A demo copy of Genuine Fractals program can be found at http://www.genuinefractals.com.

Bear in mind that you're often creating a larger image because you want a picture that can be viewed from a greater distance. Consequently, super-fine detail is not so important. If you're creating a big image that will be viewed from several feet away, then be sure to evaluate your prints from several feet away. Don't get hung up on trying to see fine detail at close distance.

SHARPENING

With everything else done and your image at its final output size, you're finally ready to apply any necessary sharpening. As with resizing, you don't want to sharpen too early as you'll run the risk of accentuating noise and other unwanted artifacts. Also, you won't know how much sharpening you need until you've adjusted the image's contrast – after all, a more contrasty image looks sharper – and until you've resized the image. If you shrink an image, it's going to get sharper, while if you enlarge it, it will almost always get softer. Consequently, sharpening will be the last step you take before outputting the image.

Photoshop includes a number of sharpening filters. In addition to these, there are third-party sharpeners as well as procedural techniques you can use to sharpen your image. Unfortunately, Photoshop does not offer editable sharpening layers. Once you apply your sharpening effects, that's it. Consequently, it's a good idea to save a copy of your image before you sharpen, or to duplicate a layer before you sharpen it. By sharpening a duplicate, you can always throw it out and go back to your original if you change your mind.

Your biggest concern when you sharpen, however, is to not sharpen too much. Oversharpening can create a number of undesirable artifacts.

HOW SHARPENING WORKS

Photoshop, like most image editors, has several sharpening filters. Sharpen, Sharpen More, Sharpen Edges, and Unsharp Mask can all be found under the Filter>Sharpen menu. However, the Unsharp Mask (USM) filter is the only one of these that you ever need to consider. The rest are simply to uncontrollable and destructive for quality sharpening.

Unsharp Mask gets its name from a darkroom sharpening technique wherein a blurry copy of a negative (an "unsharp" copy) is sandwiched with the original negative and a print is made using a doubled exposure time. The unsharp mask negative and lengthened exposure time serves to darken the dark side of an edge and lighten the light side, causing the edge to exhibit a halo. This renders the edge more pronounced and the image appears sharper.

The USM filter works the same way. When you apply the filter, your image is examined one pixel at a time. Obviously, the filter can't really tell what counts as an edge in your image, so it looks for sudden changes in contrast. If there is a sudden change in value between two adjacent pixels, then that's probably an edge. The darker pixel will be darkened and the pixels around it will be ramped down, while the lighter pixel will be lightened and the pixels around it ramped up.

If you look at an edge in an image that has had a USM filter applied, like the one in Figure 13.22, you'll see that one side of the edge is darker, while the other side is lighter. The result is a bit of a halo. As long as this halo isn't distractingly strong, the image will appear much sharper.

FIGURE *If you look closely at a sharpened image, you can see the halos that the Unsharp*
13.22 *Mask process creates along the edges of shapes to make them appear sharper.*

The key to good unsharp masking is to know when to quit. Too much sharpening and your image will appear unrealistically sharp, and the edge halos will be bright enough to be distracting.

Photoshop's Unsharp Mask tool provides three controls: amount, radius, and threshold. (Figure 13.23) This is typical of USM controls, so even if you're using a different image editor, its unsharp mask tool probably offers the same options.

FIGURE   *Photoshop's Unsharp Mask filter provides three simple controls for sharpening your*
13.23   *images.*

- **Amount** simply controls how much the pixels along an edge will be darkened and lightened. The higher the number, the more the USM filter will change the pixels. Too much of a change and your edge will become unnaturally contrasty and will possibly posterize.
- **Radius** determines the width of the halo that will be created. The wider the radius, the more pixels that will be altered around an edge to create a halo.
- **Threshold** determines what the filter will consider an edge. A higher threshold value requires more contrast between two pixels. With a high threshold, USM will find fewer edges and perform less sharpening.

To learn what makes good sharpening, it's worth spending some time looking at some professional photos. Notice that even images that have lots of detail and contrast are not necessarily razor sharp. Your image editor can actually sharpen an image far beyond what looks realistic. At the same time, your eyes like contrast so it can be very tempting to add a little more sharpness.

When you use a USM filter, start with a high Amount setting – 300 to 400% and a very small Threshold. Then start trying to find a Radius that produces minimal halos. (Figure 13.24) Sharpening is a subjective process, of course, so find a level of halo that suits you. However, be sure to consider your entire image. As you'll see in Figure 13.24, the same sharpening setting can have very different effects on different subjects.

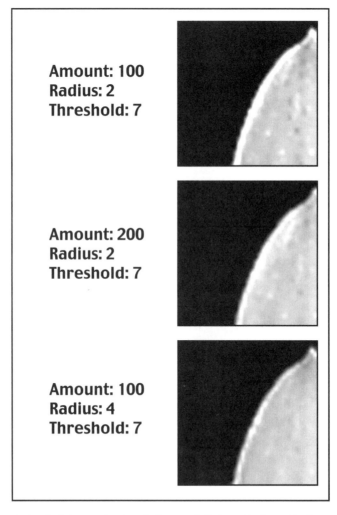

**Amount: 100
Radius: 2
Threshold: 7**

**Amount: 200
Radius: 2
Threshold: 7**

**Amount: 100
Radius: 4
Threshold: 7**

FIGURE *The right level of sharpening is a balance of all three Unsharp Mask parameters.*
13.24

Once you've found a Radius that is right, you can back off the Amount and increase the Threshold. Your goal is to use these two sliders to apply your desired radius to the appropriate amount of edge detail in your image.

NOT ALL SHARPNESS IS CREATED EQUAL

Note that some subjects sharpen faster than others. Foliage, and small, very detailed background elements, for example, usually don't stand up to a good deal of sharpening. If these types of objects are mixed with flatter subjects with less detail, then consider sharpening these elements separately. Build a mask to separate detailed objects from less complex shapes and use different levels of sharpening for each. Obviously, you want a mask with a strong feather to ensure a smooth transition.

Similarly, although you may have gone through a lot of noise reduction earlier, there's a chance that shadow areas, skies, and other areas of flat color might still have some noise in them. Because you don't want to exaggerate this noise through sharpening, it's a good idea to mask these areas out before you sharpen.

You can also control the sharpening in your image by sharpening individual color channels. For example, if you've got a noisy Blue channel, then leave it alone (or de-noise it, as explained earlier) and sharpen just the Red and Green channels.

Similarly, you can convert your image to Lab mode and sharpen just the L channel to protect any subtle color texture from oversharpening.

Going to the Web? Need small files? Go easy on the sharpening. *If small file size is your highest concern, then don't sharpen your images too much. As you sharpen, you increase contrast which means your files won't compress as small as they will if left a little soft.*

Another technique is to upsample you image to about 150% of its regular size using a wavelet compression program such as Genuine Fractals. In Photoshop, apply a very strong Unsharp Mask and then use Genuine Fractals to downsample your image back to its regular size. This is a very aggressive form of sharpening that is not appropriate for most images. If you have a very soft image, though, you might give this method a try.

TIP

Shooting VGA and XGA? Don't bother sharpening. *To shoot produce lower-resolution VGA or XGA images, many cameras shoot at full-resolution and then downsample the image before storing it. Consequently, images at these resolutions are usually plenty sharp thanks to the camera's downsampling.*

Your sharpening goal at this point should simply be to get your image on-screen to the level of sharpening that you'd normally expect from a photo. Once you start printing, you may find you need more sharpening (and occasionally, less sharpening). Because too much sharpening can wreck your image, it's a good idea to always apply sharpening to a copy of your image. If you mess up, you can always go back to your original.

CHAPTER

14

Special Effects

In This Chapter

- Simulating Depth of Field
- Stitching Panoramas
- Converting Color Images to Grayscale
- Adding Texture, Grain, and "Film" Look

Initially, most of your image editing work centered around correcting and adjusting the image to correct problems caused by your camera, or to taking advantage of exposure strategies that you may have chosen when you were shooting.

Your editor is capable of much more than simple tonal corrections, of course. By now, you've probably already played with many of the filters and effects tools in your editing application, and have begun to see just how much you can manipulate an image.

In this chapter, you'll learn some of the typical special effects that, as a digital photographer, you might want to use and explore. The techniques herein should help you get started, and should provide you with a basic set of common special effects procedures.

SIMULATING DEPTH OF FIELD

To the experienced photographer, one of the most frustrating things about a typical digital camera is the limited depth of field. As you learned earlier, the tiny focal lengths on most prosumer cameras prohibit shallow depth of field effects. Fortunately, through some clever blurring, you can use your image editor to add a depth of field effect.

One of the most important things to remember about depth of field is that it is a *depth*. That is, the area in focus begins at one point and ends at another and is centered around the focal point of the image. A shallow depth of field doesn't simply mean that your background will be blurry, it can also mean that part of your foreground will be blurry. In addition, different planes in your background will be more or less blurry depending on how far away they are.

SHORTENING DEPTH OF FIELD IN AN IMAGE

TUTORIAL

Figure 14.1 shows an image with very deep depth of field – everything in the image is in focus. In this tutorial, we're going to create a very, very shallow depth of field that will blur both the foreground and background.

STEP 1: OPEN THE IMAGE

ON THE CD

Open the image cosmo.tif located in the Tutorials>Chapter 14>dof folder on the Complete Digital Photography CD-ROM. In any portrait, you want the eyes of your subject to be in focus, so we're going to use the dog's eyes as the focal point of this shot. Your goal is to create an effect like the one shown in Figure 14.2.

FIGURE   *This image has a very deep depth of field. It's time to make it more shallow.*
14.1

FIGURE   *Your goal is to create a depth of field that defocuses both in front of and behind the*
14.2   *dog's eyes.*

STEP 2: PREPARE A GRADIENT

The blurring effect is actually very easy; we'll simply use the Gaussian Blur filter. However, we want the blur to increase gradually in both directions as it extends away from our focal point. Consequently, we'll want to apply our blur filter through a mask.

In Photoshop's Channels palette, create a new channel by clicking on the New Channel button at the bottom of the palette. Our masking needs are very simple for this project. A simple gradient should be all that we need.

Type "D" on your keyboard to select black and white as your default foreground and background colors. Click in the gradient sample on the Photoshop toolbar to open the Gradient Editor. Figure 14.3 illustrates the settings you will need.

FIGURE *Use Photoshop's Gradient Editor to build a custom gradient.*
14.3

You want a gradient that goes from white to black to white. Click on the bottom left stop and change its color to white. Change the bottom right stop to black and drag it toward the center of the gradient. Now click on the right end of the gradient sample to create a third stop, and set its color to white. When you're finished, your gradient should like the one in Figure 14.3. Name the gradient and click OK to save it.

STEP 3: APPLY THE GRADIENT TO YOUR MASK

With your new channel selected in the Channels palette, click on the eyeball icon next to the RGB channel in the Channels palette. This will allow you to see your image normally, but your actions will only affect your new alpha channel.

Click on the Gradient tool in the main tools palette and drag the tool in a diagonal line from upper left to lower right to mask the dog's eyes. Your gradient will appear on-screen as a red tint over your image. Position your gradient so that it looks like Figure 14.4. It may take a few tries, but each time you drag with the Gradient tool, the new gradient will replace the old, so it's easy to quickly try a bunch of different gradients.

FIGURE   *You want your gradient to blend into and out of the dog's eyes.*
14.4

STEP 4: APPLY THE BLUR

Now click on the RGB channel to select it and drag the alpha channel to the Load Channel as Selection button at the bottom of the dialog box to load your alpha channel as a selection. Apply a Gaussian blur filter by selecting Filter>Blur>Gaussian Blur. Enter a Radius of 7 pixels. The foreground and background of your image should go blurry.

Although the effect looks good, the hand in the background looks conspicuously in focus. It's on a much deeper plane than the dog's eyes and so it should not be in focus. Undo the blur and click on your alpha channel in the Channels palette to select it. We're going to do a little mask alteration.

STEP 5: ALTER YOUR MASK

Right now the hand is being masked because it lies on the same line as our gradient. We want to unmask it so that it will blur. Click the eyeball next to the RGB channel in the Channels palette so that you can see your image and your mask.

The thumb is masked an appropriate amount; we just need to get the rest of the hand to match. Using the eyedropper, click on the thumb to sample its color. This is the color you'll use to paint the rest of your mask. Click on a paintbrush and paint over the hand, up until it bumps the dog. Use a very soft-edged brush.

When you're finished, click off the eyeball next to the RGB layer so that you can see just your mask. It should like something like Figure 14.5.

FIGURE *After editing, your new mask should look something like this.*
14.5

STEP 6: APPLY YOUR FINAL BLUR

Load your new mask and re-apply your blur. Now your image should look something like Figure 14.2. With the hand blurred, the depth of field effect is much more realistic.

Create Planes of Depth

Typically, when you choose to shoot with a shallow depth of field (if your camera is capable) the goal is to soften the background to bring more attention to the foreground.

If all of the objects in your background are a good distance behind your subject, then you can usually get away with simply blurring the entire background (Figure 14.6).

FIGURE   *Depth of field can be easily added to this image by blurring the background.*
14.6

If, however, the background elements in your image recede from your foreground subject, simply blurring the background will look weird. In Figure 14.7, the blurred background reduces the image to two planes of depth, the foreground and the blurred background. It almost looks as if the woman is standing in front of a blurry backdrop of a street. Because the background recedes into the distance you need to control the *falloff* of the blur so that it gets stronger for objects that are farther away.

The top image in Figure 14.8 was created using a simple layering process.

- Duplicate your base layer (the layer to which you want to add the depth of field effect).
- Apply a blur to the upper layer. Choose a blur that is appropriate for the farthest elements in your image.

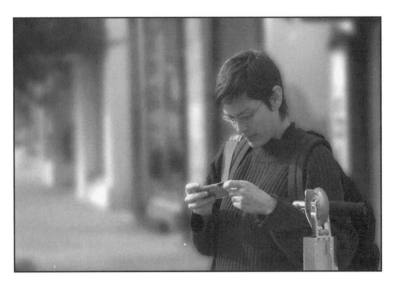

FIGURE *Simply blurring the background of this image looks weird, because everything in the*
14.7 *background is equally defocused. Because the background recedes, the defocusing*
should increase with distance.

- Now add a layer mask to the upper layer that reveals the entire layer. Your image will appear blurry.
- Using the Gradient tool and a paintbrush, mask the blur to reveal the underlying sharp image. In the case of Figure 14.8, a gradient was used to create a depth of field that gets stronger from right to left.
- Unfortunately, the gradient blended the background tree and buildings the same amount. In reality, the tree should appear closer (less blurry) than the buildings that are next to it in the image. A paintbrush loaded with 70% gray was used to paint over the tree in the layer mask. This resulted in the tree only getting 70% of the blur.

If your image has very distinct planes in the background, you can use separate layers for each plane, blurring each by different amounts, and building layer masks to reveal the appropriate parts of each layer.

STITCHING PANORAMAS

In Chapter 9 you learned about panoramic images, multiple shots that can be stitched together to create wide, panoramic pictures. Good panoramas require some thought when you shoot, but they often require a little image editing before stitching.

FIGURE *This depth of field effect works much better because of the more complex, hand-*
14.8 *painted mask. In addition to a receding sense of depth, objects at different planes are blurred appropriately.*

Your camera probably came with stitching software, (Figure 14.9) but if it didn't – or if you're not happy with it – then consider one of the third-party offerings such as MGI's PhotoVista. (For a comprehensive list of panoramic software, check out www.completedigitalphotography.com/panotools.)

FIGURE *Many cameras ship with panoramic stitching software such as Canon's PhotoStitch.*
14.9

No matter what software you use, your images might need a little clean-up before you start stitching. Variations in exposure from one image to the next can cause color banding and shift in your final panorama. Hopefully, you tried to compensate for this when you were shooting (see Chapter 9) but even the best laid plans sometimes end up incorrectly exposed.

Before you stitch, open up your panoramic shots and examine them for exposure differences. Are some images darker or lighter than others? Skies are particularly susceptible to saturation and hue changes from shot to shot. If you do see variations from one shot to the next, then you'll need to color correct your images. Typically, Levels or Curves adjustments are all you'll need. When you correct, consider the following:

- Choose the image you like most as a base image, and correct your other images to match.
- If the first or last image is very over- or underexposed (which sometimes happens because the sun is in the first or last image) then consider throwing it out altogether and creating a smaller panorama.
- If you're having trouble matching tones and color from one image to the next, try stitching and then performing corrections on the completed panorama.

Because you typically shoot panoramic images with a very wide-angle focal length, your individual images may suffer from barrel distortion. *Don't* try to correct this before stitching – let the stitching software worry about that.

Also, don't worry about spotting or removing dust or other aberrations. It's better to do this after you've stitched the panorama.

Most stitching programs offer a combination of automatic and manual controls. If your images were well-shot (and after reading Chapter 9, how could they not be?) then your program's automatic functions may be all you need. At other times, though, you may have to resort to manual control.

Manual stitching controls simply ask you to find corresponding points within an image. These points are then used to guide the software's stitching efforts. Typically, you need to identify two pairs of points along each seam. Try to pick pairs of points that are close to the top or bottom of the images. (Figure 14.10)

Finally, after stitching, your panoramic software may want to crop the image to eliminate uneven boundaries at the top and bottom of the image. These boundaries often create a nice frame and frequently include image elements that you'd like to keep. Rather than letting your stitching software crop your panorama, leave the image uncropped. You can always crop it yourself in your image editor.

FIGURE   *Some programs let you manually specify points for stitching.*
14.10

Know your focal length. *Some stitching programs want to know the focal length of the lens (in 35mm equivalency) that was used to shoot the panorama. If your camera has a fixed zoom lens, then you may not know what the exact focal length was. If you were shooting at full wide (which you should usually do for panoramas) then you can simply enter the widest angle that the lens provides (usually around 35mm). To be certain, use an EXIF reader to examine the header information in one of your images (see Chapter 8). Many cameras store focal length in the EXIF header.*

After stitching, you may find that your image needs some more correction. Again, skies can be especially problematic. If the sky in two of your images differ, then you'll see a short gradation from one color to the next along the seam of your panorama. Odds are, you won't be able to completely match the two images, but you might be able to create a smoother blend by adding a gradated Levels or Curves adjustment. Add the adjustment as an adjustment layer, and use the Gradient tool to create a smooth transition.

This is also the best time to remove dust, spots, or other aberrations.

Free Stitching. *If you don't have any stitching software, or if you want to try some very good stitching software, then check out Panorama Tools, available for free download at http://www.fh-furtwangen.de/~dersch/. Be warned, though, this software is very technical and very difficult to use. Its toolset, though, also provides excellent features for correcting lens distortion. For the theoretically-inclined, the site includes a lot of good technical information on panoramic stitching.*

CONVERTING COLOR IMAGES TO GRAYSCALE

Although your camera may do a great job of reproducing color, there will be times when you'll want to convert your color images to black and white, either for printing purposes, or simply for artistic intent. Photoshop, and most other image editors, allows you to convert an image to grayscale simply by selecting a new color mode (in Photoshop you can do this by selecting Image> Mode>Grayscale). This type of conversion works by using a stock recipe for mixing the image's Red, Green, and Blue channels to produce a grayscale result. In theory, the recipe produces an image that is well suited to the eye's different color and luminance sensitivities.

Often, this is the best way to convert your image; however, you may find that the resulting image lacks solid blacks and bright whites. With its color removed, your image may be less punchy. Fortunately, there are several other methods which provide more control and, frequently, better results.

CONVERSION METHODS

Some of the methods presented below might be better for some images than others. You'll probably want to try several approaches side-by-side to see what works best. Also, be sure that you perform your conversions on a *copy* of your image. Although you may want the image in black and white now, you never know when you might need to go back to your original color version.

Before using any of these methods, go ahead and color correct your image. This may sound strange since you're just going to remove all of the color, but an image that is more color accurate will usually produce a more pleasing grayscale image.

Figure 14.11 shows an image converted using each of the following methods.

Channeling

You may have discovered this already, but sometimes one of the individual color channels in your image actually makes for a very good grayscale image. Just click through the individual channels in the Channels palette and see which, if any, looks best. Depending on the color content of your image, any channel might look good, although the Red and Blue channels might suffer from noise.

If you find a channel you like, simply choose Image>Mode>Grayscale and Photoshop will toss out the other channels, leaving you with a grayscale image of your chosen channel.

Converting to Luminance

Just as you can select a single color channel in RGB mode, you can convert your image to Lab mode and select just the Luminance channel. This will throw out all of the color information in your image. After you convert to Lab mode, just click on the Lightness channel in the Channels palette and select Image>Mode>Grayscale.

Desaturating an Image

When you were playing with the Hue/Saturation control, you may have discovered that it is possible to completely desaturate an image to grayscale, simply by dragging the Saturation slider all the way to the left. Photoshop provides a Desaturate command (Image>Adjust>Desaturate) which performs the same function.

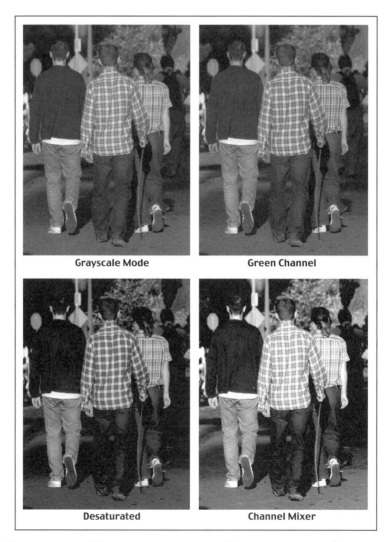

FIGURE *There are many different ways to convert a color image to grayscale. Here are*
14.11 *samples of the four methods discussed.*

Mix your Own Color Formula

As explained earlier, your image editor can convert your image to a Grayscale
mode by using a stock formula for combining the Red, Green, and Blue channels in your image. If that formula doesn't produce the image you want, you can
always mix your own combination using Photoshop's Channel Mixer
(Image>Adjust>Channel Mixer).

The Channel Mixer provides simple slider controls for adjusting how much of
each channel (in percentages) will be used to create the final image. Be sure to
check the Monochrome text box at the bottom of the dialog box. Be aware that

all three channels need to add up to 100%, or you'll lose luminance in your final image. Similarly, if your mixed channels add up to more than 100%, your image will brighten.

CREATING "HAND-TINTED" IMAGES

Hand tinting a photo is a painstaking process involving special tints and a lot of hard work. Fortunately, creating such an effect in your image editor is fairly painless and involves little, or no, painting skill.

The following techniques allow you to create a hand-painted look, or combination grayscale/color images. The following procedures assume that your image is already a grayscale image, either because it was shot that way, or because you converted it to grayscale using one of the techniques discussed above.

Painting with Light Opacity

The simplest way to tint an image is simply to paint over it using a brush with a very light (20% or lower) opacity. You can paint directly on to your image, but it will be very difficult to make changes or corrections later. A better option is to create a second layer to hold the paint. If you choose this approach, then set your brush to 100% opacity and change the opacity of the layer to 20%. This won't change the look of your results, but it will make it easier to resample the colors you're using later (you can simply set the layer opacity to 100% and then sample using the Eyedropper tool). You can even create separate layers for separate colors, making for easy color changes, as well as opacity control of each color.

One problem with this approach is that it tends to lighten up shadow areas and generally lessen the contrast of your image. You can try to put some of that contrast back by stacking a Levels adjustment layer on the very top of your image, or you can choose to use a blending mode for your paint layer. Setting your painting layers to Multiply mode will cause your painted strokes to be multiplied with the underlying tones in your image. Because multiplying usually produces darker tones, your painted colors will come out darker than you were expecting, so you might have to overcompensate by choosing lighter colors. However, most of the shadow and contrast information in your image will be preserved. Color Plate 10 was hand-painted using multiplied paintbrushes.

Painting Desaturated Images

The easiest way to produce a hand-colored look is to start with a real color picture. Shoot a color image and then add a Hue/Saturation adjustment layer. In the Hue/Saturation dialog box, drag the Saturation slider all the way to the left to desaturate the image to grayscale.

With the adjustment layer selected, click on a blackpaint brush and begin painting over the parts of your image that you would like to color. The paintbrush will mask those areas of the image, protecting them from the desaturation effect. Consequently, they'll return to their full saturation.

A fully saturated color element in the middle of a grayscale photo can sometimes look a little odd. After resaturating the elements of the image that you want colored, add another Hue/Saturation adjustment layer and apply a little desaturation to the whole image to tone down the color elements. (Or, sometimes it's better to *increase* the contrast between the color and grayscale areas. Use your new Hue/Saturation layer to increase the saturation of the color areas.)

Painting with the History Brush

You can use the History brush to perform a variation of the previous method. Take a color image, convert it to grayscale, and then convert the grayscale image back to RGB. You'll still have a grayscale image, but because it's in RGB mode, it will be able to handle color information.

Select Photoshop's History brush (available from the keyboard by pressing "Y") and begin painting the areas you would like colored. The History brush paints using the information stored in the last History snapshot (the History palette shows a thumbnail view of that snapshot). If you haven't intentionally set a new snapshot, then the History snapshot should be your original, color image.

As with the previous coloring scheme, you may end up with an image that has color elements that look a little conspicuous. Consider adding a Hue/Saturation adjustment layer and then dialing down the saturation.

ADDING TEXTURE, GRAIN, AND "FILM" LOOK

After spending all of that time and money choosing the right digital camera, why in the world would you want to go to the trouble of making your images look like they were shot on film? Despite all of the advantages of digital photography, film can have a texture and feel that is more attractive than what your digital camera might produce. And, although they may not be conscious of it, most people are very used to the look of film.

There might be also be times when you want to create a film-like look – possibly an old, beat-up film look – for stylistic purposes. Whatever the reason, there are a number of things you can do to make your digital images look more like film.

Before adding any texture or grain, take a look at the color and depth of field in your image. Professional film images are usually shot with larger cameras that afford a fine control over depth of field. Consider using one of the depth of field methods discussed earlier to shorten the depth of field in your image.

Many films have very particular color and contrast characteristics. Some produce images that are very saturated, while others yield colors that are more pastel. Most of the time you can probably choose a color quality based on personal taste. However, if the image will be presented with images shot with a particular kind of film, you might want to study that film with an eye toward mimicking its color characteristics. If you are trying to represent the look of a black and white film then you'll most likely want to use the Channel Mixing method of grayscale conversion. You might also have to spend some time adjusting contrast with Levels and Curves.

All of these adjustments need to be performed before you add any texture or grain as these effects can complicate your correction process.

ADDING GRAIN

Film images have a noticeable grain caused by the clumps and particles of silver halide that are used to form the image. Films with faster ISOs have more grain, and different brands and formulations of film have different quantities and qualities of grain. Grain might sound like a bad thing but it can actually be very beautiful, both for its inherent texture and because it serves to make the image a little more abstract, allowing the viewer's imagination to kick in.

The simplest way to add grain is with a noise filter. Photoshop includes a simple Add Noise command (Filter>Noise>Add Noise) that allows you to dial in different amounts of noise. (Figure 14.12).

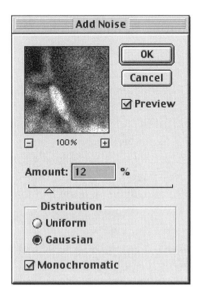

FIGURE   *With your image editor's noise filters, you can create simple film-like grain.*
14.12

Add Noise is a good choice for adding grain, but it does have limitations. First, it affects the entire image uniformly. Consequently, the resulting image can often look like it's being viewed through a simple "screen" of noise. Second, once you add noise, it's there to stay. As you saw in the last chapter, removing noise is very difficult.

TUTORIAL

ADDING GRAIN TO AN IMAGE

Although a simple Add Noise filter will let you add a layer of grain to an image, there is a better, more flexible method of achieving film-like noise in your digital pictures. Pick an image to which you would like to add grain, and then step through the following procedure.

STEP 1: CREATE A LAYER OF NOISE

First, you need some grain. Create a new layer in your document and fill it with 50% gray. You can do this in Photoshop by pressing Command-A (Control-A in Windows) to select the entire layer, and then choosing Edit>Fill. In the Fill dialog box, select 50% Gray from the Contents pop-up menu.

Now choose Filter>Noise>Add Noise. Select Gaussian Noise and check the Monochrome checkbox. The amount of noise to use depends partly on the size of your image and on how grainy you want the image to look. In general, though, 25-30% should be plenty.

After clicking OK, your image should look like a gray image full of noise. (Figure 14.13)

STEP 2: CHANGE THE BLENDING MODE

As discussed earlier, simply adding noise to your image applies the same amount of noise to every pixel, no matter how bright or dark. What's more, the noise added by the Add Noise filter is often a little too contrasty. The noise can end up looking like a layer of pixels sitting on the top of your image. We want to create a texture that will blend in with the pixels in your image.

With your noise layer selected, choose Soft Light from the Blending mode pop-up menu of the Layers palette. You should now see a very noisy version of your image.

STEP 3: LOWER THE NOISE OPACITY

As a last step, drop the opacity level on your noise level to about 25%. You should now have a very realistic-looking level of grain (Figure 14.14). You can also change the grain level by simply readjusting the opacity slider. Want to simulate a higher ISO film? Just increase the opacity. Note that you can also turn

FIGURE *A better way to add grain is to create a special noise layer and composite it with your*
14.13 *document. This will afford you more noise control and editability.*

the noise off altogether by unchecking the noise layer's eyeball icon, or by
deleting the layer altogether.

Adding Texture and Damage

You can add more complex textures to your images using a method similar to
the one described in the previous tutorial. First you need a texture such as
paper, wood, or stone. The best source for textures, of course, is your digital
camera. Although no substitute for a good scanner, it can still do a fine job of
photographing paper textures, wood surfaces, or stone. Clip-art libraries of these
types of textures are also available from stock photo agencies.

Once you've gotten your texture imported into your image editor, place it on
a layer above your image and use a Hard Light, Soft Light, or Multiply Blending
mode to merge the texture into your image. You'll typically need to set a very

FIGURE   *After compositing the noise layer using a Soft Light Blending mode and an opacity*
14.14   *adjustment, the image has a very realistic film-like grain.*

low opacity for your texture. If your texture is too strong, it will overpower your image.

Scratches, dirt, and other "damage" can be added by painting layers of damage onto a white canvas and then blending them into your image using a Multiply blending mode.

PREPARING TO PRINT

Photoshop is capable of much more than the few effects shown in this chapter. Hopefully, though, these tutorials have provided you with a few starting points for creating more complex effects as well as introducing you to some effects that digital photographers frequently need to perform.

By this point, you probably have some finished images that are ready for output. Whether your destination is paper, web, or video, the next chapter should help you with all of your outputting concerns.

Output

15

IN THIS CHAPTER

- Choosing a Printer
- Printing
- Web Output

At some point, you're going to be ready to get your pictures out of your image editor and into the real world. Whether you plan on delivering your images in print or via the web, CD-ROM, or video, you will need to take some care when you create your output. As you saw in Chapter 10, color can vary widely between devices, and you'll almost certainly find yourself returning to your color correction techniques to adjust your images for the vagaries of your target output device.

In this chapter you'll learn the specifics of those adjustments, as well as the particular concerns and issues that arise when you output to different media.

CHOOSING A PRINTER

After all of the work you've done in the preceding pages, you should be well-prepared for a discussion of printing. Fortunately, most of the color theory you learned when you were working with your camera will apply to your printer as well. This section begins with a discussion of the issues and questions you'll face when you buy a printer. Following that, you'll learn more about how to adjust your images for printing.

Your digital photography system isn't complete without a way to make prints, of course. Fortunately, today you can buy a very high-quality color printer for very little money. Even if most of your images are intended for a magazine, newspaper, or other professionally-printed material, you'll still probably want some kind of desktop printer for proofing and correction.

Your first choice when you shop for a printer is to choose a printing technology.

LASER PRINTERS

You're probably familiar with using a laser printer for printing text or simple graphics. If you already have a laser printer, or if you use one at work or at a service bureau, then you probably already know that laser printers are very speedy, quiet, and can produce very high-quality output.

Most laser printers also only print in black and white. If black and white output is your only concern, then a laser printer isn't a bad choice. However, your black and white laser printed output will be a far cry from a black and white photographic print – you won't be able to print on glossy paper and your image will not be *continuous tone*. That is, you'll be able to see the dots and patterns that the printer uses to create shades of gray. However, on a modern, high-resolution laser printer you'll have to examine your image very closely to see those dots.

If you are considering a black and white laser printer, then you'll want to select one with a high resolution – at least 600dpi, preferably 1200. Many laser printers also include special internal software for adjusting and correcting gray tones when you print. This built-in correction can prevent banding and other laser printing artifacts and usually results in a much smoother print.

If you're hoping to use your laser printer to create Xerox-able or printable masters, then you'll want a printer whose software lets you change the printer's line screen (more on line screens later). You'll also want to be able to deactivate any of the special gray tone correction routines inside the printer.

Color laser printers have been available for years, and have recently come down in price. Just like any other color printing process, color lasers work by passing the paper through the print mechanism up to four times, and applying a different color with each pass. Until recently, color laser printers produced output with a very characteristic "sheen" that smacked of color copying. Current printers do a much better job, even on plain paper, and can produce an image that looks like it was pulled out of a magazine. A magazine photo is a far cry from a photographic print, though, both in terms of texture, finish, and image quality.

Unfortunately, one of the most notable characteristics of a laser printer is price. Even a black and white laser printer will be much more expensive than an inkjet, and a color laser printer will cost you several thousand dollars. On the upside, your cost per print will be much lower than inkjet printing, so if mass production is your goal, then a laser printer might be worth the extra money.

Whether you are buying a color or a black and white laser printer, your main concern should be image quality. Look at lots of output samples and pay attention to how well the printer reproduces color and make sure that it can reproduce all color ranges (reds, blues, purples, etc.) equally. Also look for artifacts – dots and patterns – throughout the print, but especially in the highlights and shadows. Finally, you'll want to check compatibility with your operating system, hardware, and image editing software and, if you have any special networking concerns (for workgroup use, let's say) then you'll want to evaluate the printer's networking options.

Laser printers are good choices for business printing or mass production. For fine art or hobbiest photography, they're really not appropriate.

DYE-SUBLIMATION PRINTERS

Sublimation is the process of converting a solid into a gas without passing it through a liquid stage (dry ice sublimes at room temperature, melting from a solid block into vapor without becoming liquid). A dye-sublimation printer (also called simply a dye-sub) works by using special solid dyes that can be sublimed into a gas that adheres directly to special paper.

The advantage of a dye-sub printer is that it is truly continuous tone. That is, no dots or patterns will be visible in your final print because the ink hits the paper in a diffuse, gaseous form. Dye-sub paper also looks like real photo paper, giving your prints a true "photo finish."

The downside to dye-sub printers is that they can be a little soft. The same soft, diffuse property that creates continuous tone also means that it's hard for a dye-sub printer to produce a very hard edge. Dye-sub printers are also a tad slow when you compare them to inkjets or laser printers, and they typically have a high cost per print because of their expensive, proprietary media. Also, if you're looking for a printer that can be used for other tasks – printing text, for example – then a dye-sub is definitely not for you.

That said, a dye-sub printer is a great way to go if photo-quality is your highest concern. In addition to their photo-like appearance, many dye-sub printers coat their prints with a special ultraviolet layer to protect the prints from fading and discoloring.

As with other printing technologies, when you shop for a dye-sub printer, image quality should be your highest concern. Try to look at a variety of samples that cover a full range of color and detail levels as well as a full assortment of light and shadow. Dye-sub resolutions are typically lower than laser printer or inkjet resolutions due to the nature of their printing method. 300 and 400dpi printers are common and perfectly acceptable.

Make sure the printer provides the necessary connections for your computer, and that its driver software is compatible with your operating system.

INKJET PRINTERS

The best all-around photo printing solution is a color inkjet printer. Inkjets work by shooting a tiny (*really* tiny – most inkjets use a drop that is only a few picoliters) drop of ink out of a nozzle. Think of an inkjet printer as a bunch of tiny graffiti artists spray-painting your image onto the page.

Inkjet printers have a number of advantages over other printing technologies. They typically have a bigger color gamut than a laser printer, they can produce sharper images than a dye-sub printer, and they can print many more kinds of media than can either a laser or dye-sub printer. They're also often faster than laser or dye-sub because they can lay down a full-color image in a single pass. With the right paper, a good inkjet printer can create an image that's indistinguishable from a photographic print.

Inkjet printers are typically far cheaper than a laser, or even a dye-sub, although their cost per print can be expensive – up to $2/page for a photo-quality print. However, because of their flexibility in handling different media, you can also create lower-quality, less-expensive prints.

Inkjet printers can currently be divided into two major categories: 4-color printers and 6-color printers. Four-color printers use the same cyan, magenta, yellow, and black colors that an offset printing press uses. Six-color printers add an extra cyan and extra magenta cartridge to beef up the dark tones and provide smoother light tones.

Your first decision when you choose an inkjet printer, then, is to decide what type of printing you want to do. If you want a general-purpose printer capable of printing good images and text, then you'll need to go with a 4-color printer. If photo-quality printing is your highest concern, then you'll definitely want to go with a 6-color printer. If this sounds like a difficult choice, be aware that a 4-color printer can do a very good job of printing photo-quality prints, especially when it is used with quality paper. However, a 6-color printer will be able to do a better job of printing lighter colors and will be able to achieve better dynamic range in the darker tones.

If you choose a 6-color printer, then you'll next need to decide if you want a printer that can produce archival-quality prints. The dye-based inks used by the typical inkjet printer are not very durable. Print an image, hang it in direct sunlight, and it will be noticeably faded and discolored within a few weeks. Even if you stick the image in a photo album it will still discolor and fade, as dye-based inks are greatly affected by humidity.

Pigment-based inks are far more durable and are typically shown to last anywhere from 20 to 200 years. If fine-art printing is your primary application – and certainly it is if you hope to sell your prints – then it's worth spending the extra money for an archival-quality printer. If you are more of a hobbiest – that is, if you'll be making prints for your own enjoyment and for giving to family and friends – then a non-archival, dye-based inkjet should be fine.

You'll also want to consider paper size when you choose an inkjet. Although most printers offer standard letter-size printing, you can also get models (with 4four six colors, dye-based or archival) that print larger. Larger desktop inkjet printers typically support sizes up to 13 x 19 inches (also known as A3 or SuperA3 size). Although a standard letter-size printer is capable of printing an 8 x 10" print, if you're interested in fine-art printing, you may want to go for a larger printer. You'll pay more for the extra size, of course - usually about twice as much.

TIP

Really Big Printing. *If you need to print really big images with print sizes over 13 x 19", then you'll need to go with a large-format printer. These giant inkjet printers range in size from 24" wide to over 50" wide and typically accept sheets or rolls of paper, allowing you to create huge images. They also come with huge price tags. Don't expect to get a large-format printer for under $2,000. For more information, see www.completedigitalphotography.com/largeformat.*

Inkjet printers come in a number of different resolutions and, certainly, a higher resolution is often better. However, as with cameras, it's important not to get hung up on the printer's resolution as the final arbiter of print quality. There are many things that determine the quality of a printer, and a printer with a higher resolution won't necessarily do a better job than a lower-resolution competitor.

When you choose a printer, you'll want to look at a lot of output, including output on different kind of media. Try to find samples printed on the paper you think you're most likely to use. If you think you're going to do most of your printing on ordinary copier paper (not the best choice), then you'll want to look closely at the printer's plain-paper printing ability. If quality is your highest concern, then you'll want to examine output printed on photo-quality glossy paper. If you have special printing needs – the ability to print on watercolor paper or cloth, for example – then be sure to examine output on those media as well. Just because a printer prints well on one kind of media doesn't mean it will do as well on another.

Of course, you'll want to determine if the printer provides the type of connectivity and networking that your computer requires, and you'll want to be certain that it includes a driver for your operating system. Print speed can vary greatly from model to model and from quality setting to quality setting, so if you think you have speed concerns (perhaps you need to print a high volume) then you'll want to assess the printer's print speed.

Once you've got a printer, you'll then want to consider the various ink and paper choices that are available. Typically you'll want to experiment with different kinds of media, as each will have its own imaging characteristics.

MEDIA SELECTION

You can, of course, stick any old paper in your printer, including the normal 20-pound copier paper that one typically uses for office correspondence. However, paper choice can have a huge bearing on the quality of your final image. In addition to providing a more photo-like finish, different papers respond very differently to your printer's ink. For example, some papers absorb more ink than others, resulting in colors that are more muted and muddy than what you'd get from a paper with a more "opaque" finish.

Some papers are also brighter than others, which will often yield brighter prints, while other papers will have a gloss or finish that results in a more continuous tone print and a more photo-like finish. Finally, there are papers with very unique, complex textures such as watercolor paper or handmade papers. These papers typically produce prints with darker colors and strange color textures. In addition to the texture of the paper itself, coarser papers typically absorb ink in very unique ways, resulting in smears and smudges that can be very pretty.

In general, you'll want to experiment with your paper selections to find out what works best for your intended output. Be *certain* to read your printer's manual before you shove an experimental piece of paper through your printer. Most printers have thickness limits and many printers – particularly archival-quality printers – can be damaged if you use media that wasn't specifically designed for the printer.

To get the best quality, you'll want to stick with a paper that was specially formulated for your printer. Epson printers, for example, include settings for specific types of Epson-manufactured paper. Because the printer driver knows exactly what kind of paper you're using, it can do a much better job of laying down a good image.

If archival quality is your highest concern, then you'll want to choose an archival paper. Print longevity is not determined only by the ink that you're using. Special archival papers will also greatly extend the life of your prints. If longevity is your greatest concern, you'll want to shop for the appropriate paper.

INK CHOICE

In general, you should always buy ink manufactured and certified by your printer manufacturer. There are cheaper, third-party inks out there, and these frequently work just fine. However, it's important to know that your printer head can be damaged by the ink that passes through it. More important, though, your printer driver needs to know that the ink formulations in your printer will mix and blend in a particular way. If you use a third-party ink, there's no guarantee that they will have mixed their ink correctly.

There are, however, some third-party inks that work very well and are worthy of consideration. Special archival inks manufactured by Lysen (www.completedigitalphotography.com/archivalinks) let you upgrade certain non-archival printers to archival quality. In addition to their longevity, these inks offer very good color gamuts, and performance that is often equal to the manufacturer-branded inks that they're replacing.

If you do a lot of black and white printing, then you might want to consider a set of quad-tone inks. Typically, the black ink included in a normal 4-color or 6-color printer doesn't allow for a full range of grayscale printing. Printer manufacturers get around this by trying to blend all four (or six) ink colors to create shades of gray. Unfortunately, this approach usually doesn't yield a full range of gray, and often produces a black and white image with a bad color cast.

High-quality black and white commercial printing – the kind used to print black and white photography books, for example – often uses combinations of multiple shades of black or gray ink. Such ink sets are also available for desktop inkjet printers. Typically, these quad-tone ink sets provide four shades of black ink and special drivers for printing black and white images. Check out www.completedigitalphotography.com/quadtone for more info on this type of printing.

PRINTING

Once you've color corrected, edited, adjusted, tweaked, and obsessed over your image, you might be ready to try printing it out to see what it looks like on paper. Although you can simply load your printer with paper and choose the Print command in your image editor, to get the best results, you're probably going to need to print a few test prints and do a little futzing with your image.

In Chapter 13 you learned that you should resize your image after you've performed all of your edits, but before you've sharpened. (If you're unsure of how to resize an image, you might want to re-read the section on scaling in Chapter 13.) What size to make your image, though depends largely on your printer. You can simply decide: I want an 8 x 10" image. However, your camera may not provide enough resolution to print at that size. To determine the optimal print size for your image, you need to know the optimal resolution for your printer.

CHOOSING A RESOLUTION

Before you can resize an image, (as discussed in Chapter 13) you need to know the resolution that is best for your printer. Different printing technologies have different resolution requirements, so calculating optimal resolution differs from printer type to printer type.

No matter what type of printer you use, it's important to remember one fundamental difference between your computer monitor and your printer: your computer monitor can display a single pixel that can be any one of millions of colors; your color printer, on the other hand, can print a single dot that is any one of *four* colors. In other words, there is not a one-to-one correspondence between a pixel on your screen and a dot on paper. If a pixel on your screen is defined as being dark purple, your printer has to print a combination of fifty different cyan, magenta, yellow, and black dots, all in a special pattern to reproduce that one purple dot from your monitor.

So, although your printer may claim to have 1200 dots per inch of resolution, these are 1200 printer *dots*, not 1200 pixels. Choosing a resolution, then, is dependent on how the printer collects printer dots to reproduce pixels.

Choosing a Resolution for a Laser Printer

Laser printers generate different tones – both gray tones and color tones – through a process called *halftoning*, the same method used to generate images in your local newspaper. Using traditional methods, halftoning is performed by shooting a photo of an image through a special halftone screen. The resulting photo gets broken down by the screen into a pattern of dots that can be easily printed using a single ink. For color printing, four pictures of the image are taken, each through a halftone screen and color filter. The result is four plates that can each be printed using a different color of ink.

Halftoned images are really just huge conglomerations of small patterns of dots. So, for example, to represent 40% gray, a special pattern of dots are used, for 60% gray, a different pattern. (Figure 15.1) When you stand far enough from the image, the dots blur together into smooth patterns of tone. How big the dots are depends on the frequency of the screen — that is, how tightly the screen is woven.

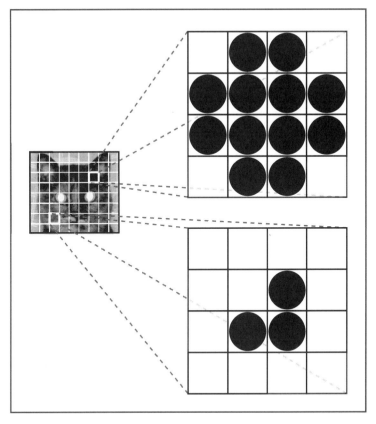

FIGURE   *A single pixel in your image corresponds to a pattern of dots on your printer. Each of*
15.1   *these halftone patterns is used to represent a pixel of a particular gray shade or color.*

When you print an image on your laser printer, the computer sends the printer its color pixel information. The printer (or the printer driver software) then figures out how to represent each dot of color using a halftone dot pattern.

Just as traditional, photo-based halftoning uses a halftone screen of a particular frequency, your laser printer bases its halftone calculations on a *line screen frequency*. For high-resolution printing (1200dpi or higher) this screen frequency is typically 133 or 166 lines per inch. This is a very fine screen that produces a magazine-quality image.

Lower-resolution printers (300 to 600) typically use a much coarser screen, usually around 85 to 100 lines per inch. Many laser printers (and most high-resolution image setters) let you specify a line screen.

Why does this matter? Because different line screens require images of different resolutions. Typically, the rule for resolution (as measured in dpi) is that your image should be 1.5 to 2 times your line screen. In other words, if your printer uses a 133-line screen, then your image needs to have a resolution of 200 to 266 dots per inch.

So, for example, if you have a laser printer that requires 200 dpi images (because it uses a 133 line screen) and you have a 2-megapixel camera that produces 1600 x 1200 pixel images, then you can print your image at 8 x 6" at 200 dots per inch – 1600/200 = 8 inches wide; 1200 /200 = 6 inches high.

Let's say, though, that you want to print an image that can be copied on a photocopier. Images for photocopying typically need to be printed with a much coarser line screen, usually around 85 lines per inch, which means your image only needs to be around 150dpi. At this resolution, the same 2-megapixel image could be printed at 10.5 x 8". (An 85-line screen is also appropriate for newspaper or phone book printing.)

Remember that, when you print to a laser printer, it's best to turn off any special gray tone correction features the printer may have.

CHOOSING A RESOLUTION FOR AN INKJET PRINTER

Inkjet printers don't use the halftone screens that a laser printer uses. Rather, they use special mezzogram patterns that are much more random than halftone screens. As such, an inkjet printer doesn't really have a screen frequency. Typically, on any inkjet printer, even a high-resolution 1200 or 1400dpi inkjet printer, your image doesn't need to be any higher than 240 dots per inch. Although you can send a higher resolution image to the printer, you probably won't notice any difference in quality, and your print times will be much longer.

At 240 dots per inch, your 2-megapixel image drops to a 5 x 6" print size. However, you can usually go down as low as 200 dots per inch (8 x 6" using the previous example) with hardly any loss in quality.

Paper quality is also a contributing factor to resolution choice. If you're printing on lousy paper, then you might be able to get away with going to a much lower resolution. The lack of resolution will often be hidden by the fact that the ink will bleed and smear when it hits the paper. Conversely, if you're using a higher-quality paper that does a better job of holding a dot, then you'll need to stick with a higher-resolution image.

CORRECTING YOUR IMAGE FOR PRINT

Once you've chosen a resolution, and corresponding print size, then you're ready to start thinking about how your image needs to be corrected for your particular printer. As you may have already discovered, images usually don't look the same on the printed page as they do on-screen. Partly this is the simple difference of looking at an image on a piece of paper as compared to looking at an image on a computer screen.

As discussed earlier, however, there are other complications as well, mostly stemming from the difficulty of converting colors represented by red, green, and blue light into colors represented by cyan, magenta, and yellow ink.

Whatever the reasons, you're going to need to make some adjustments to your image to get it to print the way you like. There are a couple of ways to make these adjustments. If you're working in Photoshop, you can simply throw an adjustment layer (or two) onto the top of your image. As you create test prints and refine your corrections, you can easily go back and tweak your adjustment layers.

If you're working in an image editor that doesn't provide adjustment layers, then save a copy of your image and use it as your printable image. If your image has many layers, you should flatten the image into a single layer before saving your printing copy, as any corrections you need to make will need to be made to the image as a whole.

Targeting the Tonal Range

You've probably already done a bunch of work to get the tone and contrast range of your image adjusted. Although the black point, white point, and gamma adjustments that you learned about in Chapter 13 have probably produced images that look good on your screen, they don't necessarily represent a contrast and tonal range that your printer is capable of printing. Fortunately, there's a pretty simple way to compress or *target* the tonal range of your image to fit your printer.

Your computer display has a bigger gamut of colors than does your printer, and most of the colors that your printer *cannot* print are in the shadow and highlight areas. Simply put, there are limits to the lightest and darkest dots that your printer can hold. If the shadow and highlight tones in your image are beyond the limits of what your printer can print, then your image prints poorly. Typically, highlights will posterize while shadows will turn to mud. (Figure 15.2)

In Chapter 12, you used the Output sliders in Photoshop's Levels dialog box to lighten an image to create an effect. We're going to return to the Output sliders now to compress the tonal range of the image into the acceptable tonal range of a printer.

FIGURE *The upper image in this figure was not targeted for this book's printing press.*
15.2 *The lower image was.*

TARGETING AN IMAGE

TUTORIAL

Although your images may look great on-screen, your printed images may often leave you unpleasantly surprised. Unfortunately, your computer monitor is capable of displaying many more colors than can your printer. Through targeting, you can adjust the tonal range in your image so that it better matches the capability of your printer.

In this tutorial, you're going to target an image for an offset printing press.

STEP 1 OPEN THE IMAGE

ON THE CD

We're going to return to an image you worked with in Chapter 11. Open the greenhouse.psd image located in the tutorials>chapter 15>targeting folder of the Complete Digital Photography CD-ROM.

Figure 15.3 shows the untargeted image. If you look at the image on-screen, you'll see that it is not nearly as dark as this printed version and has much better tone and contrast range. The printing process darkened up the image and in the process messed up the contrast.

FIGURE *Before targeting, the shadows in this image are way too dark.*
15.3

STEP 2: TALK TO YOUR PRINTER

At this stage, you would want to find out from your printer the minimum and maximum ink densities that their offset printing press can hold. In other words, what are the lightest and darkest dots that the press can hold. Typically, they'll respond with something like 5% and 95%. That is, the lightest tone the printer can print is 5% gray while the darkest is 95% gray. Anything brighter than that will simply be the white of the paper. If you're printing to newsprint or another low-quality paper, you may see numbers more like 15% and 85%.

Paper white is fine for the *specular highlights* in your image - the bright white glints and reflections that occur on very shiny surfaces and on the edges of objects. However, if the brightest spot a printer can make is 15%, then there will be a sudden change from 15% gray to paper white, which will appear as posterization in the highlights of your image. It's better to keep your white areas confined to what's printable so as to maintain control of your highlight areas.

STEP 3: TARGET THE IMAGE

The image already has two adjustment layers that serve to correct and adjust its tonal values. Add a Levels adjustment layer to the top of the layer stack. As you've already learned, the histogram in the Levels dialog box is a graph of the 256 tones in your image. We want to set the black Output slider (which currently has a value of 0) to 95%, or 13 (255-(255 x .95)). Drag the left Output slider until it reads 13. (Figure 15.4)

The white Output slider should be 5%, or 243 (255-(255 x .05)). Slide it into place.

FIGURE *After targeting, your Levels adjustment layer should look like this.*
15.4

STEP 4: EVALUATE THE IMAGE

You may think the image looks rather flat now and, certainly, it will have much less contrast than it had before. However, when it is printed, all of the tones are going to go darker at the low end, as the ink is absorbed into the paper. At the high end, this adjustment will hopefully protect your highlights (white points) from posterizing and blowing out to completely white. (Figure 15.5)

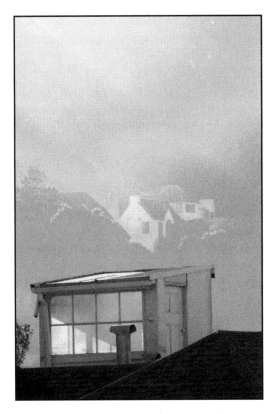

FIGURE   *After targeting, the image prints much better.*
15.5

On many images, you'll be able to perform your tonal adjustments and targeting with a single Levels command – perform your tonal corrections with the Input sliders and your targeting with the Output sliders. In this image, though, we needed a Curves adjustment between our tonal correction and image targeting.

Targeting a Desktop Printer

Targeting for your desktop printer – whether it be an inkjet, laser, or dye-sub – works exactly the same way. The only difference is, there's usually no one you can talk to about target ink densities. With some careful experimentation and observation, you should be able to determine appropriate ink densities for your target values.

Be aware that different papers will have very different minimum and maximum ink densities. As you become more experienced with targeting, you may realize that you prefer some papers over others because of their ability to hold different ink densities.

USING YOUR COLOR MANAGEMENT SYSTEM WHEN YOU PRINT

If you've been using a color management system for your editing work (see Chapter 10 for more information), then you hopefully have an appropriate printer profile installed and configured. You can use this profile for generating soft proofs as explained in Chapter 10, and you can also use it when you print from Photoshop to help ensure that the colors that come out of your printer match what's on your screen.

After selecting Print, simply choose the appropriate profile from the Profile pop-up menu located in the Print Space section of the dialog box. (Figure 15.6)

FIGURE
15.6
From Photoshop's Print dialog, you can select the appropriate printing profile for your target printer.

WEB-BASED PRINTING

There are a number of web sites that offer photo printing services. After uploading your images to these sites, they will print the images and mail them back to you. These services typically use pictrographic processes – traditional chemical-based photographic processes that expose a piece of photographic paper using a laser or LED device.

The advantage to these services is that they offer you a path to true photo quality – photo paper and continuous tone – from your digital camera. In addition, these prints are more archival than what will come out of a desktop printer, and will usually offer a lifespan of 20 years or so.

The downside is that you have to wait for your prints, and you don't know what sort of color and tonal corrections the service will make to your images. In other words, what you see on your screen may not be close to what you get in your prints. Typically, a particular printing service will be consistent about the type of adjustments that they make to their images. So, once you've figured out that prints from a service always come out green, then you can adjust your images accordingly before you submit them.

Pay close attention to a service's cropping guidelines. Some services will blow up your image to fill an entire print. If your original was a different aspect ratio than the final print, then your image will be cropped. Most services allow the option of blowing up to full print size, or padding the image to preserve your original aspect ratio.

Most services also provide photo sharing facilities. When you upload images for printing, you are usually allowed to create one or more photo albums. You can then send the address of these albums to other people who can view your images and, if they want, order prints. This can be a much faster way of distributing photos to a group of people over the web, as you only have to upload your images once. It can also save you the hassle of preparing prints for a bunch of people. They can simply order their own.

Finally, most services offer much more than simple paper printing. Coffee mugs, T-shirts, banners, cakes, and cookies can all be adorned with your photographs.

For a list of services – and recommendations – check out www.completedigitalphotography.com/webprinting.

WEB OUTPUT

Fortunately, web output is much simpler than outputting to print. Unfortunately, this is because there simply are no color controls for the web. Because there's nothing you can do but post your images and hope that your viewers are using decent monitors, you don't need to spend any time adjusting or preparing the color in your images.

Your main concern when you prepare an image for the web (or for e-mail) is file size. You probably already know what it's like to wait for a large image to download, either from the web, or from your mail server. Don't inflict the same thing on other people by posting or e-mailing really large files. Obviously, if you and your recipient have high-speed connections, then you can probably get away with creating larger files. Be aware, however, that the mail servers provided by many Internet service providers put a limit on the maximum size of an e-mail attachment. If you absolutely *have* to e-mail a large image to someone, consider segmenting it using a file compression utility.

Fortunately, images for the web tend to be very small. Most users don't have screens that are wider than 800 pixels, and most web images clock in around 300 or 400 pixels wide. Save a copy of your image (be careful not to recompress it) and resize it to an appropriate pixel size. Be sure to set the resolution to 72dpi.

The two most common graphics file formats on the web are GIF and JPEG. For photos, JPEG is really the only format you need to use. JPEG allows for varying degrees of compression and the more compression, the greater your image quality will degrade. Fortunately, Photoshop offers an excellent Save For Web option that lets you experiment with different JPEG compressions and compare the effects of different compression settings side-by-side. (Figure 15.7)

FIGURE *Photoshop's Save For Web feature makes it simple to try out different JPEG settings to*
15.7 *balance size and quality.*

If you're sending your images to someone else for them to post on their web site, consider sending them an uncompressed image. They may have their own size and compression requirements and so will want to perform their own resizing and compression. If you send them an uncompressed file, they'll be able to compress it to their specifications without introducing further image degradation.

CONCLUSION

Once you start using a digital camera, it's hard to imagine that film cameras have much of a future. Not because film cameras produce inferior results, but simply because digital cameras provide such enormous creative flexibility. Hopefully, this book has helped you understand more about the specific issues and concerns you'll face when you shoot digital as well as providing you with solutions for working around those concerns.

Your next step? Start shooting and editing! Your skill with both your camera and image editor will greatly improve as you shoot more and more pictures. Take your camera with you wherever you go and don't hesitate to fire away.

And, if you'd like to read some more about photography in general, take a look at the suggested reading list in Appendix A.

Suggested Reading

The following list will provide you with further reading on the "artistry" of photography, as well as on more specifics of digital editing and retouching.

The Camera (Ansel Adams Photography, Book 1) **by Ansel Adams, Robert Baker**. Excellent coverage of camera and photography basics. If you want to know more about exposure – particularly the zone system – this is a great place to start.

Examples: The Making of 40 Photographs **by Ansel Adams.** Whether or not you like his photos, reading details about his photographic process can be an invaluable way to learn how to think and see like a photographer.

The Ansel Adams Guide: Book 1: Basic Techniques of Photography **by John P. Schaefe**r. Written by one of the trustees of the Ansel Adams archives, this book provides a very thorough overview of the entire photographic process from cameras to developing to printing.

On Photography **by Susan Sontag.** An excellent series of essays discussing the effects that photography has had on our way of seeing the world. A must-read for any would-be photographer.

Understanding Comics **by Scott McCloud.** Essential reading for anyone who engages in any type of visual storytelling. In the form of a 200-page comic book, McCloud covers the basics of the visual literacy of comics and, in the process, presents a lot of valuable information for photographers.

Real World Photoshop **by David Blatner and Bruce Fraser.** If you want to know more about color management and printing, this is the book to read. Provides technical details for preparing your images for printing on any kind of output device.

The Rebel Angels **by Robertson Davies.** Has nothing at all to do with photography, but a very good novel, all the same.

B About the CD-ROM

ABOUT THIS CD

Whether you're a Mac or Windows user, you shouldn't have any trouble finding your way around the Complete Digital Photography CD-ROM.

IMAGES contains all of the image files from the book, many in full-color. These images can be viewed on-screen, or printed out for closer examination. Most of the figures are in PDF format and can be viewed using the Adobe Acrobat reader, included in the Software folder. Many of the sample photos are included in Photoshop and TIFF format rather than in PDF. Images are arranged in folders by chapter, and are labeled with the same figure numbers as shown in the book

TUTORIALS contains all of the files you need to complete the book's tutorials. As with images, tutorials are grouped into folders by chapter.

SOFTWARE contains demo versions of many popular applications.

Macintosh:

- Adobe Photoshop 6. If you don't already have a copy of Photoshop, you can use this demo to follow along with the tutorials in the book.
- DigiEffects Web Euphoria. This collection of Photoshop plug-ins can add all sorts of cool effects and edits to your images.
- iView Media Pro 2.0. This image cataloging app can help you keep track of your digital image library.
- nikColorEffects. This demo version of nikColorEffects lets you perform sophisticated color corrections with the click of a button.
- nikSharpenerPro. This demo version of nikSharpenerPro provides intelligent sharpening complete with batch processing.
- PhotoGenetics and Quantum Mechanic. Be sure to check out these power image-processing apps.

Windows:

- Adobe Photoshop 6. If you don't already have a copy of Photoshop, you can use this demo to follow along with the tutorials in the book.
- DigiEffects AgedFilm. Make your pictures look old, faded, scratched, and stylized with this Photoshop plug-in from DigiEffects.
- nikColorEffects. This demo version of nikColorEffects lets you perform sophisticated color corrections with the click of a button.
- nikSharpenerPro. This demo version of nikSharpenerPro provides intelligent sharpening complete with batch processing.

- PhotoGenetics, Quantum Mechanic, and Qimage Pro. Be sure to check out these power image-processing apps.

Recommended System Requirements

Macintosh: PowerPC-based Mac with 64 MB of RAM and 200 MB of free disc space; System 8.5 or later; Color monitor with 256-color (8-bit) or greater video card; Monitor resolution of 800 x 600 or greater; CD-ROM drive

Windows: Pentium processor with 64 MB of RAM and 200 MB of free disk space; Windows 98, Millenium, 2000, or NT 4.0; Color monitor with 256-color (8-bit) or greater video card; Monitor resolution of 800 x 600 or greater; CD-ROM drive

Glossary

1-bit image – An image composed of pixels that are either black or white. Called 1-bit (or single-bit) because only one bit of information is required for each pixel.

8-bit image – An image that uses 8 bits of data for each pixel. Because you can count from 0 to 255, a pixel can be any one of 256 different colors.

24-bit image – An image that uses 24 bits of data for each pixel. Because you can count from 0 to roughly 16-and-a-half million, a pixel can be any one of 16.5 million colors.

32-bit image – An image that uses 24 bits of data to store the color of each pixel and an additional 8 bits of data to store how opaque each pixel is. This transparency information is called an *alpha channel.*

35mm equivalency – What a lens would be equivalent to in terms of a standard 35mm SLR camera. Used as a standard for discussing the field of view and magnification power of a lens. In 35mm equivalency, lenses over 50mm are telephoto while lenses below 50mm are wide-angle or fisheye.

Aberrations – Irregularities in a piece of glass that cause light to be focused incorrectly. Aberrations produce artifacts and anomalies in images.

Acquire plug-in – A special type of *plug-in* that allows for communication between your image editing application and your digital camera.

Action safe area – The area of a video image that will most likely be visible on any video monitor. Essential action should be kept within the action safe area, as action that falls outside might be cropped by the viewer's screen. See *title safe*.

Active autofocus – An autofocus mechanism that achieves focus by transmitting something into the scene, usually infrared light or sonar.

Additive – Light mixes together in an *additive* process whereby, as colors are mixed, they get brighter – that is, light is added as the colors are mixed. Additive colors eventually produce white. Red, green, and blue are the primary additive colors that can be used to create all other colors.

Adjustment layers - Let you apply Levels, Curves, and many other image correction functions as a layer, allowing you to remove or adjust the effect at any time.

Aliasing – The stair-stepping patterns that can appear along the edges of diagonal lines in an image.

Alpha channel – Extra information stored about the pixels in an image. Alpha channels are used to store transparency information. This information can serve as a mask for compositing or applying effects.

Analog - As regards photography, light in the real world travels in a continuous wave. To record those continuous analog waves, your digital camera must first convert them into a series of numbers, or digits.

Aperture – An opening that is used to control the amount of light passing through the lens of a camera. Typically constructed as an expanding and contracting *iris*.

Aperture priority – A shooting mode on a camera. Aperture priority lets you define the camera's aperture. The camera will then calculate a corresponding shutter speed based on its light metering.

APS - Advanced Photography System. A fairly new format of film and cameras.

Artifacts - Image degradations caused by image processing operations. Compressing an image, for example, often results in the creation of many image compression artifacts. Different image processing tasks create different types of artifacts.

ASA - A measure of film speed. See also *ISO*.

Aspect ratio – The ratio of an image's length to its width. Most computer screens and digital cameras shoot images that have an aspect ratio of 4:3. 35mm film and some digital cameras shoot in a 3:2 aspect ratio.

Aspherical – A lens that contains some elements that are not perfect hemispheres. These non-spherical elements are used to correct certain types of aberrations.

Auto-bracketing – Some cameras include special functions that cause them to automatically shoot a series of bracketed images when you press the shutter release.

Autofocus assist lamp - See *focus assist lamp*.

Automatic exposure - A feature which will automatically calculate the appropriate shutter speed, aperture, and sometimes ISO at the time you take a picture.

Backs - In a medium, or large-format camera, the film is held in the back of the camera. The back can be removed and replaced with other backs, including digital backs.

Barrel distortion – A type of distortion caused by a lens. Causes the edges of an image to bow outward. Most prevalent in wide-angle and fisheye lenses. See also *pincushion distortion*.

Bayer Pattern – The most common color filter array.

Bicubic interpolation – A method of interpolation used in a resampling process. Usually the best interpolation choice when you scale an image.

Bilinear interpolation – A method of interpolation used in a resampling process.

Bit depth – A measure of the number of bits stored for each pixel in an image. Images with higher bit depths contain greater numbers of colors. Also known as *color depth*.

Black and white - In the film world, "black and white" is used to refer to images that lack color – that is, images that are composed of only shades of gray. In the digital world, it's usually better to refer to such images as "grayscale" as your computer is also capable of creating images composed only of black and white pixels.

Blending mode – A setting that determines how the pixels in composited layers blend together. Also known as *transfer mode*.

Blooming – A flaring, smearing artifact in a digital photo caused by a photosite on the camera's CCD getting overcharged. The extra charge spills into the neighboring photosites and creates the artifact.

Boot time – How quickly (or slowly, depending on the camera) the camera will be ready to shoot after powering up.

Bracketing – The process of shooting additional frames of an image, each over or underexposed. By intelligently bracketing your shots, you stand a better chance of getting the image you want.

Bulb mode – A special shutter mode that opens the shutter for as long as you hold down the shutter release button.

Burst – See *drive*.

Catchlight – The white highlight that appears in people's eyes.

CCD – Charge-coupled device, the image sensor used in most digital cameras.

Center-weight metering – A light metering system similar to *matrix metering*, but that lends more analytical weight to the center of the image.

Channel – One component of a color image. Different channels of color are combined to produce a full color image. For example: red, green, and blue channels are combined by your monitor or digital camera to create a full-color picture. Also known as *color channel*.

Chromatic aberrations – Color artifacts caused by the inability of a lens to evenly focus all frequencies of light. Usually appears as colored fringes around high-contrast areas in a scene. See also *purple fringing*.

Chrominance – Color information.

Clipping – When highlights or shadows suddenly cut off to completely white or black in an image, rather than fading smoothly.

Clone - See *Rubber Stamp*.

CMOS – Complimentary Metal Oxide Semiconductor. A type of image sensor. Not yet widely-used, but offers the promise of better image quality, lower cost and lower power-consumption than a CCD.

CMS – See *Color management system*.

CMYK – Cyan, magenta, yellow, and black, the primary subtractive colors that are used by a printing process to create all other colors. Although cyan, magenta, and yellow are subtractive primaries, it is impossible to create perfectly pure pigments. So, black ink must be added to create true blacks and darker colors.

Coating – Special chemicals applied to a lens that serve to reduce flares and reflection.

Color calibration - The process of calibrating your input and output devices, as well as your monitor, so that color is accurately displayed on each.

Color channel – See *channel*.

Color depth - See *bit depth*.

Color filter array – The colored filters that are placed over the photosites on an image sensor. Because image sensors can only "see" in grayscale, a color filter array is required for them to capture color information.

Color gamut – The range of colors that can be described by a particular color model. Also known as *gamut* or *color space*.

Color Management System (CMS) – A set of software components that work together to compensate for the differences in your monitor, printer, and scanner so that your images appear as accurately as possible on your display.

Color matching engine – The software component of a color matching system that performs the translations from one color space to another.

Color model – A method of representing color. RGB, CMYK, and Lab are all color models and each takes a different approach to representing color. Also see *color gamut.*

Color space – See color gamut.

Color temperature – Different lights shine at different temperatures, measured in degrees Kelvin (°K). Each temperature has a different color quality.

CompactFlash – A type of reusable, removable storage. The most common form of storage used in digital cameras.

Compositing - The process of layering images on top of each other to create composite images. Compositing is used for everything from creating simple collages to performing complex image correction and adjustment.

Continuous Mode – See *drive.*

Continuous autofocus – An autofocus mechanism that constantly refocuses as new objects move into its focusing zone.

Continuous tone - A printed image that is made up of continuous areas of printed color. Photographic film prints are continuous tone. Inkjet printers, laser printers and offset presses use printing methods that don't print continuous tone. If you look closely at a print from one of these devices, you can see that it is made up of small patterns of dots.

Contrast detection – An autofocus mechanism that determines focus by measuring contrast in a scene. The mechanism assumes that maximum contrast means sharpest focus. Contrast detection is a method of *passive autofocus.*

Contrast filters - Filters that you can add to the end of a lens to increase contrast in an image.

Contrast ratios - The ratio of the darkest to lightest tones in an image. The higher the ratio, the more contrast there is in the image.

CRT - Cathode ray tube.

Dark frame subtraction – A method of reducing noise in long-exposure digital photos.

Demosaicing – The interpolation process that a CCD uses to calculate color. The color of any individual pixel is determined by analyzing the color of the surrounding pixels.

Depth of field – A measure of the area of an image that is in focus. Measured as depth from the focal point of the image.

Destructive effects - Filters that actually modify the pixels in your image. Unlike non-destructive effects, there's no easy way to go back and change a destructive effect's settings, or undo their effects if you change your mind about them later.

Device-dependent color space – A color space that represents colors as combinations of other colors. RGB and CMYK are device-dependent color spaces because accurate color representation in these spaces is dependent on the quality of your primary colors.

Device independent color space – A color space (such as Lab color) that records what a color actually looks like, rather than how it is made.

Device profile – A description of the color qualities of a particular device such as a printer, scanner, digital camera, or monitor. Also known as *profile* or *ICC profile.*

Digital photography - In this book, the term digital photography is used to refer to images shot with a digital camera.

Digital zoom – A feature on many digital cameras that creates a fake zoom by capturing the center of an image and blowing it up to full image size.

Digitizing – The process of converting something into numbers (digits). In a digital camera, an image sensor captures an image that is then converted into numbers, or digitized.

Diopter – An optical control that lets you adjust the viewfinder on a camera to compensate for nearsightedness.

Downsample – The process of reducing the size of an image by throwing out data.

DPI – Dots per Inch, a measure of resolution.

Drive – A special shooting mode for shooting a sequence of images in rapid succession. Also known as *burst* or *continuous*.

Drybag – A sealable, waterproof bag that will keep your camera dry even if it gets submerged.

Dual-axis focusing zone – An autofocus mechanism that measures contrast along both horizontal and vertical axes.

Dynamic range – The range of colors that a device can represent. A digital camera with larger dynamic range can capture and store more colors, resulting in truer, smoother images.

Effective pixel count – The actual number of pixels that are used on an image sensor. In many digital cameras, some of the pixels on the camera's sensor are masked away or ignored.

Electron Gun – The image on a CRT screen or television screen is created by three electron guns that paint the screen with three different streams of electrons. Separate guns are provided for the red, green, and blue components of a color image.

Electronic TTL viewfinder – An eyepiece viewfinder that uses a tiny LCD screen instead of normal optics, and that looks through the lens. (This is the same mechanism you'll find on most video camcorders.)

Element – One individual lens. Most camera lens are composed of many different elements.

Emulsion - The light-sensitive chemical coating on the surface of a piece of film.

EXIF – Exchangeable Image File. A digital image file format used by most digital cameras. Notable because it includes special header information where all of an image's parameters (shutter speed, aperture, etc.) are stored.

Exposure – The combination of aperture, shutter speed, and ISO settings that determine how much light will be recorded at the focal plane.

Exposure compensation – A mechanism for adjusting the exposure on your camera that is independent of any particular exposure parameter. In other words, rather than specifically changing the aperture or shutter speed, you can simply use exposure compensation to over or underexpose an image. The camera will calculate the best way to achieve the compensation.

Exposure lock – A mechanism that lets you lock the exposure on your camera independently of focus.

External flash sync connection - Allows you to connect an external flash (usually a specific model) to the camera using a small cable.

Falloff – How quickly an effect changes. For example, a depth of field blur may have a quick falloff, meaning it the blur goes from sharp to blurry very quickly.

Fast shutter mode - Forces a large aperture to facilitate a fast shutter speed. Sometimes called *sports mode*.

Feather - The process of blurring the edge of a selection to create a smoother blend between an edit and the rest of an image.

Fill flash – Allows you to force the flash to fire to provide a slight fill light. Also known as *force flash*.

Film – A quaint, 19th-century analog technology for recording images. Requires lots of hazardous chemicals, a lot of patience, and doesn't offer cool features like Levels dialog boxes or Rubber Stamp tools. Not for the impatient. Does have the advantage that the recording and storage mediums are included in the same package.

Filter factor – Most lens filters are documented with a filter factor which will inform you of the exposure compensation (in stops) required when you use that filter.

Filters – Either colored plastics or glass that you can attach to the end of your camera's lens to achieve certain effects, or special effects that you can apply to your image in your image editing program (see *plug-ins*).

Firewire – A type of serial connection provided by many computers and digital cameras. Can be used for transferring images between camera and computer. Much faster than USB. Also called *IEEE-1394* or *i.Link*.

Fisheye – An extremely wide-angle lens that creates spherical views.

Flash compensation – A control that allows you to increase or decrease the intensity of your camera's flash. Usually measured in stops.

Flash memory – A form of non-volatile, erasable memory. Used in digital cameras in the form of special memory cards.

Focal length – The distance, usually measured in millimeters, between the lens and the focal plane in a camera.

Focal length multiplier – Many digital SLRs use an image sensor that is smaller than a piece of 35mm film. If you attach a lens to one of these cameras, its 35mm equivalency will be multiplied by the focal length multiplier. For example, if your digital SLR has a focal length multiplier of 1.6x, then a 50mm lens mounted on your camera will have an effective focal length of 80mm.

Focal plane – The point onto which a camera focuses an image. In a film camera, there is a piece of film sitting on the focal plane. In a digital camera, a CCD sits on the focal plane.

Focus assist lamp – A small lamp on the front of the camera that the camera can use to assist autofocusing. Also known as *autofocus assist lamp.*

Focus Ring – The ring on a lens that allows you to manually focus the lens. Most smaller digital cameras lack focus rings, which can make them difficult to manually focus.

Focus tracking – An autofocus mode provided by some cameras that can track a moving object within the frame and keep it in focus. Sometimes called *Servo focus.*

Focusing spot – See *focusing zone.*

Focusing zone – An area in the camera's field of view in which the camera can measure focus. Most cameras only have one focusing zone. The camera will focus on the object in this zone. Some cameras have multiple zones.

Force flash - See *fill flash.*

F-stop: Sometimes synonymous with *stop*, more specifically a measure of the size of the aperture on a camera. F-stop values are the ratio of the focal length of the lens to diameter of the aperture.

Gamma – The mid-point (between black and white) in a tonal range.

Gamut – See *color gamut.*

Gels – Thin pieces of plastic that are usually placed in front of lights to create colored lighting effects.

Gigapixel – Dream on.

Grayscale - An image composed entirely of shades of gray, rather than color. (Basically a fancy name for "black and white.")

Group – Multiple elements cemented together in a lens.

Halftoning – A process used for printing photos that begins by shooting a photo of an image through a special halftone screen. The resulting photo gets broken down by the screen into a pattern of dots that can be easily printed using a single ink. Your computer can generate halftone output from a laser printer, allowing you to skip the photographic halftoning step.

Hardware calibration - Special devices that measure the color of an output device. The data gathered by the device is then used to create a color profile of the device. This profile is, in turn, used by color management software to ensure accurate color output.

Histogram – A graph of the distribution of tones within an image.

Hot shoe – A mount for attaching an external flash to a camera.

ICC profiles - See *device profile.*

i.Link – Sony's name for *firewire.*

IEEE-1394 – The official name for *firewire.*

Image buffering – The ability of a camera to temporarily store images in an internal memory buffer before writing them out to a memory card. A large image buffer facilitates the rapid shooting of multiple frames as the camera doesn't have to stop shooting to offload images to storage.

Image stabilization – Some telephoto camera lenses offer special optics that can stabilize the tiny shakes and jitters that can be caused by your hand.

Interpolation - The process of calculating missing data in an image based on data that is already there.

Iris – A mechanism that can expand and contract to create circular apertures to control the amount of light passing through a lens.

ISO – A measure of a film's "speed" or light sensitivity. The higher the ISO, the more sensitive the film. The sensitivity of digital camera sensors are also rated using the ISO scale.

JPEG – Joint Photographic Experts Group. More commonly, the name of a popular lossy image compression scheme.

L*A*B color: See *Lab color.*

Lab Color – A color model created by the Commission Internationale de l'Éclairage. Lab color describes colors as they actually appear, rather than by how they are made. As such, Lab color makes a great reference space for performing color management and calibration.

Latitude – How far colors in an image can be pushed or pulled.

LCD - Liquid Crystal Display.

Lens flares – Bright color artifacts produced in a lens by reflections within the lens itself.

Line screen frequency – The density of the screen that is used in a halftoning process. A screen with more density yields an image with smoother tones and more detail.

L-Ion – Lithium Ion. A type of rechargeable battery.

Linear array – A digital camera mechanism that uses a single row of sensors that makes three separate filtered passes over the imaging sensors to create a full-color image.

Lossless – Indicates that a particular process does not result in any loss of quality.

Lossy – Indicates that a particular process results in loss of quality.

Luminance – Brightness information.

Macro – A special type of lens used for photographing objects at extremely close distances.

Manual mode - A shooting mode on a camera that allows you to set both the aperture and shutter speed, giving you full control over the camera's exposure.

Matrix meter – A light meter that analyzes many different areas of your scene to determine proper exposure.

Megapixel – A million pixels. Usually used as a measure of the resolution of a digital camera's sensor.

Memory Stick – A type of reusable, removable storage developed by Sony, not yet adopted by any other camera vendors.

Metering - The process of measuring light with a light meter (or by eye) so as to determine proper exposure for a shot.

MicroDrive – A tiny hard drive that fits in a Type II CompactFlash slot on a camera. Note that a camera usually has to be approved for use with a MicroDrive.

Mirror lock-up – The ability to lock a camera's mirror into the "up" position to reduce vibration when shooting long exposure images. Some higher-end cameras also provide a lock-up feature to aid in cleaning the camera's sensor.

Multiple array – A digital camera mechanism that uses three separate CCDs for capturing a color image, one each for red, green, and blue.

Multi-segment meter – See *matrix meter*.

Multi-spot focus - An autofocus mechanism on a camera that can focus on one of several different places within an image.

Nearest neighbor – A method of interpolation used in a resampling process.

Neutral density filter – A filter that cuts down on the light entering your camera's lens, without altering the color of the light. Enables you to use wider apertures or faster shutter speeds in bright light.

NiCad – Nickel Cadmium. A type of rechargeable battery. Not recommended for use in a digital camera.

NiMH – Nickel Metal Hydride. A type of rechargeable battery.

Nodal point – The optical center of a camera's lens.

Noise - The bane of all digital photographers. Noise appears in an image as very fine-grained patterns of multi-colored pixels in an area. Shadow areas are particularly susceptible to noise as are images shot in low-light. Noise is very different-looking than the grain found in film photos. Unfortunately, it's also far less attractive.

Normal lens– A lens that has a field of view that is equivalent to the field of view of the human eye. Roughly 50 mm.

Overexposed – An image that was exposed for too long. As an image becomes more overexposed it gets brighter and brighter. Highlights and light-colored areas wash out to completely white.

Parallax - The easiest way to understand parallax is simply to hold your index finger in front of your face and close one eye. Now close the other eye and you'll perceive that your finger has jumped sideways. As you can see, at close distances, even a change of view as small as the distance between your eyes can create a very different perspective on your subject. A camera that uses one lens for framing and another for shooting faces the same problems. Parallax is not a problem at longer ranges as the parallax shift is imperceptible.

Passive autofocus – An autofocus mechanism that achieves focus by analyzing the camera's view of the scene.

PC Card adapter – A special adapter that lets you insert a storage card from your camera into the PC card slot of your computer.

PC cards - Small, credit-card-sized peripheral cards that can be inserted into a PC Card slot on a laptop computer, or into a special PC Card drive on a desktop computer. PC Card adapters are available for most kinds of digital camera media, allowing you to insert media directly into your PC Card slot.

PCMCIA - See *PC cards.*

Phase detection - See *phase difference.*

Phase difference – An autofocus mechanism that uses measurements taken through different parts of the camera's lens to determine focus. Also known as *phase detection.*

Photosite – A tiny electrode that sits on the surface of an image sensor. There is one photosite for each pixel on a sensor.

Picture elements – The smallest area of color information that can be displayed on a computer monitor. Also the smallest area of color information that can be detected by a digital imaging sensor. Also known as *pixels*.

Pincushion distortion – A type of distortion caused by a lens. Causes the edges of an image to bow inward. Most prevalent in telephoto lenses. See also *barrel distortion*.

Pixel – See *picture elements*.

Pixellate - Sometimes, the individual pixels in an image can become visible, a process called pixellation.

Plug-ins – Special bits of code – usually effects or image processing filters – that can be added to your image editing application. Most plug-ins conform to the Photoshop plug-in standard.

Polarizers – Special filters that can be fitted onto the end of a lens. Polarizers only allow light that is polarized in a particular direction to enter your lens. Polarizers can completely remove distracting reflections from water, glass, or other shiny surfaces. Polarizers can also be used to increase the contrast in skies and clouds.

Posterization – Reduction of the number of tones in an image. As a particular tonal range gets posterized, it will appear more "flat."

PPI – Pixels per Inch, a measure of resolution.

Prefocus – The process of autofocusing, metering, and white balancing that occurs when you press your camera's shutter release button halfway.

Prefocus time – How long it takes a camera to perform its prefocus steps (autofocus, metering, and white balance).

Prime lens – A lens with a fixed focal length.

Profile - See *device profile*.

Proportional zoom control – A zoom control whose rate of zoom changes depending on how far you push or pull the control.

Prosumer - A marketing term for a camera that sits somewhere between the professional and consumer market.

Purple fringing – A color artifact specific to digital cameras with resolutions greater than two megapixels. Appears in an image around the edges of high-contrast objects, usually shot with wide-angle lenses. Usually confined to the edges of the screen. See also *chromatic aberrations.*

Quantization – In JPEG compression, the process of averaging the colors in one 64-pixel square area.

Quantizing – The process of assigning a numeric value to a sample. Part of the digitizing process.

Rangefinder – A viewfinder mechanism on a camera. A fixed-focus or zoom lens is used for imaging, while a separate optical viewfinder is used for framing your shot.

Raw data – Pixel data that comes directly from the CCD with no further processing. Processing is usually performed later using special software. Raw files offer quality equivalent to an uncompressed image, but require much less space.

Read-out register – The mechanism that reads the signals from each row of photosites on an image sensor. The read-out register amplifies the signals from the photosites and sends them to the camera's analog-to-digital converter.

Reciprocity – Exposure parameters have a reciprocal relationship so that different combinations of parameters produce the same exposure. For example, setting your camera to a shutter speed of $1/250^{th}$ of a second at f8 is the same as setting it to $1/125^{th}$ at f16.

Rectilinear – A type of wide-angle lens that includes corrective elements that prevent barrel distortion.

Recycling – The time it takes a camera to reset itself and prepare to shoot another shot.

Red-eye reduction – A special flash mode that attempts to prevent red eye by firing a short initial flash to close down the irises in your subject's eyes.

Red-eye – When the flash from a camera bounces off a subject's eyes and back into the camera's lens, the subject will appear to have bright red eyes. Most prevalent in cameras where the flash is very close to the lens.

Registration - When primary color channels are positioned over each other so that a full-color image is produced, the images are said to be "in registration."

Refraction – The process of slowing and bending light using a transparent substance such as air, water, glass, or plastic.

Refractive index – The amount of refraction produced by a substance.

Refresh rate – How often the image on a camera's LCD viewfinder is redrawn. An LCD with a higher refresh rate will produce an image with smoother motion.

Resampling – The process of computing new pixel information when resizing a document in your image editing application. If you are resizing upward, then the resampling process will generate new pixels. If you are resizing downward, then the resampling process will discard pixels.

Resolution – In a monitor or digital camera, the number of pixels that fit into a given space. Usually measured in pixels per inch (ppi) or dots per inch (dpi). In a printer, the number of printer dots that fit into a given space, usually measured in dots per inch (dpi).

RGB – Red, green, and blue, the additive primary colors that are used by your computer monitor and digital camera to produce all other colors.

Sampling – The process of analyzing something to determine its content. A digital camera samples light to determine how much, and what color the light is, at any given point in a scene.

Saturation - A characteristic of color. Colors that are more saturated are typically "deeper" in hue and often darker. As saturation increases, hue shifts slightly.

SCSI - Small Computer System Interface. An older, high-speed computer interface for attaching hard drives, scanners and other peripherals.

Servo Focus See *focus tracking*.

Sharpening - The process of using software to increase sharpness in a digital image. Sharpening can happen inside a digital camera or through post-processing on your computer.

Shutter – A mechanism that sits in front of the focal plane in a camera and that can open and close to expose the image sensor or film to light. Many digital cameras do not have physical shutters, but instead mimic shutter functionality by simply activating and deactivating their image sensors to record an image. Cameras that do have shutters typically use a two-curtain mechanism. The first curtain begins to slide across the focal plane to create a gap. It is followed – usually very quickly – by a second shutter that closes the gap. As the gap passes across, the entire CCD is exposed.

Shutter lag – A delay between the time you press the shutter release button on a camera, and the time it actually shoots a picture.

Shutter priority – A shooting mode on a camera. Shutter priority lets you define the camera's shutter speed. The camera will then calculate a corresponding aperture based on its light metering.

Shutter speed - The length of time that it takes for the shutter in a camera to completely expose the focal plane.

Single array system – A digital camera mechanism that uses a single image sensor for imaging. Sometimes called a "striped array."

Single lens reflex – A camera whose viewfinder looks through the same lens that your camera uses to make its exposure. Also known as *SLR*.

Single-axis focusing zone – An autofocus mechanism that measures contrast along a single axis only, usually horizontal.

Slow sync mode – A special flash mode that combines a flash with a slow shutter speed to create images that contain both still and motion-blurred objects.

SLR – See *single lens reflex*.

SmartMedia – A type of reusable, removable storage.

Soft proof – An on-screen proof of a color document.

Specular highlights - The bright white glints and reflections that occur on very shiny surfaces and on the edges of objects.

Spot meter – A light meter that measures a very narrow circle of the scene.

sRGB – An RGB color space defined by Microsoft and Hewlett Packard. It is intended to represent the colors available on a typical color monitor. A little too small for digital photography work.

Step-up ring – An adapter that attaches to the end of a lens and allows for the addition of filters or other lens-attachments. Serves to change the thread size of the lens.

Stitching – The process of joining and blending individual images to create a panoramic image.

Stop – A measure of the light that is passing through a camera's lens to the focal plane. Every doubling of light – either through changes in aperture, shutter speed, or ISO – is one stop. See also *f-stop*.

Striped array – See *single array system*.

Subtractive – Ink mixes together in a *subtractive* process whereby as colors are mixed together they get darker – that is, light is subtracted as the colors are mixed. Subtractive colors eventually produce black. Cyan, magenta, and yellow are the primary subtractive colors that can be used to create all other colors.

Telephoto – A lens with a focal length that is longer than *normal*. As a lens gets more telephoto, its field of view decreases.

TFT – See *Thin Film Transistor*.

Thin Film Transistor – A technology used to create LCD screens. Typically used for the LCD viewfinder/monitors included on the backs of many digital cameras.

Three-shot array – A digital camera mechanism that uses three *single arrays*, one each for red, green, and blue.

Through the lens – See *TTL*.

Title safe – A guide similar to the *action safe* area. The title safe area is slightly smaller.

Transfer mode – See *Blending mode*.

Trilinear array – A digital camera mechanism that uses three *linear arrays* stacked on top of each other to create a full-color image in a single pass over the image sensor.

TTL – A viewfinder mechanism that looks through the same lens that is used to focus the image onto the focal plane. Short for *through the lens*.

Underexposed – An image that was not exposed enough. In an underexposed image, dark, shadow areas turn to completely black.

Upsample – The process of enlarging an image by calculating (interpolating) new data.

USB – Universal Serial Bus. A type of serial connection provided by many computers and digital cameras. Can be used for transferring images between camera and computer.

VGA resolution - 640 x 480 pixels.

Video LUT Animation – A feature available in some versions of Photoshop that allows for real-time, on-screen viewing of color corrections and changes.

Video RAM – The memory in a computer that is used for displaying images on-screen. The more video RAM, the larger your images can be, and the greater the bit depth they can have. Also known as *VRAM*.

Vignetting – A darkening of the image around the edges.

Virtual Reality Movie – See *VR Movie*.

VR Movie - A digital movie that lets you pan and tilt in real-time to explore and navigate a virtual space.

Wavelet compression – A new fractal-based compression scheme. Converts your image from a series of raster dots into a collection of tiny fractal curves.

White balance – A color calibration used by a camera. Once a camera knows how to accurately represent white it can represent all other colors. Because white can look different under different types of light, a camera needs to be told what white is, a process called *white balancing*.

Wide-angle – A lens with a focal length that is shorter than *normal*. As a lens gets more wide-angle, its field of view increases.

XGA resolution - 800 x 600 pixels.

Zone system – A method of calculating exposure.

Zoom lens – A lens with a variable focal length.

Index